Access® 97 Essentials
Level III

John Preston
Eastern Michigan University

Robert Ferrett
Eastern Michigan University

Sally Preston
Washtenaw Community College

**An Imprint of Macmillan
Computer Publishing**

Access 97 Essentials Level III

Library of Congress Catalog No: 97-65614

ISBN: 1-57576-804-6

00 99 98 97   4 3 2 1

Interpretation of the printing code: the rightmost double-digit number is the year of the book's printing; the rightmost single-digit number, the number of the book's printing. For example, a printing code of 97-1 shows that the first printing of the book occurred in 1997.

Screens reproduced in this book were created using Collage Plus from Inner Media, Inc., Hollis, NH.

Publisher: Robb Linsky

Publishing Director: Charles O. Stewart III

Product Marketing Manager: Susan Kindel

Managing Editor: Nancy E. Sixsmith

Development Editor: Jan Snyder

Production Editor: Susan Hobbs

Copy Editor: Ed Metzler

Technical Editor: Asit J. Patel

Editorial Assistant: Beth Montano

Book Designer: Gary Adair

Production Team: Cynthia Fields, Janelle Herber, Linda Knose, Malinda Kuhn

Indexer: Chris Wilcox

Composed in *Stone Serif* and *MCPdigital* by Que® Education and Training

About the Authors

John Preston is an Associate Professor at Eastern Michigan University where he teaches microcomputer application courses at the undergraduate and graduate levels. He has been teaching, writing and designing computer training courses since the advent of the personal computer, and has authored books on Microsoft Word, Excel, Access and PowerPoint.

Robert Ferrett is the Director of the Center for Instructional Computing at Eastern Michigan University. His center provides computer training and support to faculty at the university. He has authored or co-authored books on Access 1.1, PowerPoint 4.0, Word 2.0 and Word 6.0, Access 2 and Access 7 for Windows 95, and PowerPoint for Windows 95. He has a BA in Psychology, an MS in Geography, and an MS in Interdisciplinary Technology from Eastern Michigan University. He is currently enrolled in a Ph.D. program in Instructional Technology at Wayne State University.

Sally Preston is a professional trainer who combines her extensive business experience as a bank vice president in charge of branch operations with her teaching skills in Microsoft Excel, Access, Word and PowerPoint. She teaches computer courses part-time for Washtenaw Community College and provides corporate training through the Institute for Workforce Development at the college.

Trademark Acknowledgments

Preface

Que Education and Training is the educational publishing imprint of Macmillan Computer Publishing, the world's leading computer book publisher. Macmillan Computer Publishing books have taught more than 20 million people how to be productive with their computers.

This expertise in producing high-quality computer tutorial and reference books is evident in every Que Education and Training title we publish. The same tried-and-true authoring and product-development process that makes Macmillan Computer Publishing books bestsellers is used to ensure that training materials from Que Education and Training contain the most accurate and up-to-date information. Experienced and respected software trainers write and review every manuscript to provide class-tested pedagogy. Quality-assurance editors check every keystroke and command in Que Education and Training books to ensure that instructions are clear and precise.

Above all, Macmillan Computer Publishing and, in turn, Que Education and Training have years of experience in meeting the learning demands of adult users in business and at home. We offer tiered courseware that

> ➤ provides broad-based, flexible training for novices through expert users.

> ➤ is anchored in the practical and professional needs of adult learners.

> ➤ includes trainer support in fully annotated *Instructor's Manuals*.

The "Essentials" of Hands-On Learning

The *Essentials* of applications tutorials are appropriate for use in both corporate training and college classroom settings. The *Essentials* workbooks are ideal for short courses—from a few hours to a full day or more—and meet the needs of adult learners. They can also be used effectively as computer-lab applications modules to accompany Que Education and Training's computer concepts text, *Computers in Your Future*, by Marilyn Meyer and Roberta Baber, both of Fresno City College; and *Using Computers and Information*, by Jack Rochester of Plymouth State College. The *Essentials* workbooks enable users to become self-sufficient quickly; encourage self-learning after instruction; maximize learning through clear, complete explanations; and serve as future references. Each *Essentials* module is sized at 8½×11 inches for maximum screen-shot visibility. Each text contains a disk with the data files needed to complete the tutorials and end-of-chapter exercises.

Project Objectives list what learners will do and learn from the project.

"Why Would I Do This?" shows learners why this material is essential.

Step-by-Step Tutorials simplify the procedures with large screen shots, captions, and annotations.

If you have problems... anticipates common pitfalls and advises learners accordingly.

Inside Stuff provide tips and shortcuts for more effective applications.

Key Terms are highlighted in the text and defined in the margin when they first appear.

Jargon Watch offer a layperson's view of "technobabble" in easily understandable terms.

Checking Your Skills provides true/false, multiple choice, and completion exercises.

Applying Your Skills contains directed, hands-on exercises to check comprehension and reinforce learning.

Data disks contain files for the text's step-by-step tutorials.

Instructor's Manual

If you have adopted this text for use in a college classroom, you will receive, upon request, an *Instructor's Manual* on disk at no additional charge. The manual contains suggested curriculum guides for courses of varying lengths, teaching tips, answers to exercises in the "Applying Your Skills" sections, test questions and answers, data files needed to complete each exercise, and solution files. Please contact your local representative or write to us on school letterhead at Macmillan Computer Publishing, 201 West 103rd Street, Indianapolis, IN 46290-1907, Attn: S. Kindel.

Also available is a printed *Instructor's Manual,* which is an ideal companion guide to workbooks in the *Essentials* series. It includes teaching concepts and procedures, strategies for structuring content and organizing the class, ideas for adapting the material for various audiences, pre-training assessment and post-class evaluation tools, and much more. The backbone of the *Instructor's Manual* is a heavily annotated student workbook that serves as an indispensable resource for trainers. New instructors will appreciate the tips that help them teach a topic successfully for the first time. Experienced trainers will appreciate fresh approaches to teaching familiar topics.

Que Education and Training
Publishing for tomorrow...*today*

Table of Contents at a Glance

Table of Contents

Note to the Learner

Welcome to *Access 97 Essentials Level III*! The *Essentials* series consists of student workbooks and instructor manuals for use in instructor-led classes.

If this is your first experience with instructor-led training, you're in for a real treat. Instructor-led, hands-on training is the fastest and most efficient means of teaching software applications. Your instructor is an expert in this application, so he or she can answer your questions and pass on valuable advice about using the software.

What all this means is that with the use of these materials, you'll be up and running in the shortest amount of time possible.

Who Should Use This Book?

The *Essentials* workbooks are designed to be used in the classroom and corporate-training environment. The projects in the *Essentials* workbooks are designed to teach only the "bare essentials"—just enough for you to get the job done.

How to Use This Book

Because an instructor will be present in the classroom, the *Essentials* workbooks contain a minimum of explanation and the maximum of step-by-step directions. As you begin each project, you are told what you want to accomplish and why. Realistic examples are given, so that you can quickly relate to the task and see the value of completing the project.

Each project is a series of separate lessons with detailed instructions to guide you through the completion of a task. After each numbered step, a brief explanation of the action is given to help you really understand "why you just did that." At the end of each lesson, tips and shortcuts are given to satisfy the more curious reader. A Project Summary table is included to give you a quick reference to use when you need a quick refresher.

To make your learning experience as enjoyable as possible, the projects are task-oriented and use real-world business examples.

Task-Oriented Lessons

The workbook lessons are *task-oriented*, which means that you actually accomplish a task as you work through the lesson. For example, rather than merely *reading* about moving and copying text, you learn how to rearrange your text by moving and copying sentences in a paragraph. Likewise, you learn how to format documents by changing the margins, changing the line spacing, setting justification, changing the font and font size, and adding page numbers and a header.

Once you get past the first two projects, the remainder are independent of each other—they can be completed in any order. If your time is limited, you can pick and choose your projects, depending on which concepts you need to learn right away.

Real-World Examples

Concepts are illustrated with realistic situations that you would encounter in a workplace. The more realistic the examples are, the easier it is for you to relate to the situation. For example, in the lesson in which you complete a newsletter, the sample file contains information that you would find in a typical corporate newsletter. You work with letters to conference attendees, status reports, annual reports, and job descriptions instead of letters to book clubs or public-domain documents (such as the Declaration of Independence).

Conventions Used in This Book

The *Essentials* series uses the following conventions to make it easier for you to understand the material:

➤ Text that you are to type appears in a **special font and boldface.**

➤ Underlined letters in menu names, menu commands, and dialog-box options appear in **bold**. Examples are the **F**ile menu, the **O**pen command, and the File **n**ame list box.

➤ Important words or phrases appear in *italic* the first time they are discussed.

➤ *Key terms* are defined in the margin as soon as they are introduced.

➤ On-screen text and messages appear in a special font.

Project 1

Project

1

Making the Input Form More User-Friendly

Adding color and customizing controls can enhance a form

In this Project, you learn how to:

➤ Change the Color of Text, Backgrounds, and Borders Using Buttons

➤ Copy Formats between Individual Controls and Format Many Controls at Once

➤ Change Colors and Align Text Using Properties

➤ Add Status Bar Instructions in the Form View

➤ Add Customized ControlTips to Controls

➤ Customize a Toolbar with Predefined Buttons

➤ Add a Button to a Toolbar to Run a Macro

Why Would I Do This?

Customizing the appearance and functions of Access helps to personalize the database, while at the same time making it more interesting, informative, and easier to use. Effective use of colors, buttons, and help features can make the difference between a boring database and a professional-looking product.

Most data entry is done in the Form View. Changing the color of the text, background, and border colors can improve the look of the form and can also be used to provide important information to the user. You can use colors, for example, to warn the user of required fields.

Control
A general term that includes objects such as text boxes, label boxes, and calculated fields.

Changing the format or adding new features to each *control* on a form can be time-consuming. Access contains a rapid format feature that can save a great deal of time.

Access gives you the option of adding customized help for the user. You can place instructions on the Status Bar, and you can even add ControlTips to the controls on a form.

It is also possible to customize any of the toolbars. Predefined buttons that are included with Access can be added to any toolbar, and seldom-used buttons can be removed. The order of the buttons can be rearranged. You can also attach Access macros to your own buttons.

In this project, you learn how to change the appearance of various parts of the database to give the user more information and to make your database look professional.

Lesson 1: Changing the Color of Text, Backgrounds, and Borders Using Buttons

The first thing you need to do is to copy the database file included with this book. Once you have copied and renamed the file, you will be ready to complete the first lesson.

To Open the Federal Census Database

1 **Make a copy of the student data file Proj0101.**

2 **Rename the copy Federal Census.**

Include the .mdb extension only if you can see the extension on the Proj0101 file.

3 **Launch Access 97.**

4 **Open the Federal Census database.**

The database window should now be open to the Tables area. If not, click on the Tables tab (see Figure 1.1). Keep the database open for the next exercise.

Figure 1.1
The database window displays the Tables area of the Federal Census database.

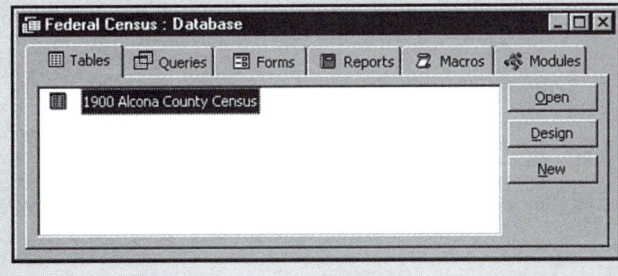

You can make the form easier to read through a restrained use of color. Try not to overdo the use of colors. Too many different colors on a screen can be very distracting, and bright colors with high contrast can be very hard on the eyes. You can also use colors as cues for the user.

In this section you will learn how to change the colors of the text (foreground), background, and control borders in a form using buttons on the Form Design toolbar.

To Change the Color of Text, Backgrounds, and Borders Using Buttons

❶ Click the Forms tab.

The 1900 Alcona County Census form should be highlighted.

❷ Click the Design button. Maximize the Design window and the Access window if necessary (see Figure 1.2).

The 1900 Alcona County Census form is ready for design changes.

Figure 1.2
The design window displays the design area of the 1900 Alcona County Census database.

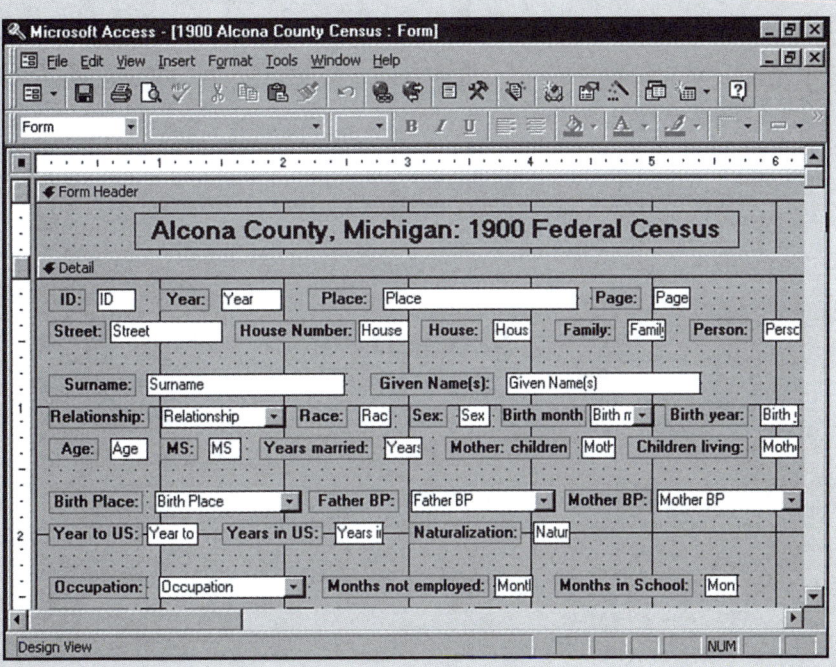

continues

To Change the Color of Text, Backgrounds, and Borders Using Buttons (continued)

3 **Click the title "Alcona County, Michigan: 1900 Federal Census" to select it.**

Handles should appear around the title.

4 **Click the down-arrow on the Font/Fore Color button, which is on the Form Design toolbar.**

The Font/Fore Color drop-down box appears. The Font/Fore Color button could, in this case, be called the Text Color button, although it can change the color of any foreground. The left side of the button shows the current text color. The down-arrow button is used to display a menu of optional colors.

5 **Choose dark blue.**

The dark blue color, which appears in the sixth box to the right in the second row would be a good choice (see Figure 1.3).

Figure 1.3
The Font/Fore Color drop-down menu offers a variety of colors for text.

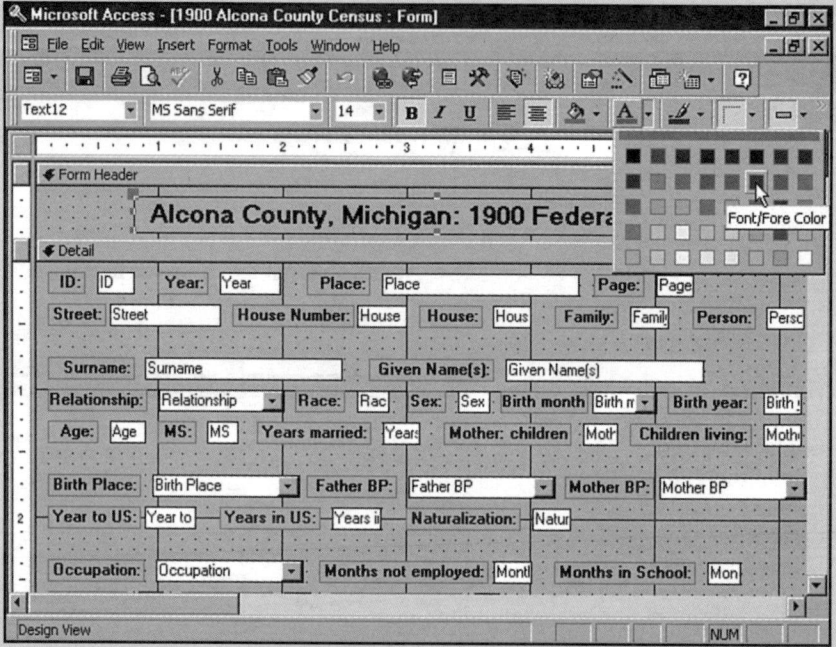

6 **Click on the gray background area to the left of the title in the Form Header area. Click the down-arrow on the Fill/Back Color button on the Form Design toolbar.**

The Fill/Back Color drop-down box appears.

7 **Choose a light blue background.**

A background color that goes well with dark blue text is the fifth box to the right in the fifth row (see Figure 1.4).

Figure 1.4
The Fill/Back Color drop-down menu offers a variety of colors for the background.

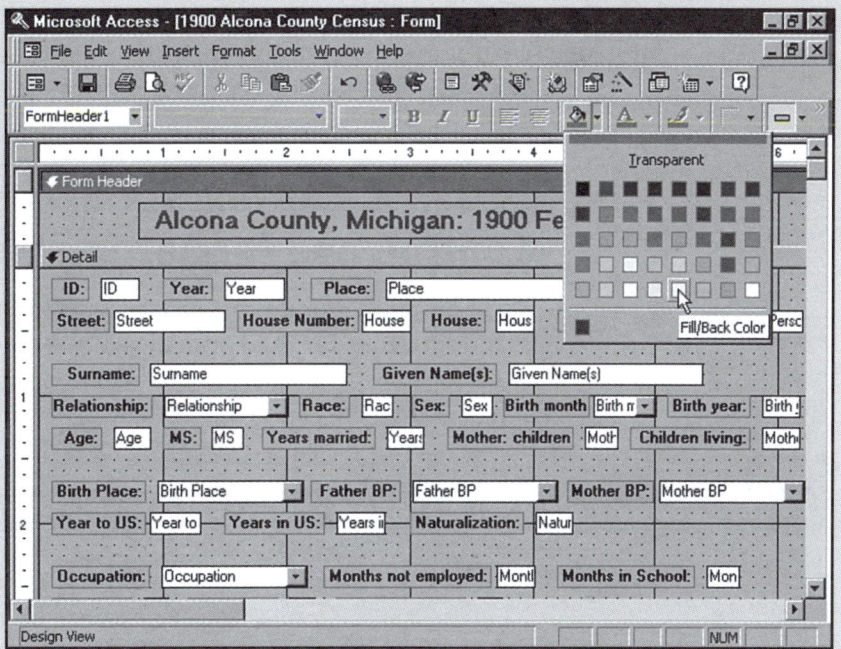

Notice that the background of the title is still gray.

8 Click anywhere on the title to select it.

The title should show a border with handles as it did when selected before.

9 Click the Down-arrow on the Fill/Back Color button and click the ___Transparent choice.

When you want the background of a box to be the same as the background color of the area behind it, you can make the background of the box transparent.

10 Click the down-arrow on the Line/Border Color button.

A drop-down menu appears. This menu shows 40 colors, and is identical to the one found under the Fill/Back Color button.

11 Choose the same shade of dark blue you selected for the title text.

The menu of colors shows the most recently selected colors at the bottom of the menu. You can select the dark blue color from this area as well as its original location on the menu.

12 Click the View button.

You leave the Design View and open the Form View. Notice the color combination in the Form Header area.

13 Save the changes and close the form. Keep the database open for the next lesson.

Once you choose a color for the foreground, background, or lines it becomes the default choice for that button on the toolbar. The color of the button changes to indicate the current default and you may apply that color to a selected object by clicking the left side of the button.

Lesson 2: Copying Formats between Individual Controls and Formatting Many Controls at Once

You can easily copy the format from one control to another. The Format Painter button, on the Form Design toolbar, can be used in several ways to copy formats from one control to one or more other controls. You can also select many fields and format them all at once.

To Copy Formats between Individual Controls and Format Many Controls at Once

❶ In the Federal Census database, click the Forms tab and <u>O</u>pen the 1900 Alcona County Census form.

Look at the way your form appears.

❷ Click the View button.

This switches from the Form View to the Design View. Maximize the form, if necessary.

❸ Click the label for the ID field (ID:).

Handles should appear around the label control box but not the field text control box.

❹ Use the Font/Fore Color, Fill/Back Color, and Line/Border Color buttons to change the colors to those you used for the title in Lesson 1.

Just change the ID label box on the left, not the ID text control box on the right. Simply click the left side of each button to apply the same colors you used in the previous lesson. If the default color for one of the buttons has been changed, use the drop-down arrow on the right of the button and choose the color the way you did in Lesson 1.

❺ Click the Format Painter button in the Form Design toolbar.

The pointer changes shape, adding a paintbrush to the normal arrow (see Figure 1.5).

Figure 1.5
The Format Painter pointer has a paintbrush added to the arrow.

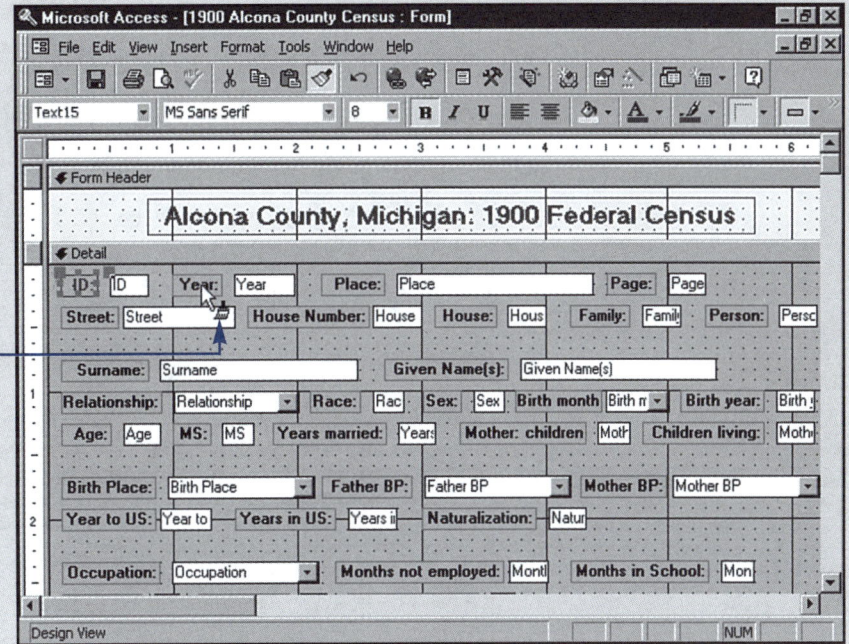

Mouse pointer for the Format Painter

6 **Click the label for the Year control box (Year:).**

The Fore Color, Back Color, and Border Color now match the ID label. Notice that the pointer no longer has a paintbrush attached.

The Format Painter will also apply the settings for font style, point size, and alignment.

7 **Double-click the Format Painter button with the ID label still selected.**

Double-clicking will lock the button on for repeated use.

8 **Click the label control box for the Place field.**

The Fore Color, Back Color, and Border Color now match the ID field label. Notice that the pointer still has a paintbrush attached. You can continue to "paint" as many label and field text controls as you want.

9 **Click two or three other labels.**

Notice that the paintbrush remains with the mouse pointer.

10 **Click the Format Painter button once to turn off the Format Painter.**

There is an even faster way to change the format of several controls at once.

11 **Move the pointer to the vertical ruler, immediately to the left of the ID field.**

The pointer turns into an arrow pointing to the right.

continues

To Copy Formats between Individual Controls and Format Many Controls at Once   (continued)

12 Click and hold down the left mouse button.

A thin line appears through the first row of controls.

13 Drag the pointer down until it is to the left of the Age field.

A thin line should appear through the row of fields that begin with the Age field, and the ruler will be black between the two lines (see Figure 1.6).

Figure 1.6
The vertical ruler turns black to show the selected area.

Vertical ruler ——→

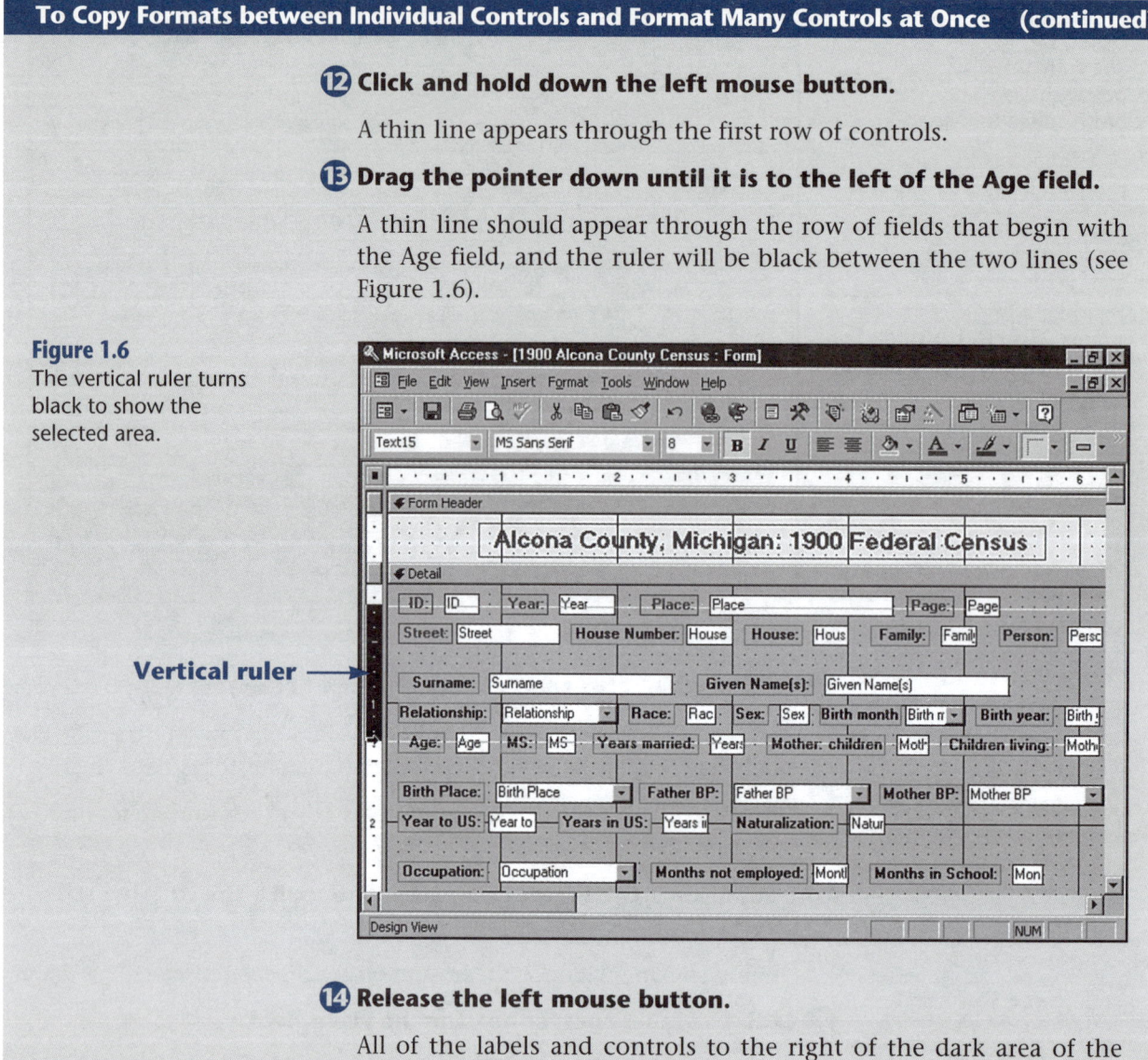

14 Release the left mouse button.

All of the labels and controls to the right of the dark area of the ruler are selected (see Figure 1.7).

Figure 1.7
Many controls can be
selected at once.

Selected controls

(15) **Use the Font/Fore Color, Fill/Back Color, and Line/Border
Color buttons to change the colors to those you used in step
4 of this lesson.**

The background, text, and border of the selected labels and controls
should be changed. Notice that this method enables you to select
the formats separately and does not change the font alignment.

(16) **Repeat steps 11–15 to change the colors of the rest of the
controls in the Detail area of the form.**

The background, text, and border of all of the labels and controls
should now match the Form Header area.

(17) **Click in a blank area of the Detail section.**

(18) **Use the Fill/Back Color button to change the background of
the unused portion of the Detail area to the same light blue
you used for the Form Header area.**

(19) **Click the View button.**

Notice the color combination of the form. Also notice that the
Combo Box buttons remain gray and black, as do the perimeter
portions of the screen, such as the Status Bar and the scroll bars.

(20) **Save your changes and close the form.**

The previous procedure involves several steps to select all of the components of
the Detail area. If you know that all of the objects on the form will be formatted
the same, you can use the Select **A**ll option from the **E**dit menu. If you are
going to format most of the objects the same way, you can use the Select **A**ll
option, then hold the [⬆Shift] key down and click the ones you don't want to format to deselect them.

continues

continued

If you use the Format Painter to copy the format of a label onto a text box, you will not see any immediate problem. However, when you use the form, the text box will show a gray background instead of white when you tab to it to enter data.

Lesson 3: Changing Colors and Aligning Text Using Properties

In Lesson 2, you used the buttons on the Form Design toolbar to change the color of the background, text, and borders. Using the Properties dialog box to change color gives you many more colors and shades from which to choose. This is especially important if, for example, you are attempting to make your form colors match your company's colors. There are other formatting options available in the Properties dialog box.

In this lesson, you will use the Properties dialog box to change the color of the three required fields in this form. This will warn users that these fields are "special" in some way. You will also align the label text of one of the fields.

To Change Colors and Align Text Using Properties

1 **Highlight the 1900 Alcona County Census form on the Forms tab, click the Design button, and maximize the form, if necessary.**

2 **Right-click the Surname label control box.**

A shortcut menu appears.

3 **Choose Properties from the shortcut menu.**

4 **Click the Format tab, if necessary.**

5 **Scroll to the bottom of the Format area to display the Fore Color box.**

The last format option to appear should be Text Align (see Figure 1.8).

Figure 1.8
The Format tab in the Properties dialog box offers a variety of text formatting features.

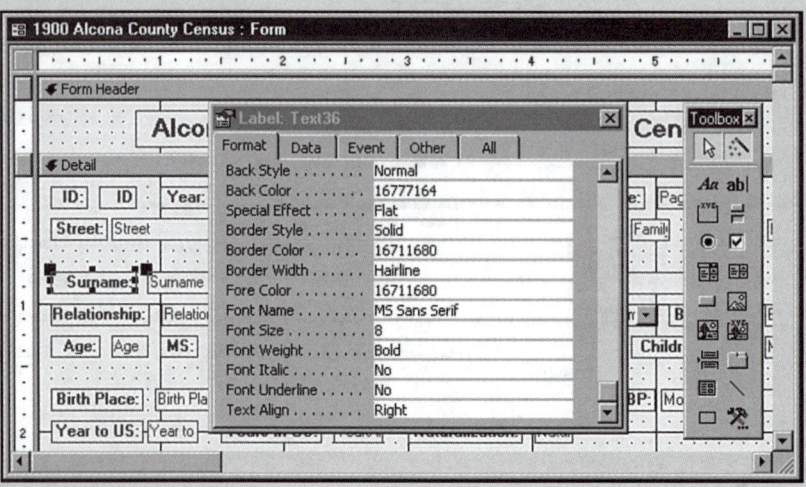

6 **Click the Fore Color box.**

A Build button appears on the right side of the Fore Color box.

7 **Click the Build button.**

The Color dialog box appears.

8 **Click the Define Custom Colors button.**

The Color dialog box expands to include a box showing a range of color options. The current color is indicated by an arrow on the right-hand slide and by crosshairs at the top edge of the multi-colored box (see Figure 1.9).

Figure 1.9
The Color dialog box has been expanded to show custom colors.

Crosshair

Color arrow

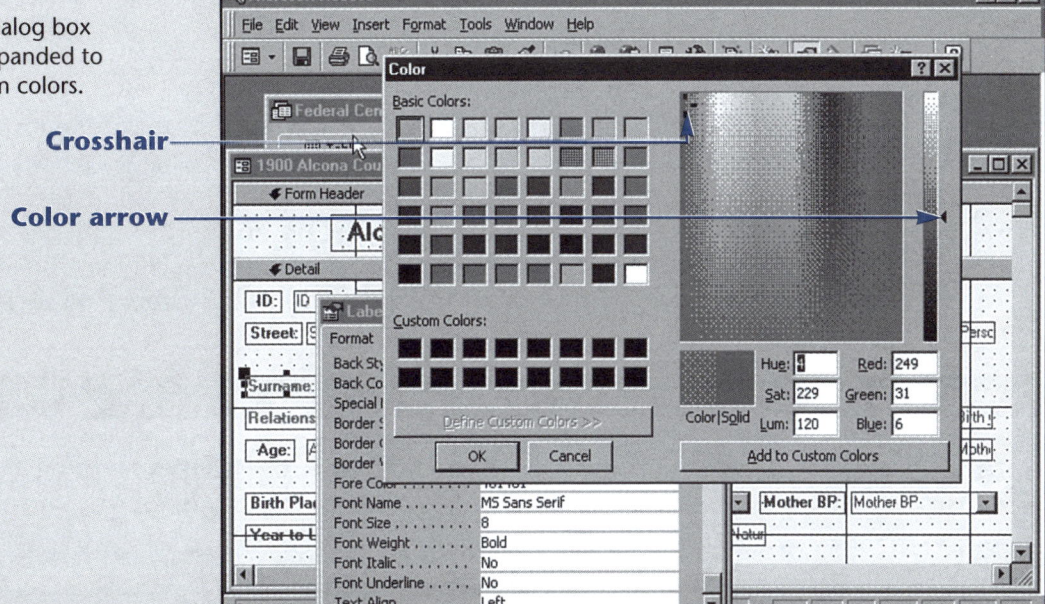

9 **Click on a bright red area of the multi-color box and click OK.**

10 **Click in the Text Align box.**

The Surname label will change color when you move to another area of the Properties box. Notice that the Surname label is right-aligned and does not look correct.

11 **Choose Left from the Text Align drop-down box.**

12 **Close the Properties dialog box.**

You have now warned the user that the Surname field is special in some way (you will let them know exactly what is special about it in a later lesson). You will now copy the format of the Surname label to the other two required fields.

13 **With the Surname label control still selected, double-click the Format Painter.**

continues

To Change Colors and Align Text Using Properties   (continued)

14 **Click the Given Name(s) and Relationship label controls to change the color of the text to match the color of the Surname label.**

15 **Click the Format Painter button again to turn it off.**

 16 **Click the View button.**

Notice that the three required fields stand out on the screen.

17 **Save your changes and close the form.**

Lesson 4: Adding Status Bar Instructions in the Form View

In Lesson 3, you learned how to give the user a visual cue that there was something special about a field. If you want to make the form easy to use, you may also need to give the user help on what to put in the field, and also give information on any special characteristics of the field. There are several ways to help the user, ranging from printed instructions to Status Bar messages to custom ControlTips. In this lesson you will add help to the Status Bar. Lesson 5 shows you how to create custom ControlTips.

To Add Status Bar Instructions in the Form View

1 **Highlight the 1900 Alcona County Census form on the Forms tab, click the Design button, and maximize the form, if necessary.**

2 **Right-click the Surname text control box.**

A shortcut menu appears.

3 **Choose Properties from the shortcut menu.**

4 **Click the Other tab.**

5 **Click the Status Bar Text box.**

If you have problems...

If you don't see the Status Bar Text box, you probably right-clicked the Surname label control box instead of the Surname text control box in step 2. Leave the Properties box open and click the Surname text control box. The Properties box will display the properties of the currently selected object.

6 **Type in the following text:**

```
Enter the person's surname. If unreadable, type in ?; if
blank, type in "not given".
```

This is the text that will appear in the Status Bar when the cursor is in the Surname field (see Figure 1.10). The Properties box in Figure 1.10 has been expanded to show the entire label in the Status Bar Text box.

Figure 1.10
Whatever is typed into the Status Bar Text box will appear in the Status Bar.

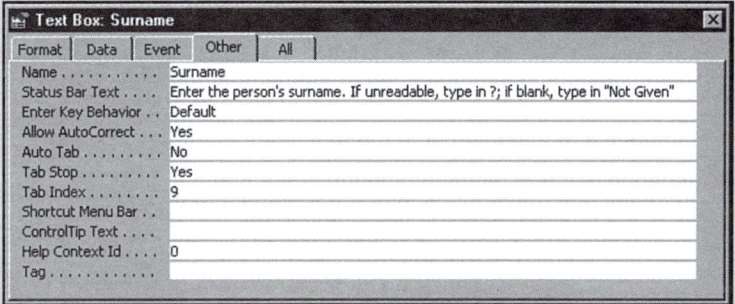

Text Box: Surname	✕

Format | Data | Event | **Other** | All

Name	Surname
Status Bar Text	Enter the person's surname. If unreadable, type in ?; if blank, type in "Not Given"
Enter Key Behavior . .	Default
Allow AutoCorrect . . .	Yes
Auto Tab	No
Tab Stop	Yes
Tab Index	9
Shortcut Menu Bar . .	
ControlTip Text	
Help Context Id	0
Tag	

❼ Click the Text box of the Given Name(s) field. Enter the following text in its Status Bar Text box:

```
Enter the given name(s). If unreadable, type in ?; if
blank, type in "not given".
```

This message is slightly altered from the text used for the Surname field. The word "person's" was removed because that made the text too long for the space allowed in the Status Bar.

❽ Click the Relationship Text box and place the following text in the Status Bar Text box:

```
Enter the relationship. If unreadable, type in ?; if
blank, type in "not given".
```

❾ Close the Properties box.

❿ Click the View button, then click the Surname text box.

The message you typed should appear in the Status Bar (see Figure 1.11).

continues

To Add Status Bar Instructions in the Form View   (continued)

Figure 1.11
The Status Bar displays the text entered into the Status Bar Text option of the Properties dialog box.

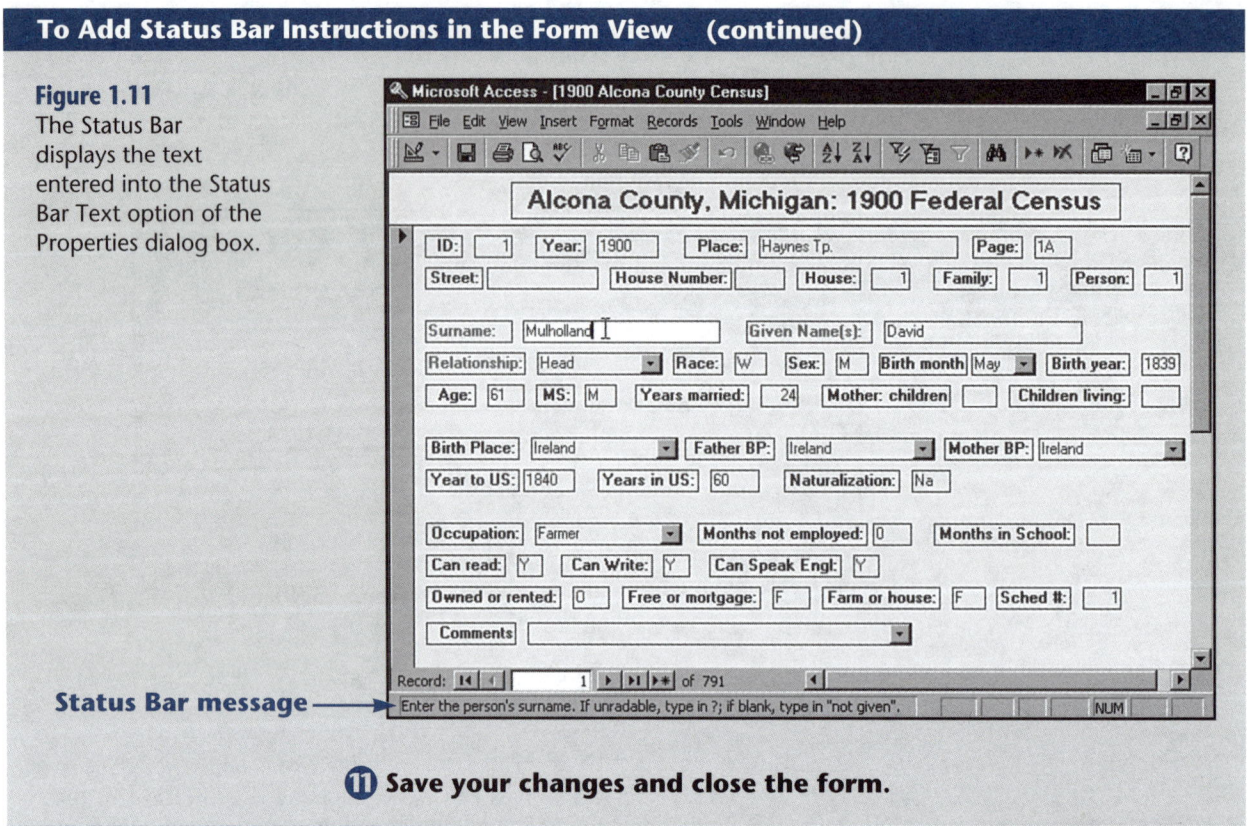

Status Bar message ──────► Enter the person's surname. If unradable, type in ?; if blank, type in "not given".

⑪ **Save your changes and close the form.**

It might seem that the Format Painter could be used to copy Status Bar text. The Format Painter, however, works on those functions that change the appearance of an object. It does not work on any of the customized features that require that text be entered. If you are entering identical (or similar) text to the Status Bar for several fields, type the text into a field, highlight it, then use the copy and paste commands to place the text in the Status Bar Text areas of subsequent fields. (You will have to use the keyboard shortcuts or the right mouse shortcut menu to copy and paste because the menu and toolbar versions of copy and paste apply to the selected object, not the boxes in the properties menu.)

Lesson 5: Adding Customized ControlTips to Controls

ControlTip
A pop-up tip that can be added to a control; similar to a ToolTip.

In Windows 95, when you move the pointer over a button on a toolbar and leave it there for a short time, a ScreenTip appears, telling you what the button does. You can add the same feature to the controls on your forms, which can help make the form easier to use. In a form, these ScreenTips are known as *ControlTips*.

In this lesson, you add ControlTips to augment the Status Bar messages you created in Lesson 4. You will also use a ControlTip to tell the user how to change a default value.

To Add Customized ControlTips to Controls

1 **Highlight the 1900 Alcona County Census form, click the Design button, and maximize the form, if necessary.**

2 **Right-click the Surname text control box.**

A shortcut menu appears.

3 **Choose Properties from the shortcut menu.**

4 **Click the Other tab.**

5 **Click the ControlTip Text box.**

6 **Type in the following text:**

> Do not leave this blank. Check the Status Bar on the bottom of the screen for further instructions.

This is the text that will appear in the ControlTip when the pointer is moved over the Surname field. The Properties box has been widened to display the entire text of the ControlTip (see Figure 1.12).

Figure 1.12
Whatever is typed into the ControlTip Text box will appear when the pointer is held over the field.

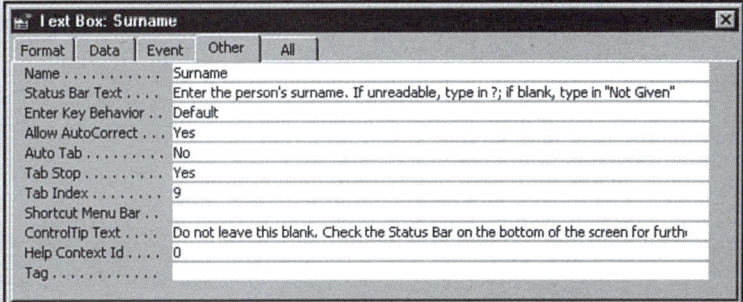

7 **Click the Given Name(s) text box. Locate the ControlTip Text box in the Properties box and enter the same message.**

8 **Repeat step 7 to place the identical text in the ControlTip Text box of the Relationship text control box.**

In each case, the ControlTip tells the user how to find more information. The same procedure can be used to give instructions for anticipated problems. In this database, for example, the Place field has a default value. As the user moves from township to township, this default value has to be changed.

9 **Repeat step 7 for the Place field, but enter the following text in the ControlTip Text area:**

> To change the Place default value, close this form and move to the Tables tab. Select the 1900 Alcona County Census table and click the Design button. Select the Place field, then type the new Default Value in the Field Properties area.

There is a limit of about 200 characters for a ControlTip message. This message is about the maximum size.

continues

To Add Customized ControlTips to Controls (continued)

⑩ **Close the Properties dialog box.**

⑪ **Click the View button. Click the Surname field and leave the pointer over the Surname field.**

Look at the ControlTip and the Status Bar (the cursor is in the Surname field). These types of messages can be very helpful, especially to a new user (see Figure 1.13).

Figure 1.13
Status Bar and ControlTip messages can be of great help to the new user.

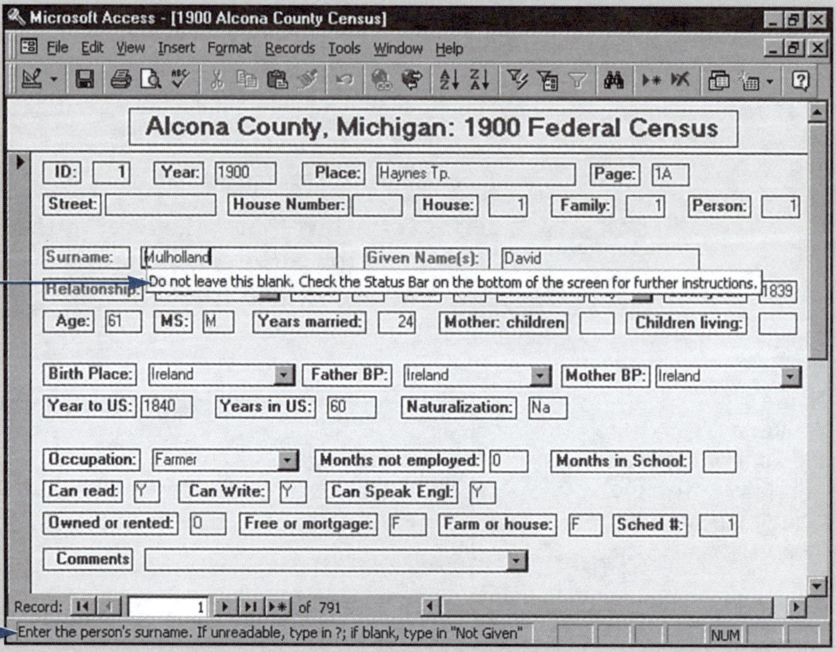

Control Tip

Status Bar message

⑫ **Save your changes and close the form.**

The ControlTip is linked to the pointer while the status bar is linked to the cursor. If you have the cursor in one box and point at another, they will not refer to the same box.

Lesson 6: Customizing a Toolbar with Predefined Buttons

The toolbars associated with the various components of Access are helpful to both the database designer and the end-user. While the end-user will seldom use any of the buttons associated with the various design views, there are always tasks that can be performed using toolbars, such as sorting, filtering, and printing. There are more buttons available than are shown in the default toolbars. These buttons can be added to toolbars, and unused buttons can be removed.

Datasheet View
A Form View that is similar to the Table View. It displays data in a row and column format.

When entering information like that in the Federal Census database, the user must often look at several records at once to see previous entries. This can be done by changing to the form's *Datasheet View*. In this lesson you will remove unused buttons and add buttons to make it easy for the user to toggle between the Form View and the Datasheet View.

To Customize a Toolbar with Predefined Buttons

1 **Highlight the 1900 Alcona County Census form, click the Open button, and maximize the form if necessary.**

2 **Right-click on the Form View toolbar.**

A shortcut menu appears.

3 **Choose Customize from the shortcut menu.**

The Customize dialog box appears, showing tabs for three sections: Tool**b**ars, **C**ommands, and **O**ptions (see Figure 1.14).

Figure 1.14
The Customize dialog box has three sections. The Tool**b**ars section displays existing toolbars.

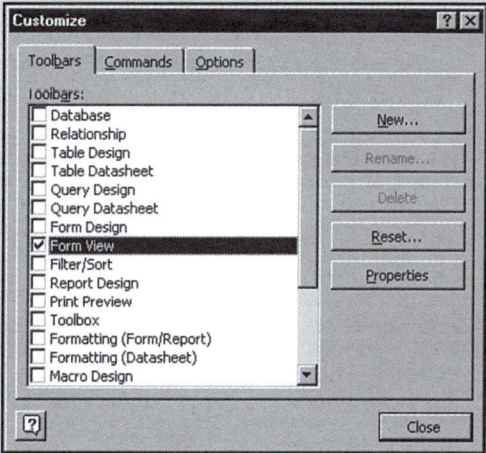

4 **Scroll down the list of toolbars and click the checkbox for the Utility 1 toolbar.**

This toolbar is normally empty and may be used to create a customized toolbar. As soon as you check the box, an extra toolbar will be added (see Figure 1.15).

continues

To Customize a Toolbar with Predefined Buttons   (continued)

Figure 1.15
The Utility 1 toolbar will be added as soon as its box is checked.

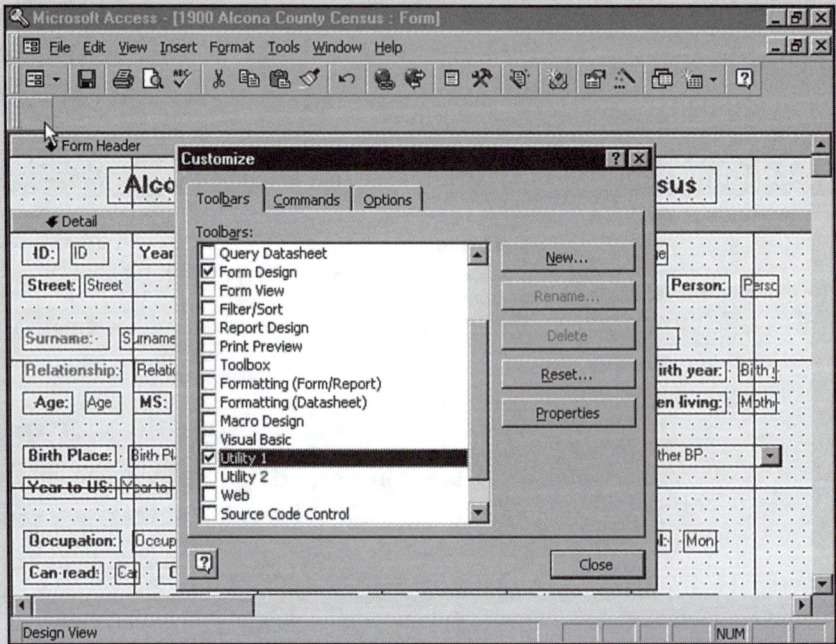

5 **Click on the Commands tab.**

There are many buttons that may be added to the toolbar. They are grouped by the categories displayed on the left and individual buttons are shown on the right.

6 **Click on Records in the Categories section.**

A list of commands that are useful for dealing with records is displayed.

7 **Click on the Filter Excluding Selection command and drag it up to the new Utility 1 menu (see Figure 1.16).**

Figure 1.16
When adding a button to the toolbar, a small button appears to be attached to the pointer arrow.

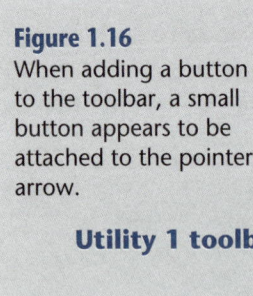

Utility 1 toolbar

Insert command pointer

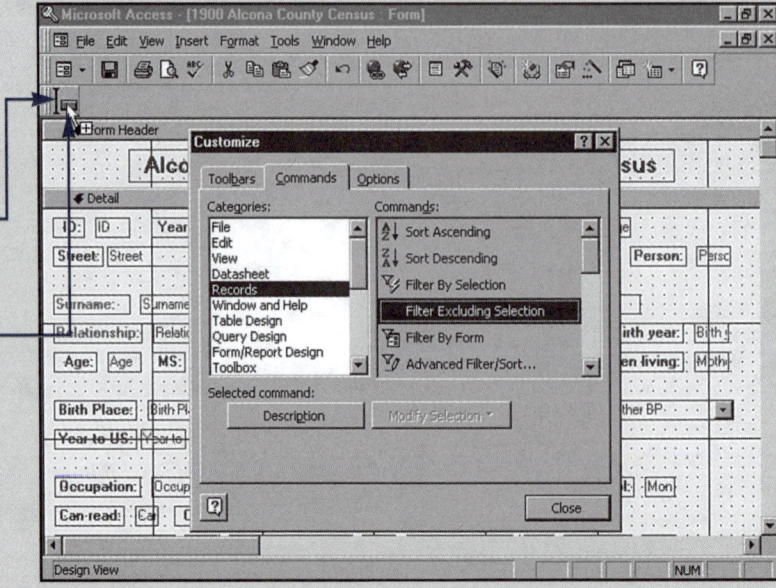

8 Release the mouse button.

The command is added to the toolbar.

9 Scroll down the list of Records commands to the Delete Record command. Drag it onto the Utility 1 toolbar to the right of the first command.

You have now added two buttons to the Utility 1 toolbar. Next we will add two more buttons and separate them from the first two on the toolbar.

10 Click the Form/Report Design category. Drag the Tab Order command to the toolbar and place it to the right of the Delete Record button.

You now have three buttons on the Utility 1 toolbar. In the next step you will create a separation mark on the toolbar that is useful for visually grouping similar buttons. In this case the first two buttons are used to manage records while the next two can be used when designing forms.

11 Click on the Tab Order button that you just placed on the toolbar and drag the pointer so that the small box attached to its end is about half off the button to the right. Release the mouse button.

This will move the button to the right and insert a vertical separating bar (see Figure 1.17).

Figure 1.17
Dragging the button slightly to the right will insert a vertical bar on the toolbar that may be used to visually separate groups of buttons.

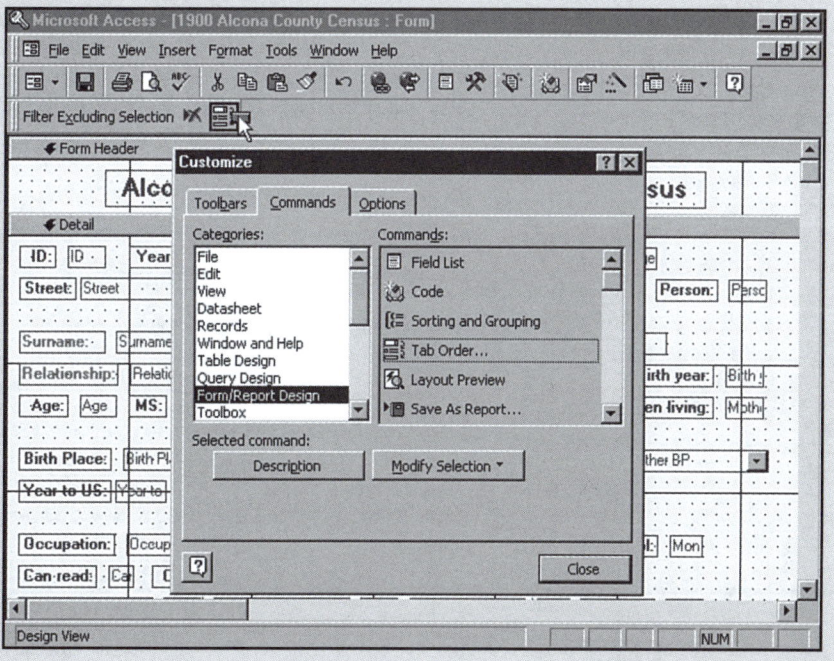

12 Drag and drop the Layout Preview and Ruler commands to the toolbar. Place them to the right of the Tab Order button you just added.

continues

To Customize a Toolbar with Predefined Buttons   (continued)

You will have to scroll down the list of commands to find the Ruler command. Your Utility 1 toolbar should look like Figure 1.18.

Figure 1.18
The Utility 1 toolbar has had five buttons added and separated into two groups.

Buttons added to the toolbar

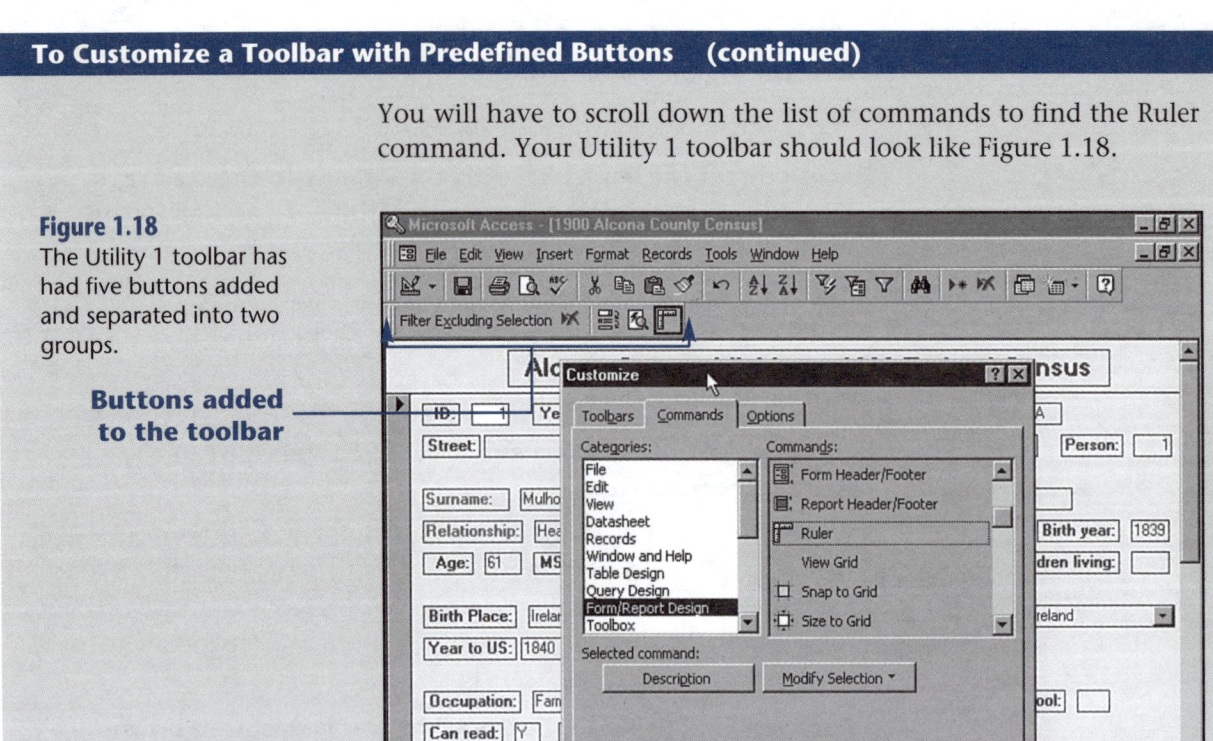

You will also need to know how to remove buttons from the toolbar. When the Customize dialog box is open, they may be removed by dragging them from the toolbar.

⑬ **Click and drag the Layout Preview button from the toolbar to any part of the screen below the toolbar.**

The button will be removed from the toolbar but still exists in the list of commands and may be placed on the toolbar again using the previously described method above.

⑭ **Close the Customize dialog box.**

⑮ **Click the View button to switch to the Design View.**

⑯ **Click the Ruler button to toggle the ruler on or off.**

The two buttons on the left of the toolbar that manage records are not active in the Design View. They can be used in the Form View.

⑰ **Close the form. Leave the database open for use in the next lesson.**

You can create additional toolbars by opening the Customize dialog box and clicking the **N**ew button on the Tool**b**ars section. You can also choose the name of the toolbar.

The toolbars are part of the Access interface, not one particular database. When you change the toolbars, it will affect anyone else who will be using the application. Do not change the standard toolbars unless you have the permission of other users or it is your personal machine.

Lesson 7: Adding a Button to a Toolbar to Run a Macro

In Lesson 6, you learned how to add predefined Access buttons to a toolbar. You can add buttons to a toolbar to run macros you have created.

In this lesson, you create a button to run a Print Preview macro, and you will learn how to customize the button design.

To Add a Button to a Toolbar to Run a Macro

❶ Select the 1900 Alcona County Census form, click the <u>O</u>pen button, and maximize the form, if necessary.

❷ Right-click on the Utility 1 toolbar.

A shortcut menu appears.

❸ Choose Customize from the shortcut menu.

The Customize dialog box appears.

❹ Click the <u>C</u>ommands tab, if necessary, then scroll to the bottom of the list of Categories and click All Macros.

All of the macros in the database (in this case, just the one created for this lesson) are displayed in the Commands area (see Figure 1.19). This macro was created to show a print preview of the main report of this database, not to show a print preview of the form.

Figure 1.19
Any macro in a database can be attached to a customized button.

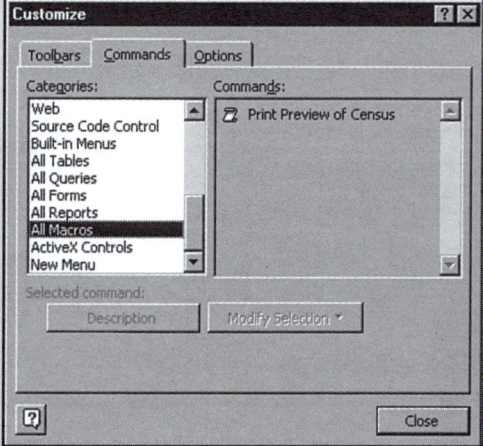

❺ Drag the Print Preview of Census macro to the Utility 1 toolbar, and drop it just to the right of the Ruler command.

A new Macro button is added to the toolbar.

❻ Drag the Print Preview of Census button slightly to the right and release it to insert a vertical separator.

If you accidentally move the button too far, it will be removed from the toolbar. Just repeat step 5 to replace it.

continues

To Add a Button to a Tooolbar to Run a Macro   (continued)

❼ Close the Customize dialog box and move the pointer to the new button.

After a short time, a ScreenTip will appear for this button (see Figure 1.20).

Figure 1.20
The newly created Print Preview button comes with its own ToolTip.

New Macro button

New Macro button ToolTip

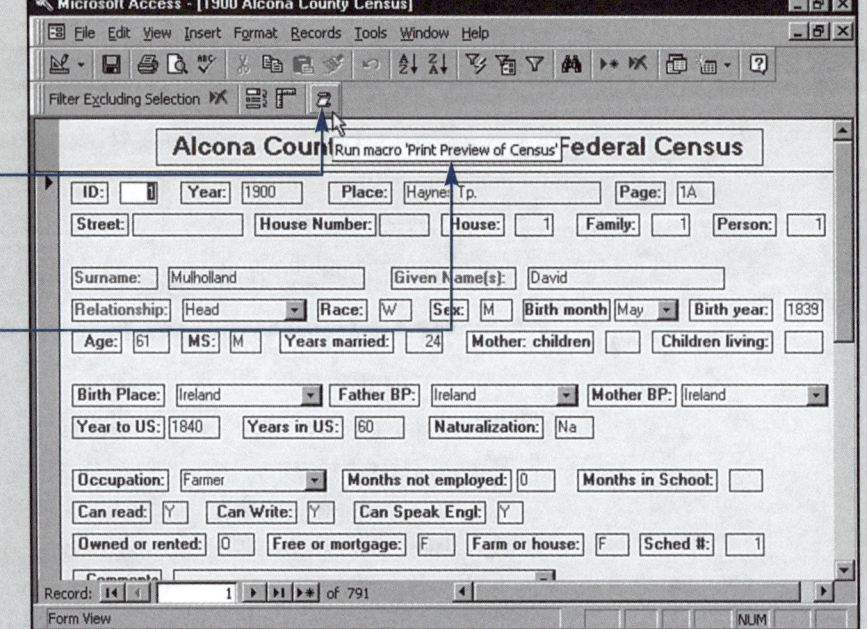

❽ Click the button you just added.

The Print Preview appears (see Figure 1.21).

Figure 1.21
The new Print Preview button gives you a pre-view of your Report while you are still in the Form View.

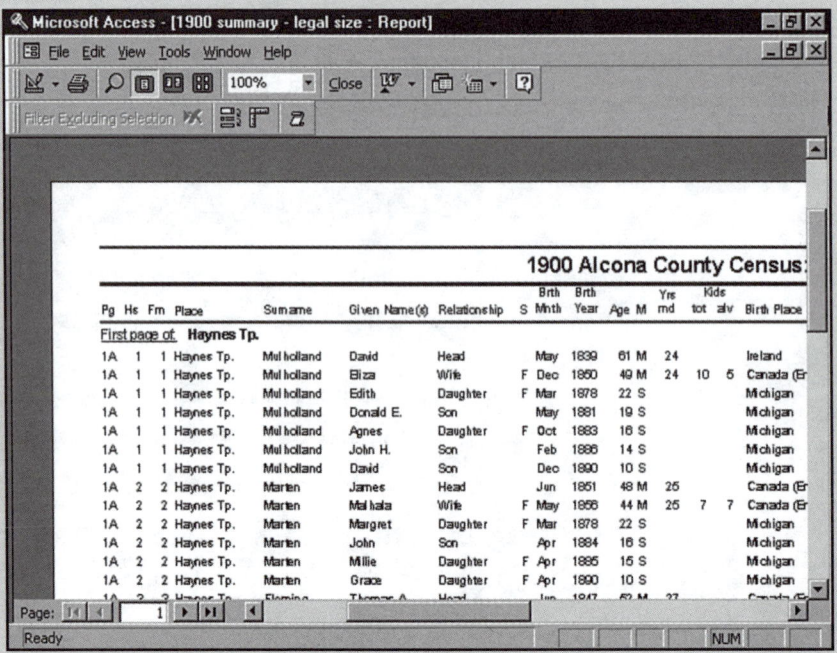

❾ Close the Print Preview.

The program takes you back to the Form View.

Now that you have added a new button, you can customize the look of the button.

❿ Right-click the Utility 1 toolbar.

A shortcut menu appears.

⓫ Choose Customize from the shortcut menu.

The Customize dialog box appears.

⓬ Right-click the Print Preview macro button you just added to the toolbar.

A new shortcut menu appears.

⓭ Select Change Button Image.

A sub-menu with 42 button design choices appears (see Figure 1.22).

Figure 1.22
This shortcut menu enables you to choose a predesigned icon or create your own.

New button image

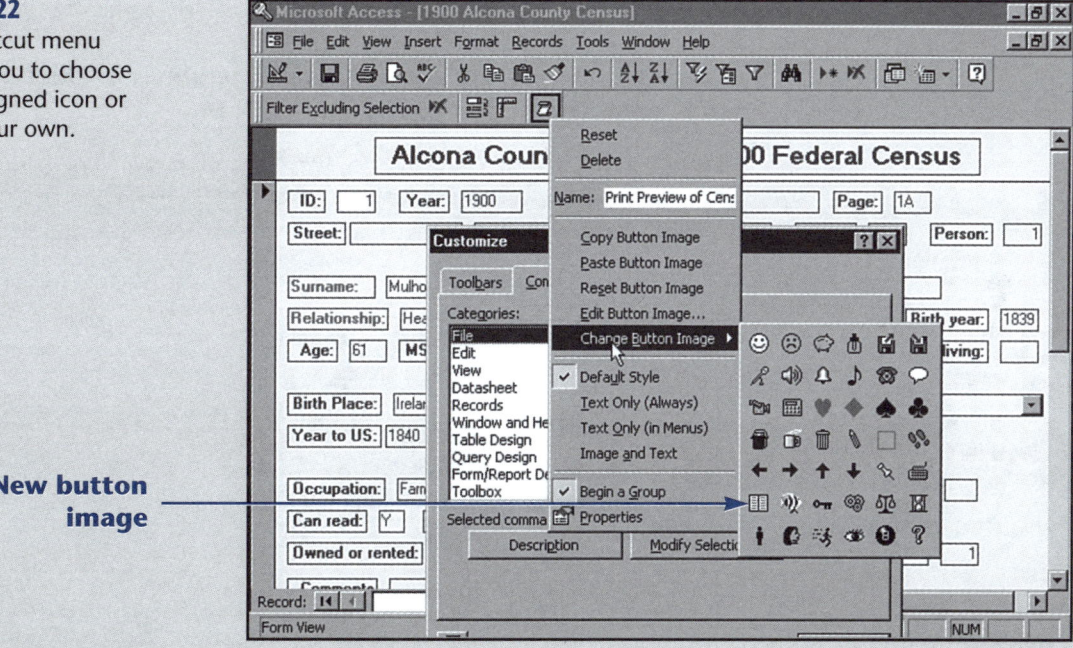

⓮ Select the icon that looks like a miniature report and click it.

Notice that when you click the image, the icon changes in the toolbar, even though the Customize window is still open.

⓯ Right-click the new button and choose Edit Button Image from the shortcut menu.

The Button Editor appears (see Figure 1.23). You can now edit each pixel in the button. You can erase everything in the Picture window and start from scratch, or you can simply change the colors of the existing icon.

continues

To Add a Button to a Tooolbar to Run a Macro   (continued)

Figure 1.23
The Button Editor enables you to redesign the figure on a button.

16 **Click on the bright red color in the Colors section, then move the pointer to the Picture area and click one of the black pixels in the centerline that separates the two pages of the report image.**

The pixel turns red.

17 **Carefully click and drag the rest of the pixels in the centerline to change their color to red and click OK.**

You can click and drag across several pixels to save time. If you change a pixel you did not want to change, click the Cancel button and start over. The centerline of the report icon should now be red (see Figure 1.24).

Figure 1.24
The Button Editor has been used to change the icon used for pre-viewing reports with a macro.

Red centerline ——

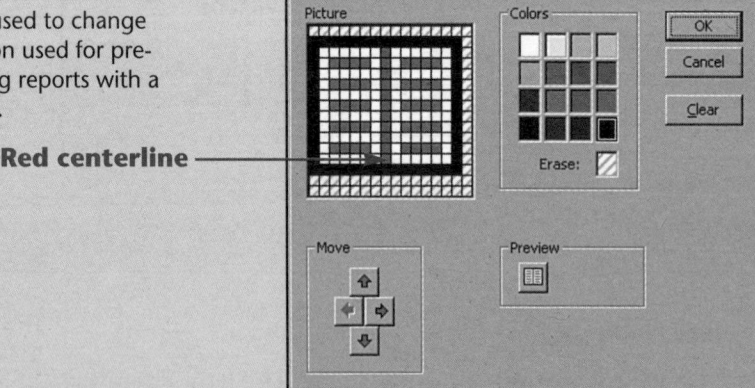

18 **Close the Customize dialog box.**

Look at your new Print Preview button. It now has a red line separating the pages.

19 **If you are sharing this application with others and do not have permission to change the toolbars, you should reset this toolbar to its original condition. Right-click on the toolbar, click Customize, select the Utility 1 toolbar and click on the Reset button.**

20 **Right-click on the Utility 1 toolbar. Click on the Utility 1 check box to deselect it.**

The toolbar will no longer appear on the screen. It may be turned on again by using the **V**iew and **T**oolbars choices from the menu bar.

21 **Close the form.**

22 **Close the Federal Census database and close Access.**

Project Summary

To	Do This
Change the color of text, backgrounds, and borders using buttons	In the Form Design View, select the control or label you want to format. Use the Font/Fore Color button to change the foreground (usually text) color; the Fill/Back Color button to change the background color; or the Line/Border Color button to change the border color.
Copy formats between individual controls and format many controls at once	In the Form Design View, select the control or label that is formatted the way you want it. Click the Format Painter button, then click the control you want to copy the format to. Double-clicking the Format Painter button keeps it active until you click the Format Painter button again.
Change colors and align text using Properties	In the Form Design View, click the right mouse button on the control or label you want to format. Choose Properties, then go to the Format tab. In the Font/Fore Color, Fill/Back Color, or Line/Border Color area, click the Build button to choose a color. Choose alignment from the Text Align drop-down box.
Add Status Bar instructions in the Form View	In the Form Design View, click the right mouse button on the control and choose Properties from the shortcut menu. Click the Other tab, then type in the desired Status Bar text in the Status Bar Text box.
Add customized ControlTips to controls	In the Form Design View, click the right mouse button on the control and choose Properties from the shortcut menu. Click the Other tab, then type in the desired ControlTip text in the ControlTip Text box.
Customize a toolbar with pre-defined buttons	Click the right mouse button on the toolbar, then choose Customize from the shortcut menu. Select the category containing the desired button(s). Drag the button to the toolbar and drop it. To remove a button, drag it off the toolbar and let go.

continues

continued

To	Do This
Add buttons to a toolbar to run a macro	Click the right mouse button on the toolbar, then choose Customize from the shortcut menu. Select the All Macros category and select the desired macro. Drag the macro name to the toolbar.

Checking Your Skills

True/False

For each of the following statements, check *T* or *F* to indicate whether the statement is true or false.

__T __F   **1.** Double-clicking the Format Painter button takes you to the Format Painter dialog box.

__T __F   **2.** One reason you might use the Properties dialog box to change a color is that this method gives you more color options than the toolbar button does.

__T __F   **3.** If you customize a toolbar, the changes will only appear when you use the database that was open when the toolbar was customized.

__T __F   **4.** To create a toolbar button for a macro, go to the Customize dialog box and drag the macro name to the toolbar.

__T __F   **5.** The number of characters you can put in a ControlTip is unlimited.

Multiple Choice

Circle the letter of the correct answer for each of the following questions.

1. To change the color of text in a form, use the _____ button.

   a. Fill/Back Color

   b. Line/Border Color

   c. Font/Fore Color

   d. Special Effects

2. The Status Bar Text option is found in the _____ tab of the Properties dialog box.

   a. Format

   b. Data

   c. Event

   d. Other

3. To remove a button from a toolbar, go to the Customize dialog box, then:

   a. drag the button below the toolbar and let go

   b. select the button, then press the Del key

   c. select the button, then choose Cut from the Edit menu

   d. click the button with the right mouse button and select Remove from the shortcut menu

4. You can change the color of each pixel in a button icon in the:

   a. Button Editor

   b. Button Builder

   c. Drawing toolbar

   d. Tools menu

5. A ControlTip is activated when you:

   a. place the cursor in the appropriate control

   b. place the mouse pointer over the appropriate control for a short time

   c. click the field with the left mouse button

   d. click the field with the right mouse button

Completion

In the blank provided, write the correct answer for each of the following statements.

1. Most data entry is done in the _____ View.

2. An easy way to copy the format from one control to another is to use the _____ button.

3. A(n) _____ is a pop-up help feature that is similar to a ToolTip.

4. To create a gap when customizing buttons, drag the button to the _____ about $\frac{1}{8}$".

5. You can add helpful information to the _____ at the bottom of the screen.

Applying Your Skills

At the end of each project in *Access 97 Essentials Level III*, you learn how to apply your Access skills to various situations. The following exercises help you practice the skills you have learned in this project. Take a few minutes to work through these exercises now.

Exploring Additional Formatting Options

In the first three lessons of this project, you learned how to change several of the characteristics in the form, such as text foreground and background color. There are many more features that can be changed.

To Explore Additional Formatting Options

1. Open the **Federal Census** database, and move to the Design View of the 1900 Alcona County Census form.

2. Change the color of the title to a bright red to match the required fields.

3. With the title still selected, go to the Properties dialog box, click the Format tab, and change the Special Effect format to Shadowed.

4. Change the Special Effect for all of the controls in the Detail area to either Raised, Sunken, or Etched (choose your favorite).

5. Italicize the title.

6. Change the text color of the three required fields to match the other text (dark blue), then set them off by changing the background color of the label control boxes for those fields only. Try several colors to come up with a readable background/foreground combination.

Exploring Additional Options for Added Help

The database you are using in this Project is one used to transcribe historical documents. Although many of the census-takers were very bad spellers, historical transcriptions must always be taken exactly as written. It is always a temptation to correct an obvious misspelling in a primary source, particularly for something like a state or country name. This makes the Access Status Bar text options very useful for constantly reminding the transcriber NOT to make changes.

To Explore Additional Options for Added Help

1. Open the **Federal Census** database, and move to the Design View of the Alcona County Census form.

2. Go to the Properties dialog box and add the following text to the Status Bar for the Birthplace field:

        Type the birthplace exactly as written; include spelling
        errors.

3. Go to the Properties dialog box and add the following text to the Status bar for the Naturalization field:

    `Na - Naturalized; Pa - Permanent Alien`

4. Add the following ControlTip to the Year to US field:

    `Year to US and Years in US sometimes don't match. If not, mention the discrepancy in the Comments area.`

Exploring Additional Options for Toolbars

The ability to customize toolbars means that you can make an Access database more user-friendly for the end-user. There are many buttons that can be added to the various toolbars, all of which can be helpful in various situations. Customized buttons with macros attached can also be very useful. These techniques, along with the capability to customize access to the database (see Project 6), will give you a great deal of control over the databases you create.

To Explore Additional Options for Toolbars

1. Add the View Grid button to the Utility 1 toolbar. Hint: It can be found in the Form & Report Design category of the Customize dialog box.

2. Use the Button Editor to create your own design for the button you just added.

3. Reset the Utility 1 toolbar you changed in this exercise if you do not have permission to change toolbars.

Project

2

Managing Changing Data

Maintaining your database by using update techniques

In this Project, you learn how to:

➤ Update Tables by Substituting New Text

➤ Update Tables Based on Selected Portions of Fields

➤ Update Tables with a Calculated Expression

➤ Update a Table Based on Values in Another Table

➤ Update Linked Tables Automatically

Why Would I Do This?

n this project, you learn how to make changes to groups of records in an existing table. You use an update query to replace text fields or parts of text fields. This is useful when a new area code is created or a part number is changed.

You also learn how to use calculations to update fields. This feature is useful if you intend to raise prices by a certain percentage for an entire line of products.

In some cases, you may have a table that has new values for many individual records in another table. In this project you learn how to update one table based on the contents of another.

Join
To form a relationship between two tables.

When you have tables that are joined, you have the option of causing changes in one table to be automatically made in related tables. Changes in customer identification numbers in one table could be automatically updated in a table of customer purchases, or those purchases could be automatically deleted if the customer's name was deleted.

Lesson 1: Updating Tables by Substituting New Text

The first thing you need to do is to copy a database file included with this book. Once you copy and rename the file, you are ready to complete the first lesson.

To Open the Cleaning Database

1 Make a copy the student data file Proj0201.

2 Rename the copy Cleaning.

Include the .mdb extension only if you can see the extension on the Proj0201 file.

3 Launch Access 97.

4 Open the Cleaning database.

The database window should now be open to the Tables area (see Figure 2.1). Keep the database open for the next exercise.

Figure 2.1
The database window displays the Tables area of the Cleaning database.

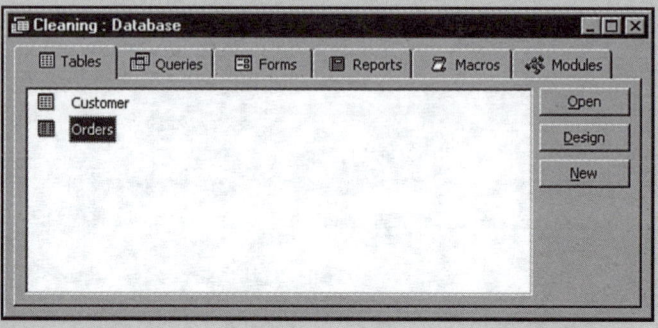

If you need to change the entire contents of a text field, such as a company's name that occurs in many records, you can use an update query.

In this example, a company that provides industrial cleaning supplies has a database that tracks its customers and their orders. We know that one of their customers, AMIX Corp., has spun off its Michigan offices into a new company named MichIx. All of the addresses for AMIX Corp. contacts in Michigan need to be changed.

To Update a Table by Substituting New Text

1 Click the Queries Tab.

The list of existing queries is displayed.

2 Click the New button.

The New Query dialog box appears.

3 In the list box, select Design View, and then click OK.

The Show Table dialog box appears (see Figure 2.2).

Figure 2.2
The Select Query design window and Show Table dialog box are displayed.

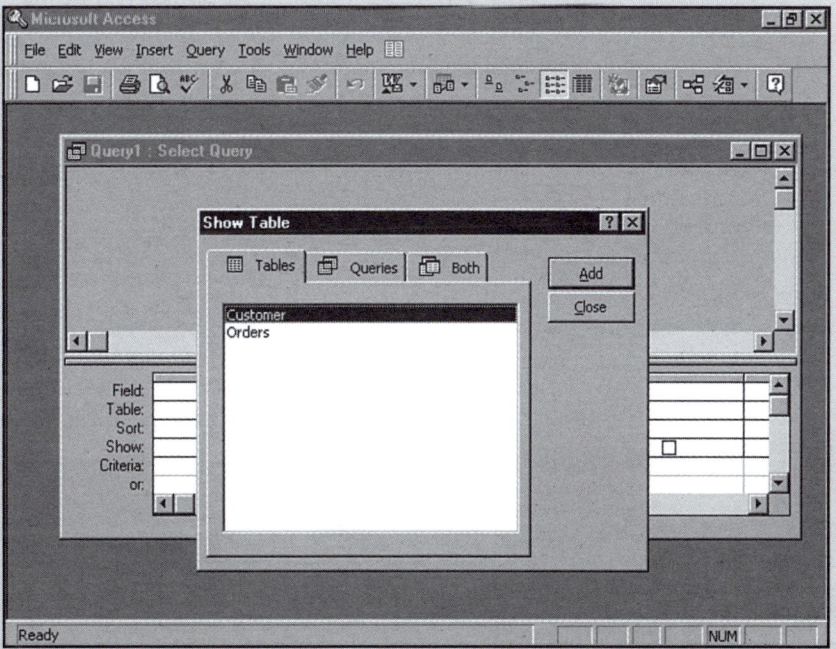

4 Click the Customer table name and then click Add.

The Customer table is added to the query design window.

5 Click Close.

The Show Table dialog box closes and the query design window is shown with the Customer table (see Figure 2.3).

continues

To Update a Table by Substituting New Text   (continued)

Figure 2.3
The Query design window is shown with the Customer table added.

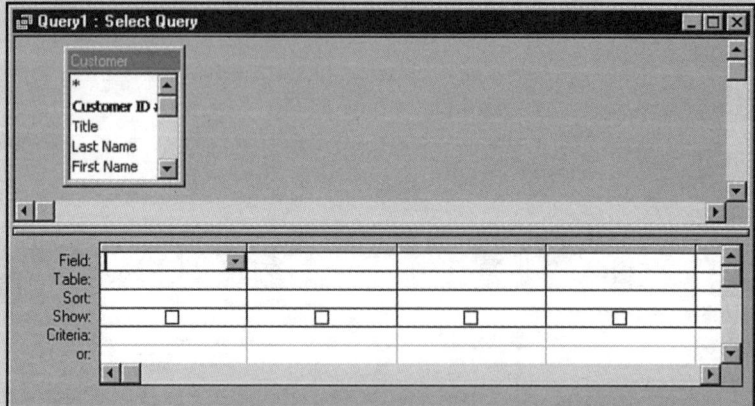

---

6 **Drag the Last Name, Company, and State fields (in that order) to the query design.**

Remember to drag each field from the Field List to the Field: row in the Query Design table.

The Last Name, Company, and State fields appear in the first three columns of the query design (see Figure 2.4). You now want to set up the query to find all of the companies named AMIX Corp. in Michigan.

Figure 2.4
The Query design is shown with the Last Name, Company, and State fields chosen.

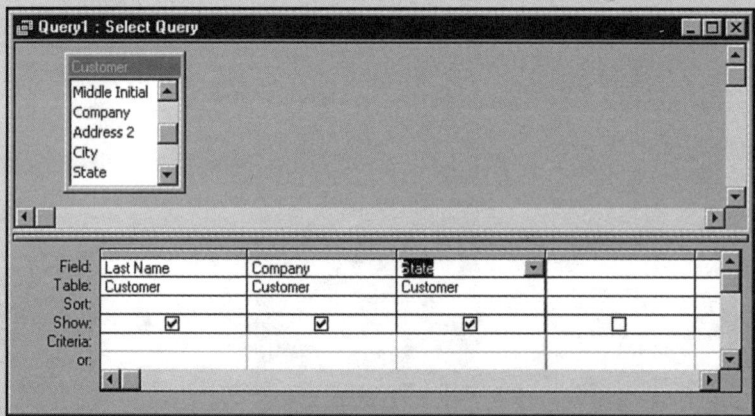

---

7 **Enter the company name AMIX Corp. in the criteria box in the Company column.**

Remember to include the period following the abbreviation for corporation.

8 **Enter MI in the Criteria box in the State column.**

The criteria for company and state should identify all of the company's contacts in Michigan (see Figure 2.5).

Figure 2.5
The Criteria for identifying the AMIX Corporation's Michigan contacts have been entered.

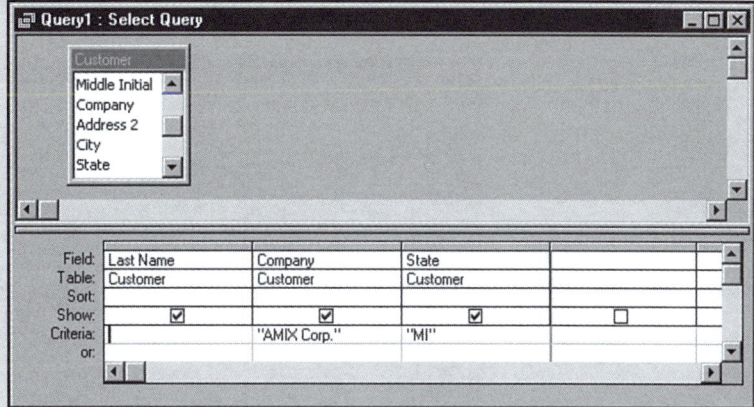

 9 **Click the View button to see if you have correctly identified the two Michigan contacts.**

We only included three of the fields in this query for simplicity. The two Michigan contacts are shown (see Figure 2.6).

Figure 2.6
The two Michigan addresses are shown.

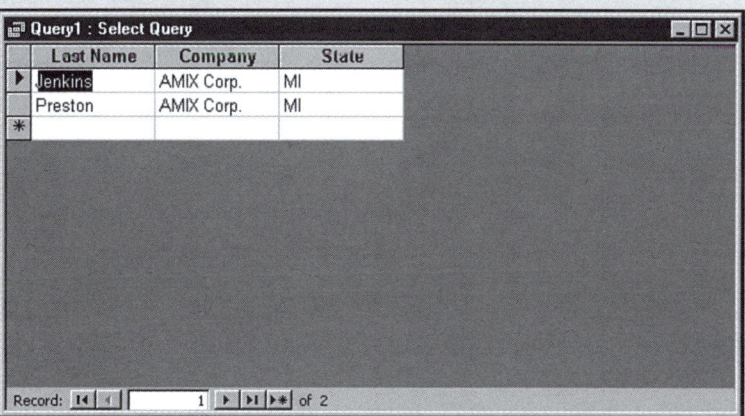

 10 **Click the View button again to return to the query design.**

 11 **Click the down-arrow on the Query Type button.**

A drop-down menu appears (see Figure 2.7).

continues

To Update a Table by Substituting New Text   (continued)

Figure 2.7
The drop-down menu
of query types.

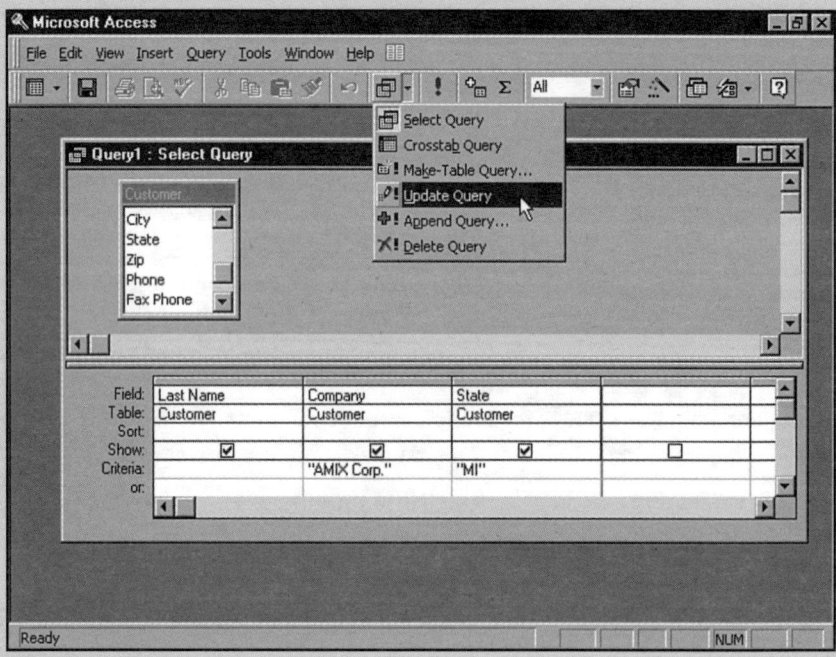

⓬ **Click the Update Query option.**

Notice that the Sort and Show rows have been replaced by the Update To row in the query design (see Figure 2.8).

Figure 2.8
The Query design win-
dow has an Update To
row added.

The Update To row ——→

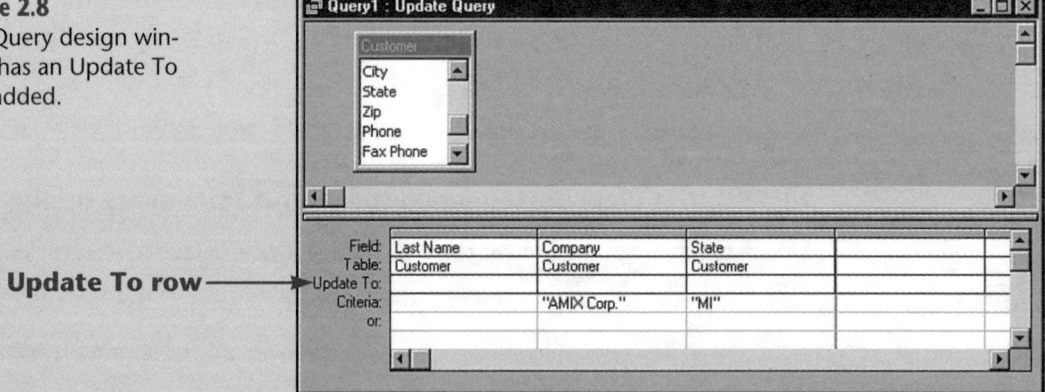

⓭ **Enter the new regional company name, MichIx, in the Update To box of the Company column.**

The new company name is placed in the Update To box in the Company column (see Figure 2.9).

Figure 2.9
The new company name appears in the Update To box.

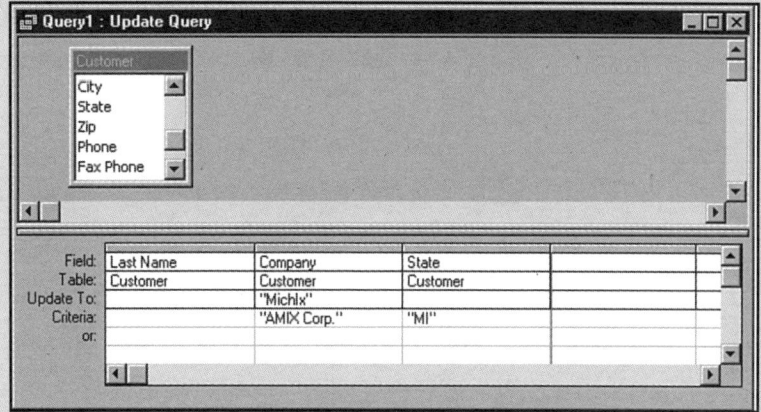

You are now ready to run the Update query to change the AMIX Corp. records in Michigan to MichIx.

⑭ **Click the Run button on the toolbar.**

A warning message is displayed, advising that you are about to make an irreversible change.

⑮ **Click Yes to update the records.**

The company names are changed. Make sure that you have made recent backups of your tables before you use this procedure on important tables.

⑯ **Close the query and save it with the name** Update Company Name.

⑰ **Click the Tables tab and open the Customer table.**

Scroll through the records to confirm that the two customer contacts in Michigan have had their company name changed from AMIX Corp. to MichIx.

⑱ **Close the table.**

Leave the database open for use in the next lesson.

Lesson 2: Updating Tables Based on Selected Portions of Fields

Some updates are based upon a portion of a field. When the telephone company creates a new area code, it will assign some of the exchanges from the old area to the new one. To automatically update your database, you may need to determine if part of the field matches a criteria and then change only part of the data in each field.

In this lesson you learn how to use expressions for selecting the left, middle, and right portions of a string of text characters and for using them in an update query.

To Update Tables Based on Selected Portions of Fields

1 In the Cleaning database, click on the Queries tab and click New.

The New Query dialog box appears.

2 In the list box, select Design View, and then click OK.

The Show Table dialog box appears.

3 Click the Customer table, and then click the Add button.

The Customer table is added to the query design.

4 Click Close.

5 Drag the Last Name, Company, City, and Phone fields to the query design table.

The query design table now has four fields (see Figure 2.10).

Figure 2.10
The Query Design View shows the phone field and three other fields.

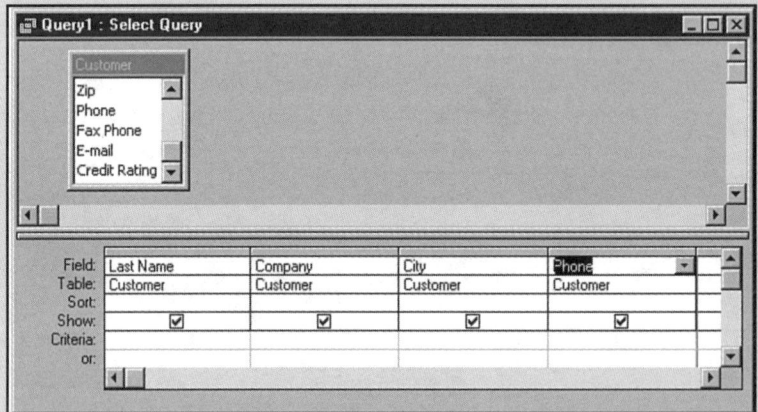

6 Enter the following expression in the Criteria box for the Phone field:

```
Left([Phone],9)="(313) 665"
```

The Left expression will extract the characters at the left end of a string of text. In this example, we wanted to identify all those phone numbers in the 313 area code that were also in the 665 exchange. We checked for the first nine characters at the left end of the phone field. Notice that we counted the parentheses and the space.

7 Click the View button to switch to the Datasheet View to confirm that the criteria found the two records that match.

The Datasheet View should show the two matching records (see Figure 2.11). If it does not show any records you have made an error in entering the expression. Make sure the proper brackets are used, and make sure there is a space after the area code.

Figure 2.11
The query has found the records that match the phone number criteria.

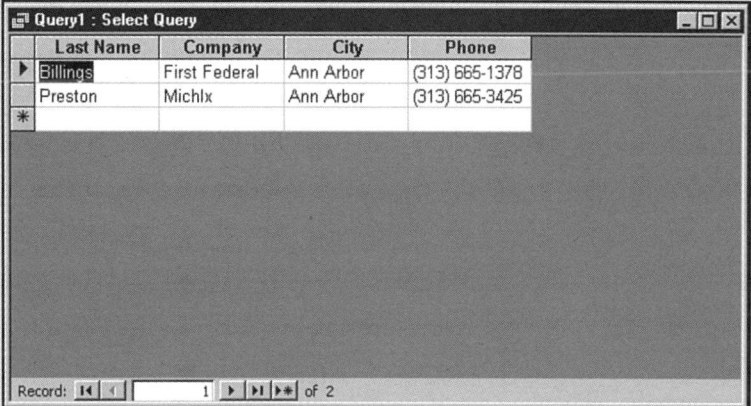

 ❽ Click the View button.

The program returns to the Design View. You will now change the Query Type and add another expression.

 ❾ Click the down-arrow on the Query Type button on the toolbar and select Update Query from the drop-down menu.

❿ Enter the following expression in the Update To box of the Phone field:

`"(311)"+Right([Phone],9)`

The purpose of this expression is to create a new phone number that begins with the new area code and the old exchange and then attaches the nine characters from the right end of the phone number (see Figure 2.12).

Figure 2.12
The Criteria and Update To expressions for replacing the area code for the 665 exchange.

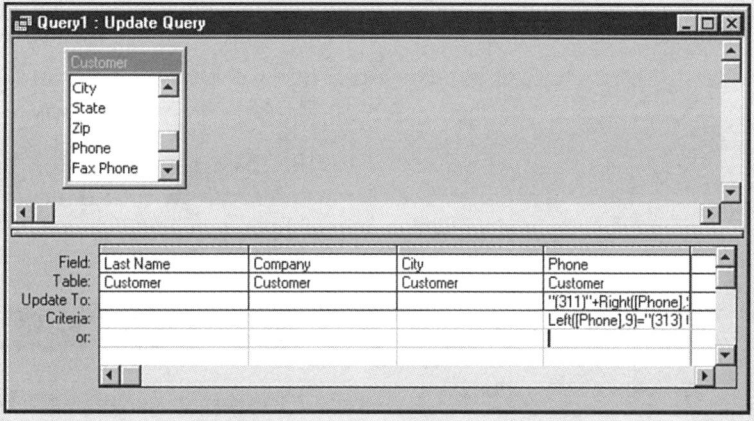

 ⓫ Click the Run button on the toolbar.

A warning message will be displayed, notifying you that you are about to make an irreversible change to two records. If it says that you are about to change more than two records, click No and look for a problem.

⓬ Click Yes to update the records.

The phone numbers will be changed.

continues

To Update Tables based On Selected Portions of Fields   (continued)

Make sure you have made recent backups of your tables before you use this procedure on important tables.

⓭ **Close the query and save it as** Update Area Code.

⓮ **Click the Tables tab and open the Customer table.**

Scroll through the records to confirm that the two phone numbers that were formerly (313) 665, are now (311) 665.

⓯ **Close the table.**

Leave the database open for use in the next lesson.

The Left and Right expressions use character counts based on the actual characters stored in the table. If the table has been designed to use an input mask, the character count will be off. In the example in this lesson, the data was entered into the table with the parenthesis, spaces, and dashes, so they were counted. The phone numbers in the Fax Phone field were entered using an input mask and do not contain the extra characters.

There is a third expression that is similar to Right and Left. The Mid expression selects characters from inside the string of characters. To select the exchange numbers 665 from a phone number in this lesson, you would use the expression Mid([Phone],7,3). It would start at the seventh character and select three characters.

Lesson 3: Updating Tables with a Calculated Expression

Some table updates are based on calculations. Numeric fields can be changed based on algebra-like expressions.

In this lesson, you increase the price on a line of products by 10%, using a calculation. You also learn how to use more than one criterion to determine if a bill is unpaid and if it is overdue.

To Update Tables with a Calculated Expression

❶ **In the Cleaning database, move to the Queries tab and click New.**

❷ **Click Design View and then click OK.**

The Show Table dialog box appears.

❸ **Click the Orders table and then click the Add button.**

The Orders table will be added to the query design.

❹ **Click Close.**

❺ Drag the Order #, Product Description, Unit Price, Date of Purchase, and Date of Payment fields to the query design table, in that order.

The query design table will have five fields (see Figure 2.13).

Figure 2.13
The query design shows the five selected fields.

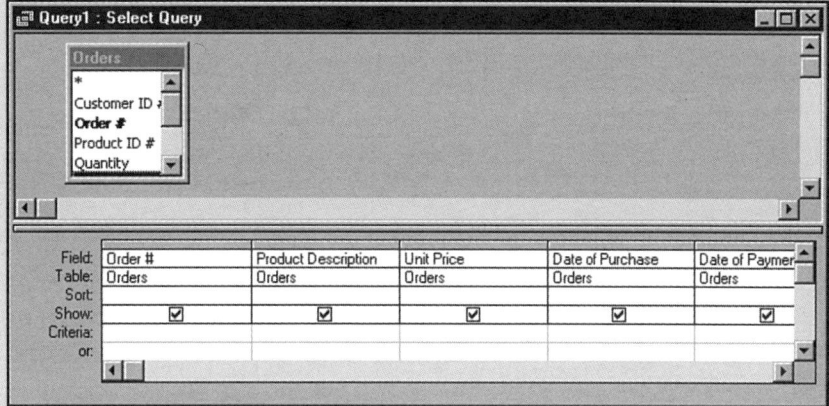

❻ Enter the following expression in the criteria box for the Date of Payment field:

Null
The absence of data—an empty field.

```
Is Null
```

If a field has no entry, it is called a null value. This is not the same as a space or zero.

 ❼ Click the View button to switch to the Datasheet View.

This allows you to confirm that the criteria found the records that have no date for the Date of Payment field.

The Datasheet View should show the thirteen matching records (see Figure 2.14).

Figure 2.14
The query has found the unpaid bills.

Order #	Product Descri	Unit Price	Date of Purcha	Date of Payme
11	Hand Cleaner	$35.00	3/10/96	
12	Polish	$11.50	6/14/96	
14	Hand Cleaner	$35.00	3/22/96	
15	Degreaser	$22.00	1/15/96	
17	Degreaser	$22.00	3/13/96	
18	Hand Cleaner	$35.00	2/14/96	
2	Hand Cleaner	$35.00	2/17/96	
20	Hand Cleaner	$35.00	1/ 4/96	
4	Polish	$11.50	3/12/96	
6	Degreaser	$22.00	3/12/96	
7	Polish	$11.50	2/10/96	
8	Hand Cleaner	$35.00	3/12/96	
9	Degreaser	$22.00	1/24/96	
*		$0.00		

Record: ◄◄ ◄   1   ► ►I ►* of 13

 ❽ Click the View button to return to the Design View.

continues

To Update Tables with a Calculated Expression   (continued)

⑨ Enter the following expression in the criteria box for the Date of Purchase field:

<2/1/96

The computer treats dates as if they were sequential numbers that increase with time. The expression shown above will select dates before February 1, 1996.

If two criteria are on the same line in the query design, they both must be met. In this case, the records selected will be those that have not been paid and were purchased before 2/1/96.

⑩ Click the View button to switch to the Datasheet View.

You can now confirm that the criteria found the records that have no date for the Date of Payment field and were purchased before 2/1/96. The Datasheet View should show the three matching records with order numbers of 15, 20, and 9. (see Figure 2.15).

Figure 2.15
The bills are shown for purchases made before 2/1/96 that have not been paid.

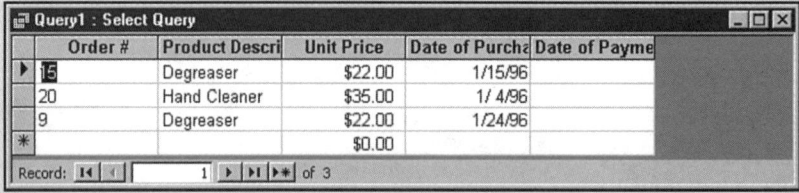

Order #	Product Descri	Unit Price	Date of Purcha	Date of Payme
▶ 15	Degreaser	$22.00	1/15/96	
20	Hand Cleaner	$35.00	1/ 4/96	
9	Degreaser	$22.00	1/24/96	
*		$0.00		

Record: ⏮ ◀ [1] ▶ ▶I ▶* of 3

⑪ Click the View button to return to the Design View.

Notice that the program has added # symbols around the date. If you ever have problems with a complex criteria where the program has not correctly identified a date you entered, enclose the date with # symbols.

⑫ Click the Query Type button on the toolbar and select Update Query from the drop-down menu.

⑬ Enter the following expression in the Update To box of the Unit Price field:

[Unit Price]*1.1

The purpose of this expression is to increase the price of the purchases that have not been paid on time (see Figure 2.16).

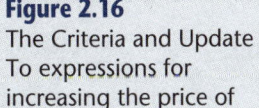

Figure 2.16
The Criteria and Update To expressions for increasing the price of purchases are shown.

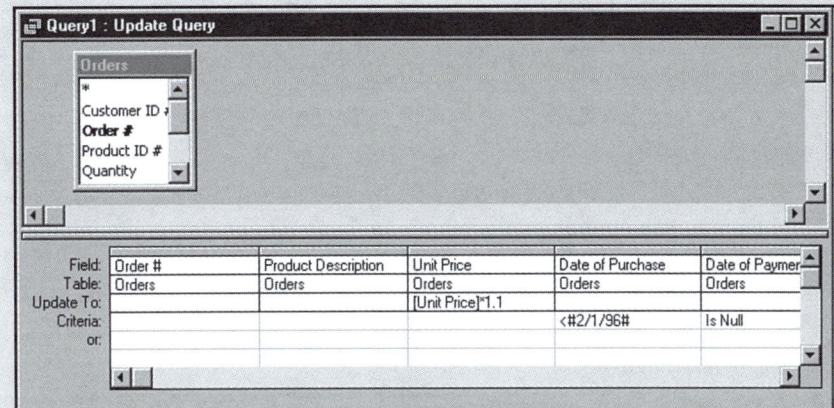

14 Click the Run button on the toolbar.

A warning message will be displayed, notifying you that you are about to update three rows.

15 Click Yes to update the records.

The Unit Price values will be changed. Make sure you have made recent backups of your tables before you use this procedure on important tables.

16 Click on the View button to switch to the Datasheet View.

Notice that the prices have been increased from $22.00 for degreaser to $24.20 and from $35.00 to $38.50.

Do not run the Update Query more than once. It will increase the price each time you run it.

17 Close the query and save it as Increase Price for Late Payment.

18 Close the table and the database.

Lesson 4: Updating a Table Based on Values in Another Table

In some cases, it is convenient to change several values in one table and then apply them to another table. In this lesson, you learn how to update the suggested sale price on a table that lists the stock on hand in a warehouse.

To Update a Table Based on Values in Another Table

1 Make a copy of the student data file Proj0202.

2 Rename the copy Auto Parts.

Include the .mdb extension only if you can see the extension on the Proj0202 file.

3 Open the Auto Parts database.

The database window should now be open to the Tables area (see Figure 2.17).

Figure 2.17
The Tables area of the Auto Parts database is shown.

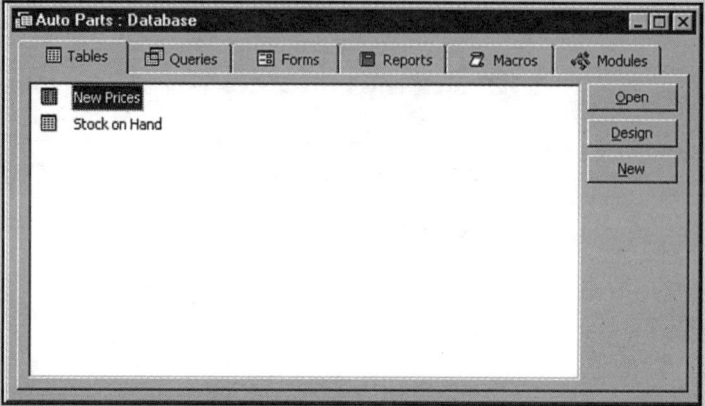

4 Highlight the Stock on Hand table and click Open.

Notice there is a field at the far right to indicate whether a particular lot of parts has been sold.

Close the table.

5 Click the Queries tab and click New.

The New Query dialog box appears.

6 Click Design View and click OK.

The query design window appears with the Show Table dialog box in front of it.

7 Click the New Prices table name and click the Add button.

8 Click the Stock on Hand table name and click the Add button.

9 Click the Close button.

The query design window will display the two tables joined by the Code field (see Figure 2.18).

Figure 2.18
The query design shows two tables joined by the Code field.

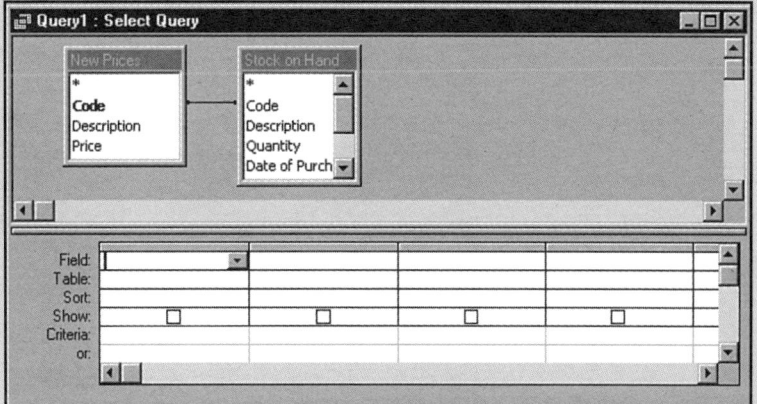

⑩ Scroll down the list of fields in the Stock on Hand table. Drag the Suggested Price and Sold fields to the query design table below.

The query design will show the Suggested Price and Sold fields (see Figure 2.19).

Figure 2.19
The Suggested Price and Sold fields have been added to the query from the Stock on Hand table.

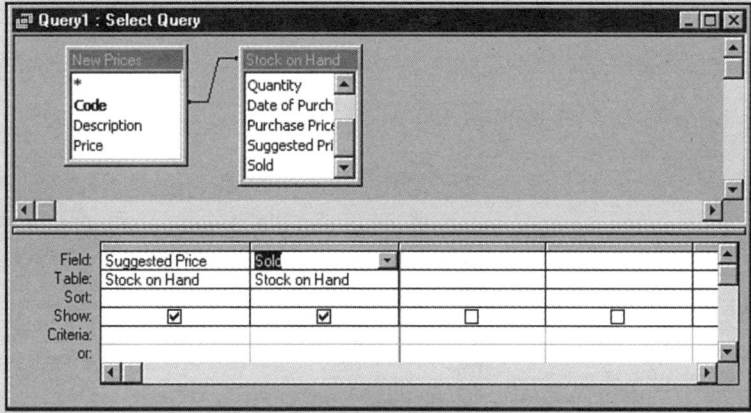

⑪ Click the Query Type button on the toolbar and click Update Query.

A row will be added to the query design for update expressions.

⑫ Enter the following expression in the Update To box in the Suggested Price column:

`[New Prices].[Price]`

The first part of the expression identifies the table, and the second part identifies the field in that table. Notice the names are enclosed in square brackets and separated by a period.

This update will replace the values in the Stock on Hand table with those found in the New Prices table.

⑬ Enter the following text in the Criteria box in the Sold column:

No

To Update a Table Based on Values in Another Table   (continued)

This condition will restrict the price changes to those items not yet sold (see Figure 2.20).

Figure 2.20
The update and criteria for changing the prices on the unsold inventory have been added.

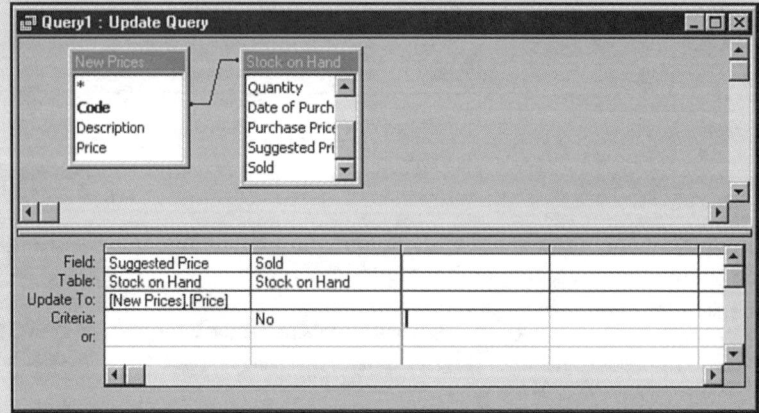

14 **Close the query and name it** Update Prices.

15 **Click the Tables tab of the database. Open the Stock on Hand table.**

Notice that the first lot of 45 axles has already been sold at $300 (see Figure 2.21).

Figure 2.21
The Stock on Hand table is shown before the prices have been updated.

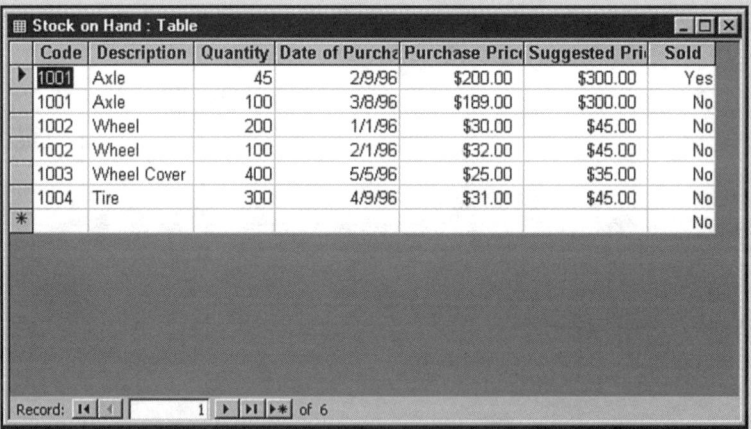

16 **Close the Stock on Hand table and open the New Prices table.**

Notice that the new price for an axle will be $285 for those that are still in stock.

17 **Close the New Prices table and Click the Queries tab.**

The Update Prices query is highlighted, since it is the only query in the database.

18 **Click Open.**

This type of query is an action query that acts like a program. When you try to open it, it performs its function. In this case, you get a dialog box that asks if you want to run the query (see Figure 2.22).

Figure 2.22
The dialog box cautions you that you are about to run an action query.

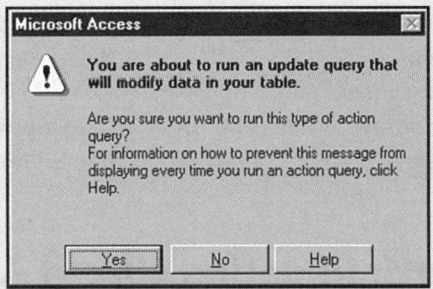

19 **Click Yes to continue.**

Another message appears, telling you you are about to make permanent changes to five rows of the table (see Figure 2.23). There were six rows in the table, but one of them did not meet the criteria we placed in the Sold column. This is an indication our query is working properly.

Figure 2.23
The dialog box informs you that you are about to make irreversible changes.

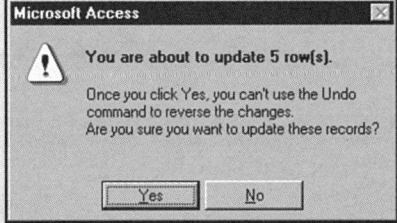

20 **Click Yes to update the records.**

The records are updated, but nothing appears to happen on the screen.

21 **Click the Tables tab and open the Stock on Hand table.**

Notice that the suggested price for the stock has changed, except for the first record that was marked as already sold (see Figure 2.24).

Figure 2.24
The Stock on Hand table is shown after the prices have been changed.

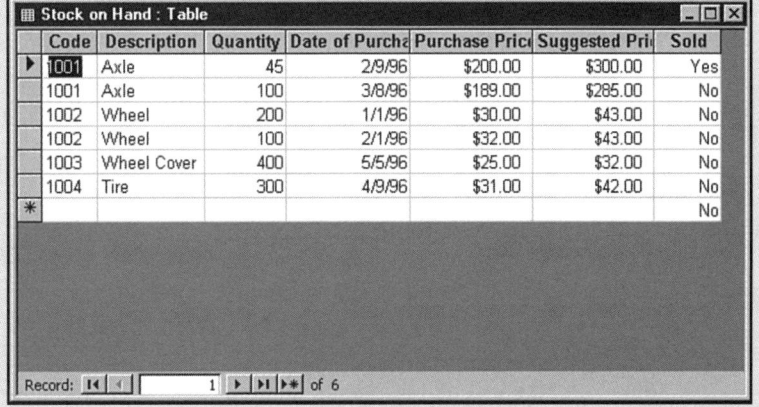

Code	Description	Quantity	Date of Purcha	Purchase Pric	Suggested Pri	Sold
1001	Axle	45	2/9/96	$200.00	$300.00	Yes
1001	Axle	100	3/8/96	$189.00	$285.00	No
1002	Wheel	200	1/1/96	$30.00	$43.00	No
1002	Wheel	100	2/1/96	$32.00	$43.00	No
1003	Wheel Cover	400	5/5/96	$25.00	$32.00	No
1004	Tire	300	4/9/96	$31.00	$42.00	No
*						No

Record: 1 of 6

22 **Close the table and the database.**

It is easy to make a mistake when you are designing an update query but very difficult to fix the results of a mistake. You can make a copy of the table before you attempt an update. In the Table tab, select the table and use the copy and paste options from the menu bar. This will give you a copy of the original table, but the program will let you give the backup table a new name. This procedure should be done before you try to update an important table.

Lesson 5: Updating Linked Tables Automatically

If two tables are linked, it is important to protect the linking fields from unexpected changes. If two companies merge and one of the companies has to change its parts codes to match those of the other system, it would be important to update the related customer records.

In this lesson you learn how to set the relationship between a primary key and a related field in another table, set referential integrity, and select automatic update options such as cascade update and cascade delete.

To Update Linked Tables Automatically

❶ Make a copy of the student data file Proj0203.

❷ Rename the copy Auto Parts 2.

Include the .mdb extension only if you can see the extension on the Proj0203 file.

❸ Open the Auto Parts 2 database.

The database window should now be open to the Tables area.

❹ Choose Tools and then Relationships from the menu bar.

An empty window titled Relationships appears, along with a Show Table window.

❺ Choose Relationships and then Show Table from the menu bar.

The Show Table window appears and displays the names of the two tables, New Prices and Stock on Hand (see Figure 2.25).

Figure 2.25
The Show Table window displays the two tables in the Auto Parts 2 database.

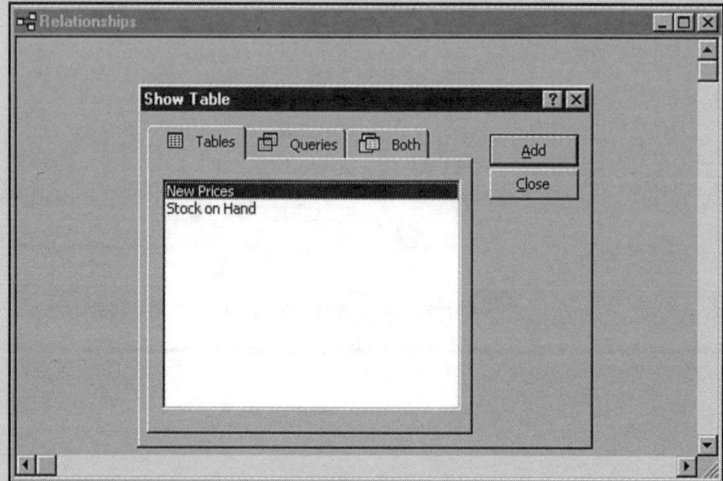

6 **Click each table name and then the Add button to add them to the Relationship window.**

You may need to move the Show Table window to see the tables as they are added to the Relationships window.

7 **Click the Close button to close the Show Table window.**

The Relationships window will display the two tables (see Figure 2.26). Notice that the Code field in the New Prices table is displayed in bold-faced type. This indicates that it is the primary key field for that table.

Figure 2.26
The Relationships window displays two tables and their fields.

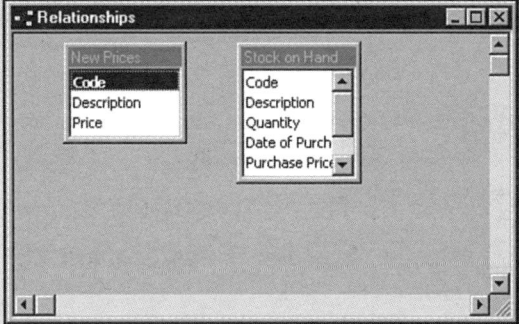

8 **Click and drag the Code field name from the New Prices table to the Code field in the Stock on Hand table.**

A Relationships dialog box appears to help you define the relationship (see Figure 2.27).

Figure 2.27
The Relationships dialog box is displayed.

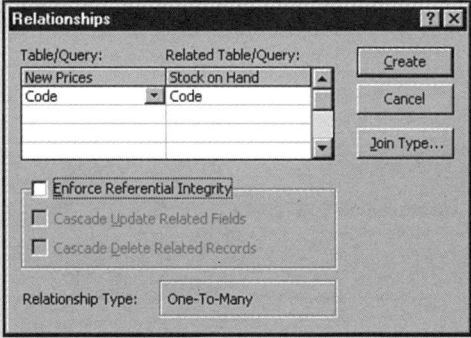

9 **Click the Enforce Referential Integrity check box.**

Two more options that were previously dimmed now become available.

10 **Click both the Cascade Update Related Fields and the Cascade Delete Related Records check boxes.**

This allows for automatic updates and deletions of the records in the Stock on Hand table if changes are made to the code field in the New Prices table (see Figure 2.28).

continues

To Update Linked Tables Automatically   (continued)

Figure 2.28
The Relationships dialog box is set for automatic updating.

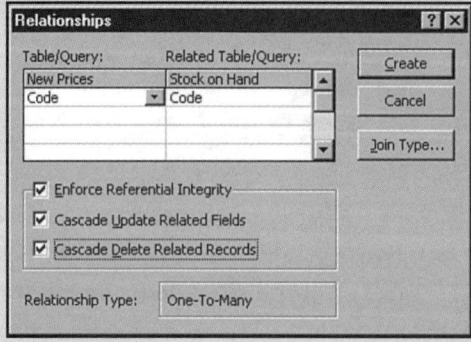

11 Click **C**reate to create the relationship.

The relationship that is created is one-to-many.

12 Close the Relationships window and save the changes to the layout.

13 Open the New Prices table.

14 Change the code for axles from 1001 to 1007 and close the table.

Because of the relationship you created, the records in the Stock on Hand table should now show that the code for axles is 1007.

15 Open the Stock on Hand table.

The code for axles was automatically changed (see Figure 2.29).

Figure 2.29
The code for axles has been updated.

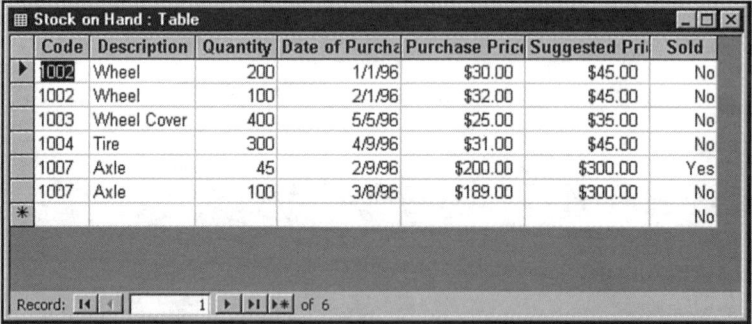

16 Close the Stock on Hand table and open the New Prices table.

17 Click the record selector for the first row to select the record for Wheel.

The first row is selected (see Figure 2.30).

Figure 2.30
The first row of the New Prices table is selected.

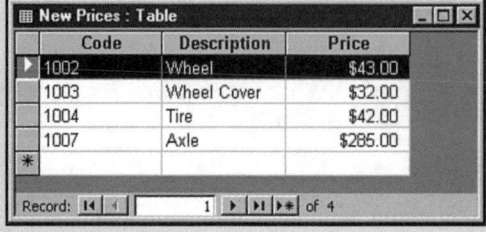

18 **Press the** Del **key to delete this record.**

A cautionary message is displayed to inform you this record will be deleted, as well as an unspecified number of records on related tables (see Figure 2.31).

Figure 2.31
A warning message is displayed when the cascade delete feature is about to delete records in related tables.

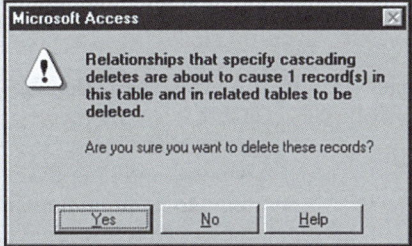

19 **Click Yes to delete the records.**

20 **Close the New Prices table and open the Stock on Hand table.**

Notice that both records that had the code 1002 for Wheels have been deleted from this table.

21 **Close the table and the database.**

Project Summary

To	Do This
Update tables by substituting text	Create a query based on the table that needs to be updated. Drag the field to be updated plus any other fields that may be used as limiting criteria to the QBE grid. Enter any necessary criteria. Click the Query Type button and select Update. Enter the new text in the Update To box. Click the Run button on the toolbar.
Update portions of fields using expressions like left, mid, and right	Create a query as in the section above. Use an expression such as Left([field name],#ofchars)= "characters" in the criteria box to find the appropriate records. Place an expression that combines new characters within quotation marks plus a portion of the existing field in the Update To box and run the query.
Update tables with a calculated expression	Create an update query as in the previous steps. In the Update To box, enter an expression that contains the field names within square brackets and uses mathematical operators, such as *,/,+,-. Run the query to update the table.
Update a table based on values in another table	Create a new update query and select both tables. The tables must be joined by a one-to-many relationship. Drag the field to be updated and any other fields to be used with criteria

continues

continued

To	Do This
	from the target table into the query design. In the Update To box, specify the table and field name by enclosing them in square brackets and separated by a period. For example: [Table].[Field]. Run the query.
Update linked tables automatically	Use the menu selections, **R**elationships and Show **T**able from the menu bar. If no relationship exists, add the two tables to the relationships window and drag the primary key field from one table to its corresponding field in the other table. (If a relationship already exists, double-click the relationships line.) In the resulting dialog box, click **E**nforce Referential Integrity and then click Cascade **U**pdate Related Fields and Cascade **D**elete Related Records. Click **C**reate and close the window.

Checking Your Skills

True/False

For each of the following statements, check *T* or *F* to indicate whether the statement is true or false.

__T __F **1.** In an Update query you can only use two fields, the one you want to update and one other field for a single criterion.

__T __F **2.** If you make a mistake in the Update Query design and update the wrong fields, you can use **E**dit and **U**ndo from the menu to undo the mistake.

__T __F **3.** The expression, Left([Name],4) would select the left four characters of a field called "Name."

__T __F **4.** The expression "Mr. "+[LastName] would produce a new string of characters that would be a combination of the title, Mr., and the last names stored in the LastName field.

__T __F **5.** If you delete a record from the table that contains the primary key field, any records that are joined to it in the other table will be deleted if you have selected Cascade **D**elete Related Records as a condition to the one-to-many join.

Multiple Choice

Circle the letter of the correct answer for each of the following questions.

1. To select the first five characters in a field, use the following expression:

    a. Left[(Name), 5]

    b. First([Name],5)

   c. Right([Name],5)

   d. Left([Name],5)

2. To update a field based on the Name field in the Customer table, use the _____ expression.

   a. [Name].[Customer]

   b. (Customer)+(Name)

   c. [Customer].[Name]

   d. Left[Customer]+Right[Name]

3. If two tables are joined with a one-to-many relationship, the _____ option will cause changes to the primary key field to be automatically made to any corresponding record in the joined table.

   a. AutoUpdate

   b. Cascade Update Related Fields

   c. Table-to-Table

   d. AutoUpdate Cascade

4. To change an ordinary Select query into an Update query, you start by clicking on the _____ button.

   a. Query Type

   b. Query View

   c. Run

   d. Preview

5. If you want to increase all of the prices by 10%, you could use the following expression:

   a. [Price] + 10%

   b. [Price]*.1

   c. [Price]*1.1

   d. [Price]/.9

Completion

In the blank provided, write the correct answer for each of the following statements.

1. The absence of data in a field is called a(n) _____ value.

2. A relationship between two tables is called a(n) _____.

3. A(n) _____ expression is used to select characters from the middle of a string of characters.

4. Action queries like Update are similar to macros in that they are activated by a _____ command.

5. When you use a field name in an expression, it must be enclosed by _____ .

Applying Your Skills

At the end of each project in *Access 97 Essentials Level III*, you learn how to apply your Access skills to various situations. The following exercises help you practice the skills you have learned in this project. Take a few minutes to work through these exercises now.

Updating a Table with a New Product Description

As you have seen, Update queries can be powerful database tools, and can save you a lot of time. In this exercise you will replace the Degreaser product description with Solvent in the Cleaning database.

To Update a Table with a New Product Description

1. Open the Cleaning database and create a new query based on the Orders table.

2. Drag the Product Description field to the query table.

3. Enter the term `Degreaser` in the criteria box.

4. Use the Query Type button on the menu bar to change the query to an Update query.

5. Enter the term `Solvent` in the Update To box.

6. Run the query.

7. Close the query, but do not save it.

8. Open the Orders table to confirm the results.

Assigning a Sale Price on All the Purchases Made after a Certain Date

Formula fields can be used for many purposes—increasing prices, setting sale prices, or even adding surcharges onto late payments. In this exercise you will create sale prices for a sale starting on a certain date.

To Assign a Sale Price on All the Purchases Made after a Certain Date

1. Open the Auto Parts database, and open a new query based on the Stock on Hand table.

2. Drag the Date of Purchase, Suggested Price, and Sold fields to the query table.

3. Enter a criterion in the Date of Purchase column that will select only purchases made after March 1, 1996.

4. Enter a criterion in the Sold field that will select records that have "No" in that field.

5. Change the query type to Update.

6. Enter an expression in the Update To box in the Suggested Price column that will multiply the Suggested Price field by .9.

7. Run the query.

8. Close the query, but don't save it.

9. Open the Stock on Hand table to see if the query worked.

Joining Two Tables and Establishing Automatic Updates and Deletions

Many large databases consist of numerous tables, many of which need to be interrelated. The Relationships feature of Access allows you to relate tables, and to have them automatically update each other. This can save an enormous amount of time and effort if done correctly. In this exercise you will join two tables and create a relationship between the Vendor fields.

To Join Two Tables and Establish Automatic Updates and Deletions

1. Copy the Proj0204 database and rename it `Plumbing`.

2. Open the database. Use the **R**elationships and **S**how Table menu options to add both tables.

3. Drag a link between the primary key in the Vendors table (Name) to the Vendor field in the other table.

4. In the dialog box, select **E**nforce Referential Integrity, Cascade **U**pdate Related Fields, and Cascade **D**elete Related Records.

5. Create the relationship, then close the Relationships window.

6. Test the relationship by changing the contents of a primary key field and/or deleting a record in the table that contains the primary key.

Project

3

Using Access Tools

Using tools to edit, modify, and control your database, and connect to other Microsoft applications

In this Project, you learn how to:

➤ Correct Spelling with the Spelling Checker

➤ Customize Data Entry Using AutoCorrect

➤ Analyze a Table

➤ Analyze Database Performance

➤ Determine Database Characteristics Using the Documenter

➤ Use OfficeLinks to Analyze Data Using Excel and Create Reports Using Word

Why Would I Do This?

Access provides a full range of tools to help you edit data, analyze components of your database, and connect to other Microsoft Office applications. These tools help you, the database designer, to control and modify your database to best suit your needs.

Access includes a Spelling Checker and an AutoCorrect tool. You may be familiar with these tools from Microsoft Word, Excel, or PowerPoint. While the need for these tools is not as obvious in a database as it is in other applications, there are certain situations where both can be useful.

Access also provides three powerful analysis tools, one for tables only and two for any database object. With the Table Analyzer, an Access wizard will help you to determine if there is redundant data in the database. If there is, it will suggest ways of splitting up the table into smaller, more efficient, related tables. The Documenter enables you to look at the structure of the components of a database and lets you print out a report showing such things as field characteristics and table relationships. The Performance Analyzer is a wizard that makes recommendations about the structures of various database components.

Finally, Access offers tools to help you use the capabilities of other Microsoft applications to analyze and report your data. You can send data to Excel for further analysis or advanced graphing. You can also send information to Word if you need a quick, attractive report.

Lesson 1: Correcting Spelling with the Spelling Checker

The first thing you need to do is to make a copy of a database file that has been included with this book. Once you copy and rename the file, you are ready to complete the first lesson. You will use this new file to correct spelling using the Access Spelling Checker.

To Open the Short Stories Database

1 Make a copy the student data file Proj0301.

2 Rename the copy Short Stories.

Add the .mdb extension only if you can see the extension on the Proj0301 file.

3 Launch Access 97.

4 Open the Short Stories database.

The database window should now be open to the Tables area (see Figure 3.1).

Figure 3.1
The database window displays the Tables area of the Short Stories database.

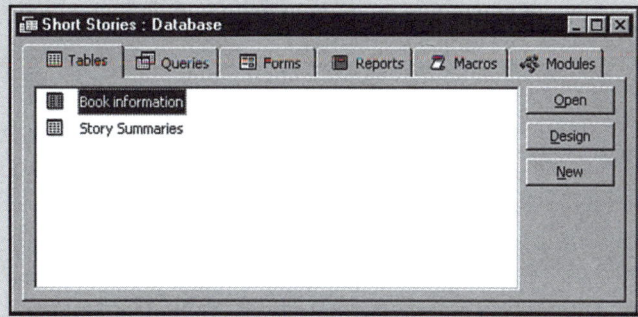

Keep the database open for the next exercise.

Spelling Checker

A tool that enables you to compare words in your database to words in a dictionary.

In some cases, such as a last name field, a city field, or a numeric field, the Access *Spelling Checker* would be of little or no use. There are times, however, when standard text is entered into a field. This would be true for fields such as memo fields in personnel databases or description fields in inventories.

In this lesson, you use a database of short story summaries. This database has a memo field that contains long (200+ character) entries, and also has six category fields. The Spelling Checker would be useful for these seven fields, and might also be useful for the source and title fields.

To Correct Spelling with the Spelling Checker

1 Click the Tables tab of the Short Stories database, if necessary.

2 Open the Story Summaries table, and maximize the window, if necessary.

For the first part of this lesson, run the Spelling Checker on only one field. To do that, you need to select the field first.

3 Move the pointer to the column heading of the Description field.

The pointer should turn into a down arrow.

4 Click the Description heading.

The Description column is now highlighted (see Figure 3.2).

continues

To Correct Spelling with the Spelling Checker   (continued)

Figure 3.2
A field can be selected by clicking in the column heading area.

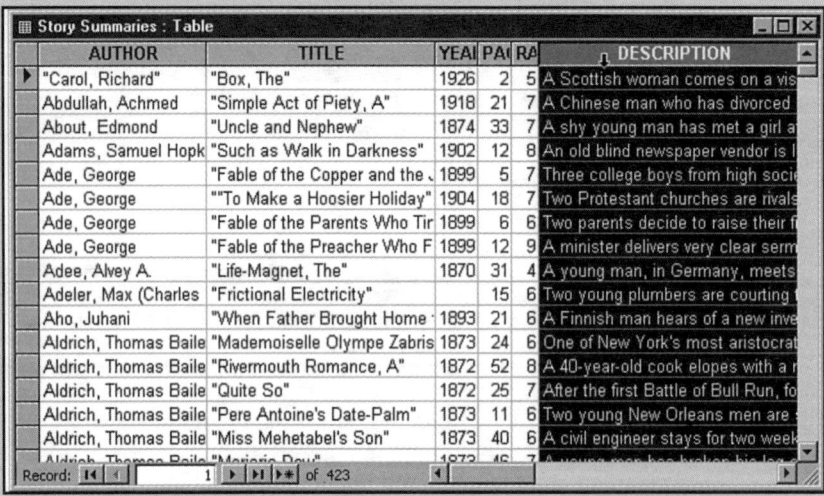

5 Click the Spelling button on the toolbar.

The Spelling dialog box appears (see Figure 3.3).

Figure 3.3
The Spelling dialog box gives you several options.

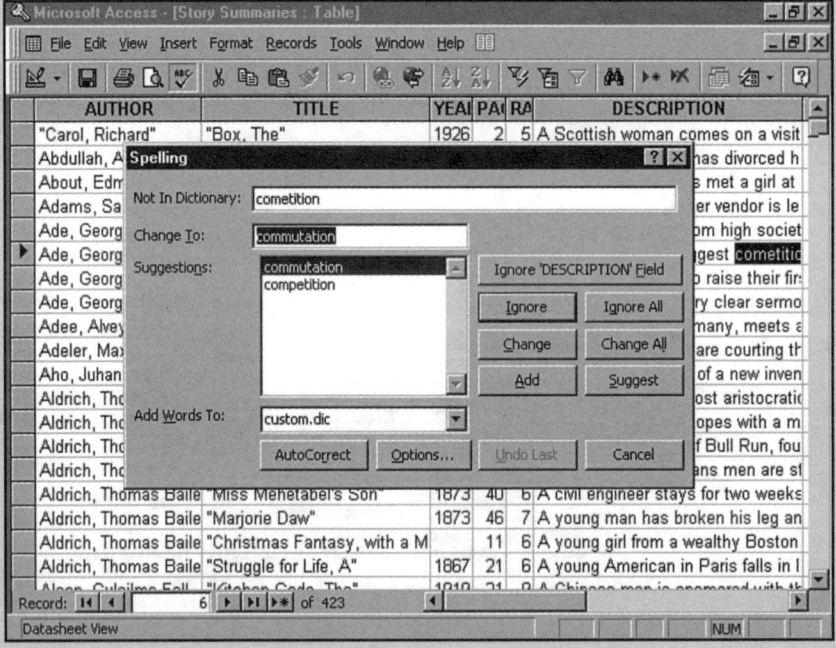

The Spelling Checker moves to the first word that does not match a word in its dictionary. It displays that word, in this case "cometition," then tries to offer suggested alternatives.

6 Click "competition" in the Suggestions area and click the Change button.

The program replaces the misspelled word with the correction, then moves on to the next unrecognized word. The next two unrecognized words are "Campbellites" and "Winesburg." Both are proper nouns that you probably will not use again.

7 **Click Ignore for the next two choices.**

8 **Correct the word "expecially" then close the Spelling Checker.**

9 **Scroll to the right so you can see the six category fields (C1 through C6).**

10 **Click the column heading for the C1 field and drag to the right to highlight all six category fields.**

Make sure fields C1, C2, C3, C4, C5, and C6 are highlighted (see Figure 3.4).

Figure 3.4
Using the click-and-drag procedure enables you to select several fields at once.

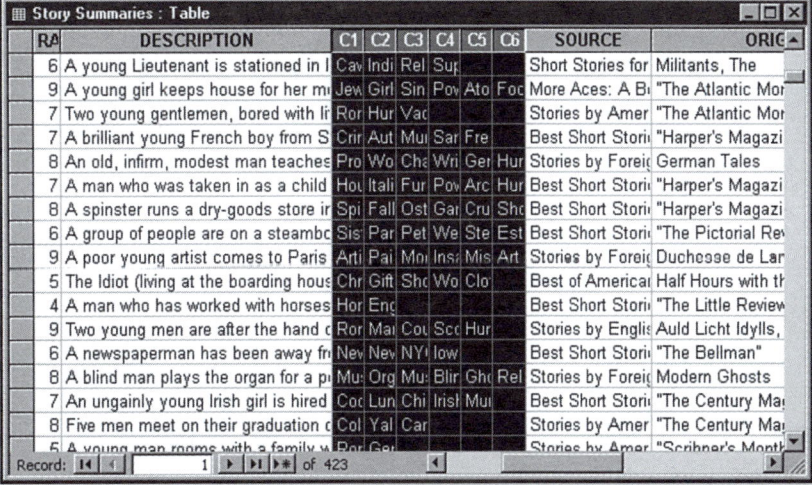

The Spelling Checker checks only the highlighted fields unless no fields are selected, in which case it checks the whole table.

11 **Click the Spelling button on the Table Datasheet toolbar.**

The Spelling Checker begins checking the first row of selected fields, then moves to the next row. In this example, the first word not recognized is 'Rasputin.' Let's assume you want to add that word to the dictionary.

12 **Click the Add button.**

The word 'Rasputin' has now been added to your Custom dictionary. This dictionary is a supplement to the main dictionary. Words added while you do a Spelling check in Access will also be available in other Microsoft Office products, since the dictionary and Custom dictionary are shared.

Another situation that occurs frequently is where a misspelled word is not recognized by the dictionary, and the correct spelling is not among the suggestions.

13 **Click Ignore on the next few unrecognized words until you get to 'Blubeard.'**

This word, which should be spelled 'Bluebeard,' is not found in the dictionary and the only suggestion, 'Bluebird,' is incorrect.

continues

To Check Spelling with the Spelling Checker   (continued)

⑭ Click anywhere in the Not in Dictionary box.

The misspelled word is placed in the Change **T**o box (see Figure 3.5).

Figure 3.5
Clicking in the Not In Dictionary box places the misspelled word in the Change To box.

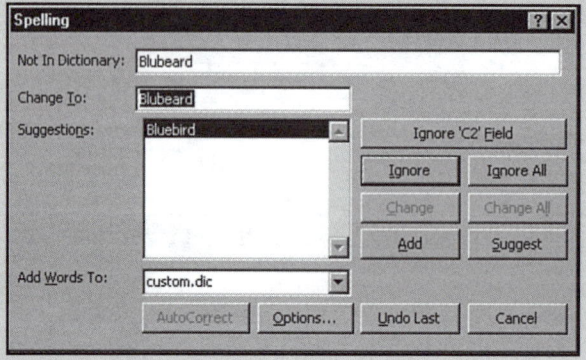

⑮ Edit the misspelled word in the Change To box, so that it is spelled "Bluebeard," then click Change.

A dialog box warns you that you are changing this word to a word that is not in the dictionary (see Figure 3.6). You are then asked if you want to make the change and continue.

Figure 3.6
The Spelling Checker warns you if you Change To a word that is not in the dictionary.

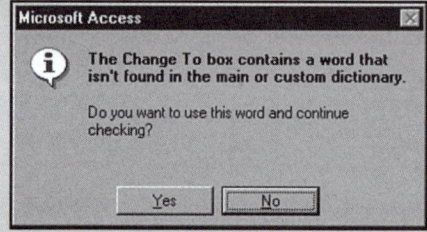

⑯ Click Yes.

⑰ Close the Spelling Checker and close the table, but leave the database open for the next lesson.

Lesson 2: Customizing Data Entry Using AutoCorrect

AutoCorrect

A tool that enables you to enter shortcuts for longer words or phrases, or to correct common typos.

Combo and List boxes offer an excellent way to create shortcuts for many data entry tasks. An alternative method for creating data entry shortcuts is to use the *AutoCorrect* feature in Access. The AutoCorrect feature is available in other Microsoft Office applications, such as Word, Excel, and PowerPoint. An advantage of using AutoCorrect rather than List or Combo boxes is that the AutoCorrect feature works in every field in which you are entering data.

To Customize Data Entry Using AutoCorrect

1 **In the Short Stories database, select the Forms tab.**

2 **Select the Short Story input form and click the Open button.**

Maximize the form if necessary. Notice that the Original field contains the name of the original source of the short story. This source is usually a magazine, often followed by a date.

3 **Choose Tools, AutoCorrect from the menu.**

The AutoCorrect dialog box appears (see Figure 3.7). Notice that there is an option to correct two capital letters at the beginning of a word. There are also options to capitalize the first letter of sentences, capitalize the days of the week, and adjust for accidental use of the Caps Lock key. The feature you will want to use is Replace Text as you type.

Figure 3.7
The AutoCorrect dialog box gives you five options.

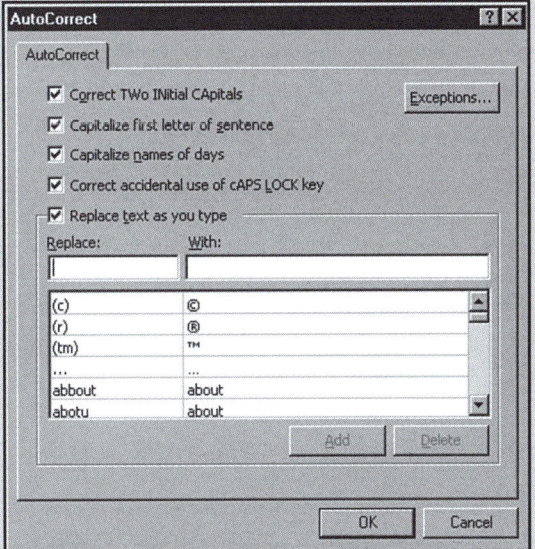

4 **Type pu in the Replace box.**

5 **Type "Putnam's Magazine," in the With box.**

Make sure you type the text exactly as shown, including the quotation marks and the comma before the final quotation mark (see Figure 3.8). (This is the way to reference a magazine as a source. The quotation marks and the comma are not required by the Access program.)

continues

To Customize Data Entry Using AutoCorrect   (continued)

Figure 3.8
In the **W**ith box, type exactly what you want to appear in the field.

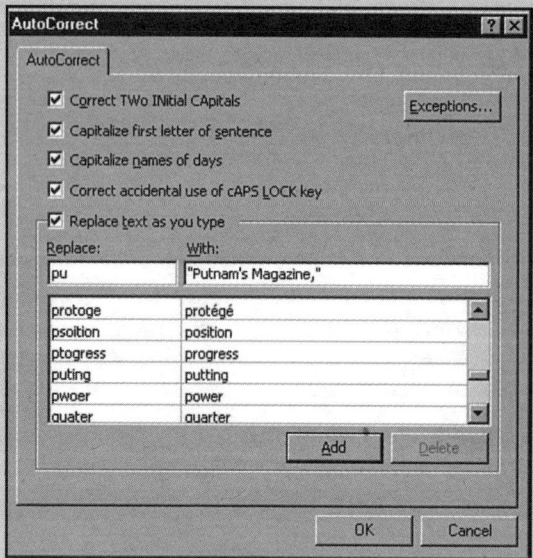

6 **Click Add, then click OK.**

The shortcut has now been added to the AutoCorrect list.

 7 **Click the New Record button at the bottom of the screen.**

8 **Click on the Original box and type pu then press** Spacebar.

Notice that the pu and the space have been replaced by "Putnam's Magazine," exactly as you typed it into the AutoCorrect list. Notice also that the cursor is still in the field, with a space after the magazine's name—exactly where you want it so you can add the date (see Figure 3.9).

Figure 3.9
The AutoCorrect tool may be used to enter commonly used words.

In order to activate the AutoCorrect feature, you must follow the shortcut with either a space or a punctuation mark. In the following steps you will check to see if your AutoCorrect addition can be used in another Microsoft program.

9 **Launch Microsoft Word and open any document (you do not need to close Access).**

10 **Choose Tools, AutoCorrect from the menu and scroll down to see if pu is there. Notice that it does, in fact, show up in the Microsoft Word AutoCorrect list. It will also appear in PowerPoint and Excel. This is because the AutoCorrect list is stored as a shared file available to all Microsoft Office products. This can be a great time-saver for you.**

11 **Close Microsoft Word and return to Access.**

When you name the shortcut, make sure it will be something you'll remember. In the first example, pu was used for Putnam's Magazine. In some cases, you will have two entries with the same initials, so you will need to use three or more letters for the shortcut.

12 **Choose Tools, AutoCorrect from the menu.**

To create a shortcut for Scribner's Monthly and Scribner's Magazine (which were two separate publications), you will need to be a little more creative.

13 **Type smo in the Replace box and "Scribner's Monthly," in the With box.**

14 **Click Add to add this shortcut to the AutoCorrect list.**

The shortcut is shown, and the **R**eplace box is highlighted.

15 **Type smag and press the Tab↹ key.**

This replaces the previous entry in the **R**eplace box, then moves the highlight to the **W**ith box.

16 **Type "Scribner's Magazine," in the With box and click Add.**

Both Scribner's publications now have shortcuts in the AutoCorrect list (see Figure 3.10).

continues

To Customize Data Entry Using AutoCorrect   (continued)

Figure 3.10
The AutoCorrect tool can store numerous shortcuts.

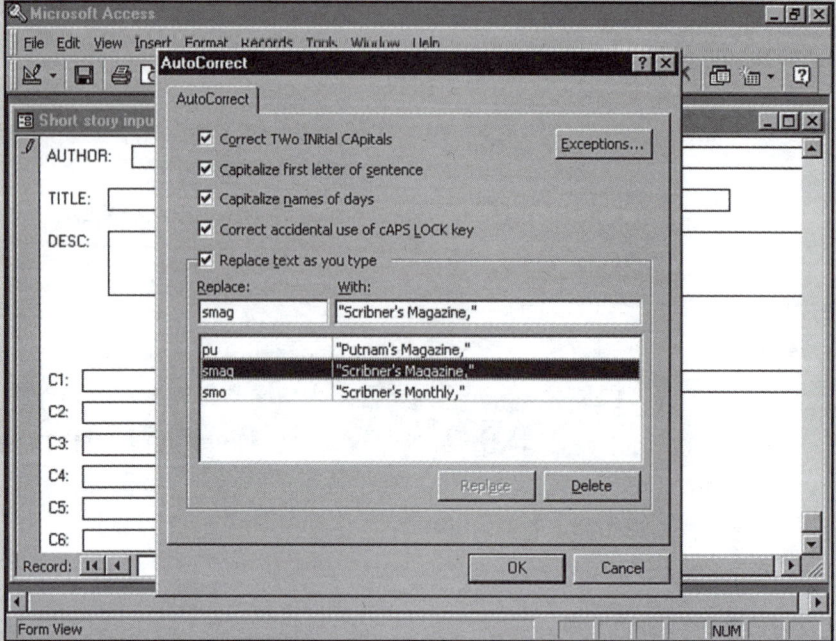

⑰ **Try out your shortcuts in the Original field.**

⑱ **Close the form, but leave the database open for the next lesson.**

Lesson 3: Analyzing a Table

Table Analyzer
A tool that looks for duplications in fields and splits tables to make them more efficient.

Access provides three analysis tools to help you fine-tune your database—a *Table Analyzer*, a Performance Analyzer, and a Documenter. These tools help you in different ways. The Table Analyzer contains a wizard that looks at a table, determines which fields contain duplicated information, then splits the large table into smaller, more efficient linked tables. If you are not interested in having the Access program determine which fields to split out of the original database, you can identify the fields yourself.

In this lesson, you analyze the tables in the Short Stories database you used in the first two lessons of this project.

To Analyze a Table

❶ **Make sure the Short Stories database is open.**

It does not matter what area you are in. The analyzers work from anywhere in the database.

❷ **Choose Tools, Analyze from the menu, then select Table.**

This wizard has two introductory screens that are optional. Compare your screen to Figure 3.11. If your screen does not match the following figure, click the **N**ext button until you reach this screen. This dialog box shows all of the tables in the database. It also enables you to turn on some introductory screens that describe the process in detail. Turn those on if you are interested, then click **B**ack to view them.

Note: The two introductory screens can be turned off by clicking the Show Introductory Pages? checkbox on the first active Table Analyzer Wizard dialog box (see Figure 3.11).

Figure 3.11
The first Table Analyzer Wizard dialog box enables you to choose a table to analyze.

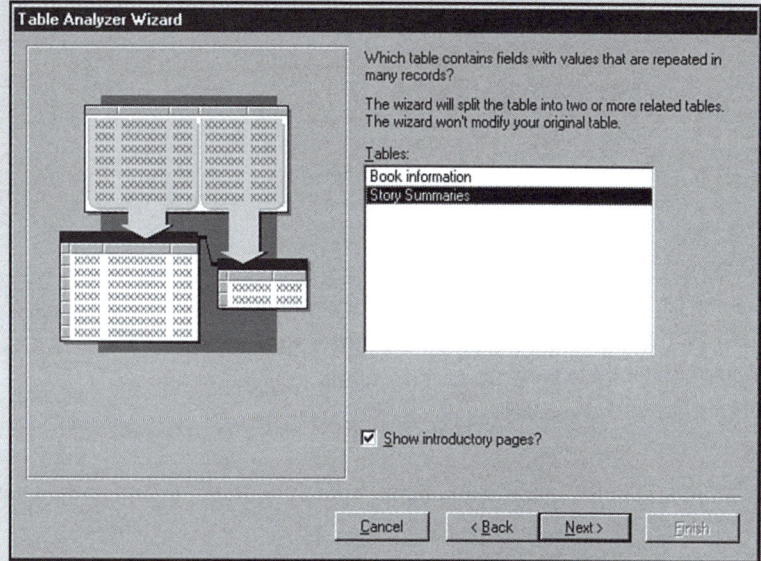

③ Choose the Story Summaries table and click Next.

The second Table Analyzer Wizard dialog box sets the program's level of control over the process.

④ Select the Yes, let the wizard decide option, then click Next.

Access decides which fields have sufficient duplication to warrant a separate table (this may take a minute or so). It sets up the structure of the resulting tables, and shows you the links it will create (see Figure 3.12).

continues

To Analyze a Table (continued)

Figure 3.12
The third Table Analyzer Wizard dialog box shows how the tables will be split and how they will be linked.

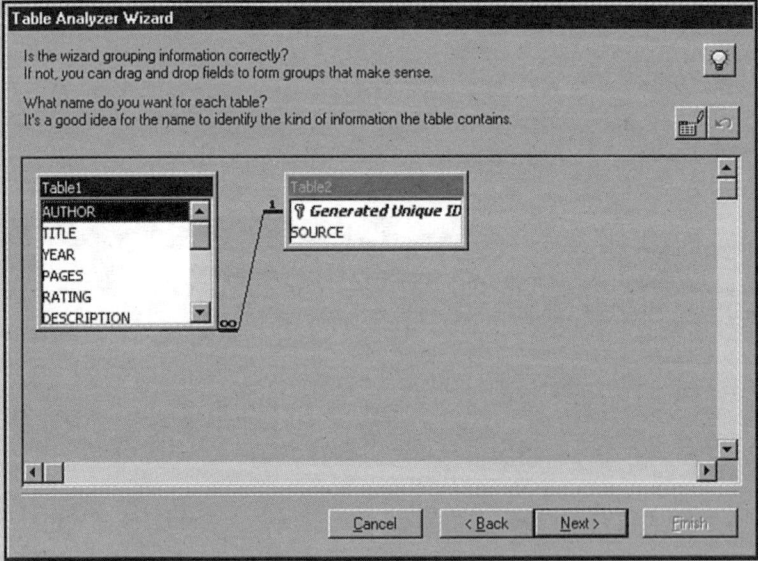

The Source field has been separated from the original table. Because the tables need to be linked, Access has created a key field called Generated Unique ID. At this point it is a good idea to rename the new tables with descriptive names.

5 **Click the title bar for Table1, then click the Rename Table button.**

A dialog box with the Table **N**ame option appears (see Figure 3.13). Note: You can also double-click on the title bar to bring up the dialog box to change the table name.

Figure 3.13
The dialog box with the Table **N**ame option enables you to give the new table a descriptive name.

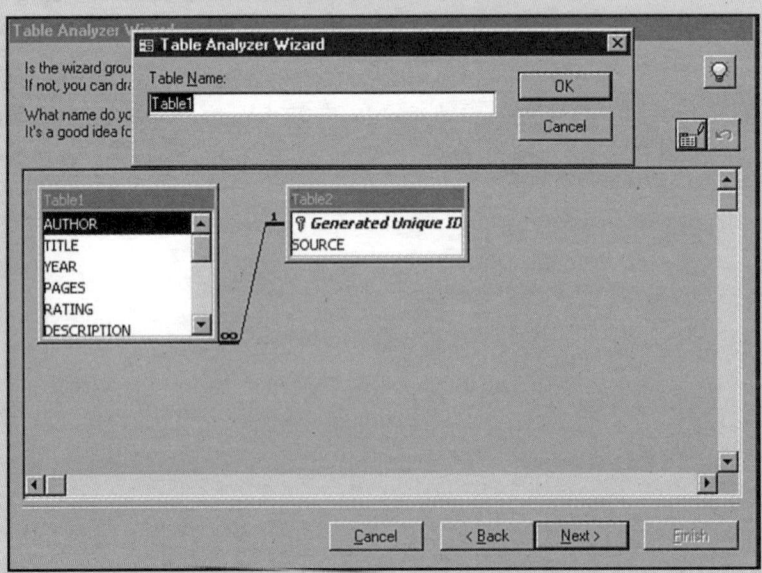

6 **Rename Table1 as** Short Story Information **and click OK.**

7 **Using the procedure from steps 5 and 6, rename Table2 as** `Short Story Sources.`

8 **Click <u>N</u>ext.**

The fourth Table Analyzer Wizard dialog box appears. This dialog box asks if you are satisfied with the primary key field chosen by the program. If not, you are told how to assign another field as the primary key.

9 **Click <u>N</u>ext.**

After a brief delay, the fifth Table Analyzer Wizard dialog box appears. This dialog box looks at the entries in the new table. In this case, the Correction column has been widened and you are looking at some of the rows in the middle of the source column. If any of the entries appear similar, or if the Wizard finds typos, it suggests changes (see Figure 3.14).

Figure 3.14
The fifth Table Analyzer Wizard dialog box looks for typos or inconsistent duplicate entries.

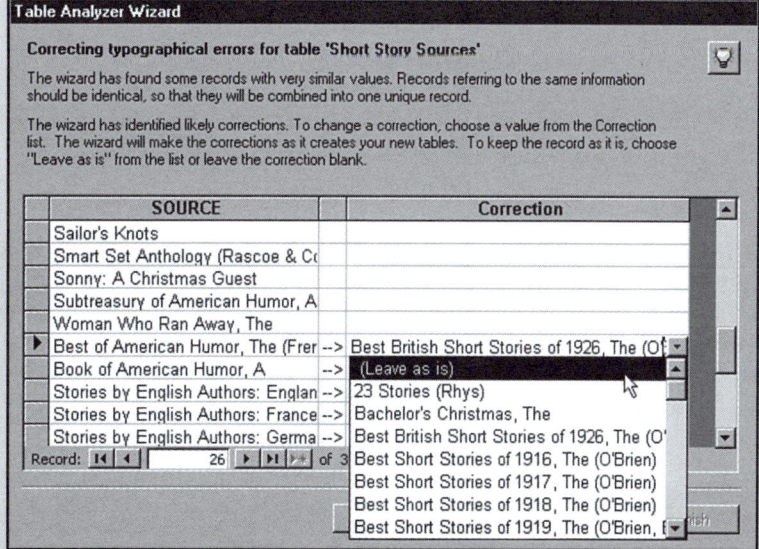

The purpose of this dialog box is to identify identical items, one or more of which might have been misspelled or entered differently. If you want to change an entry, choose a correction from the drop-down list in the Correction column, or type a new entry. There are no changes to be made to this list.

10 **Click <u>N</u>ext.**

A warning dialog appears asking if you are sure you want to move on (see Figure 3.15).

continues

To Analyze a Table (continued)

Figure 3.15
The program warns you that you have made no changes, even though changes were suggested.

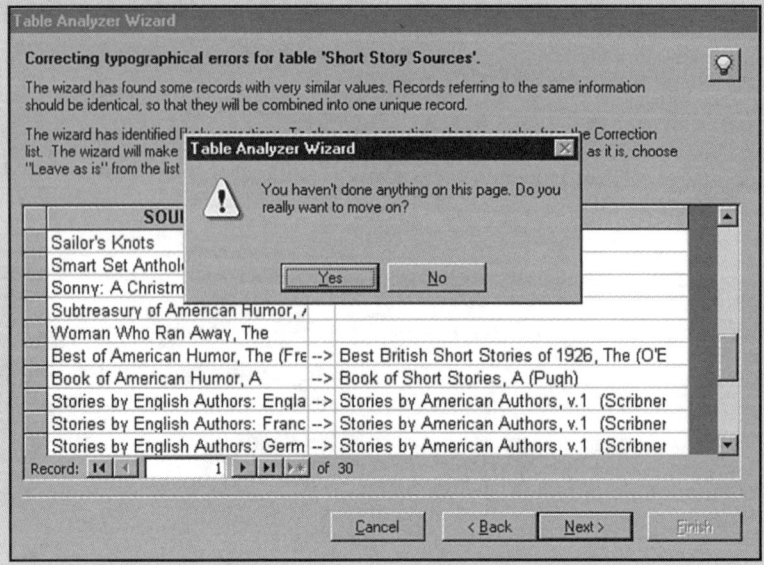

⓫ **Click Yes.**

The sixth Table Analyzer Wizard dialog box appears. This dialog box asks if you want to create a query that will look like your original table (see Figure 3.16).

Figure 3.16
The sixth Table Analyzer Wizard dialog box asks if you want to create a query similar to the original table.

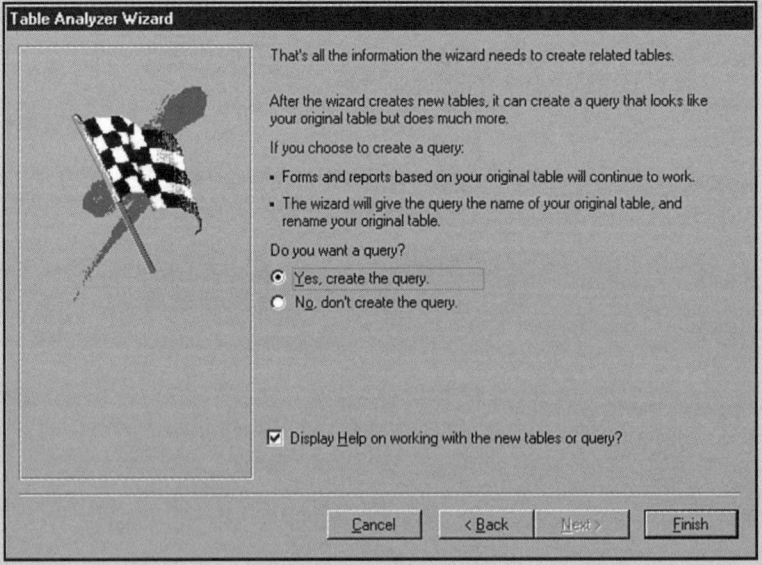

It is usually a good idea to create this query. Not only will you appear to be working from your original table, Access will also make the links to make sure all forms and reports can still find the necessary information.

⓬ **Make sure the Yes, create the query option is selected, then click Finish.**

After a brief delay, the program shows the results of the query, which should look exactly like the original table.

If you have the Display Help on working with the new tables or query? checkbox chosen, you will also be shown a help page on how to use the new query. You will need to close that window before looking at the results of the query.

⑬ Close the query.

⑭ Move to the Tables tab, if necessary, and open the Short Story Information table.

⑮ Scroll to the right until you can see the last field.

Notice that the Source is shown, and is called Lookup to Short Story Sources (see Figure 3.17). It is now a lookup field, taking its information from the Short Story Sources table. In this case, the Lookup to Short Story Sources column has been widened, so you can see the results more clearly.

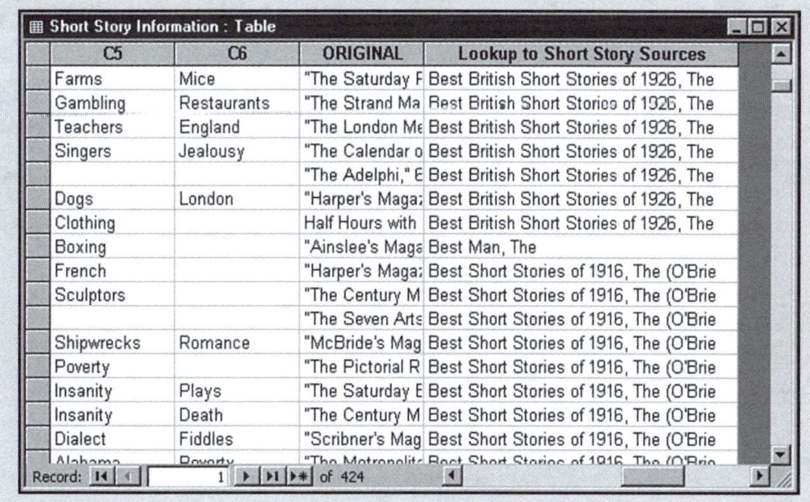

Figure 3.17
Access creates a table with a lookup field for the fields split from the original table.

C5	C6	ORIGINAL	Lookup to Short Story Sources
Farms	Mice	"The Saturday F	Best British Short Stories of 1926, The
Gambling	Restaurants	"The Strand Ma	Best British Short Stories of 1926, The
Teachers	England	"The London Me	Best British Short Stories of 1926, The
Singers	Jealousy	"The Calendar o	Best British Short Stories of 1926, The
		"The Adelphi," E	Best British Short Stories of 1926, The
Dogs	London	"Harper's Maga;	Best British Short Stories of 1926, The
Clothing		Half Hours with	Best British Short Stories of 1926, The
Boxing		"Ainslee's Maga	Best Man, The
French		"Harper's Maga;	Best Short Stories of 1916, The (O'Brie
Sculptors		"The Century M	Best Short Stories of 1916, The (O'Brie
		"The Seven Arts	Best Short Stories of 1916, The (O'Brie
Shipwrecks	Romance	"McBride's Mag	Best Short Stories of 1916, The (O'Brie
Poverty		"The Pictorial R	Best Short Stories of 1916, The (O'Brie
Insanity	Plays	"The Saturday E	Best Short Stories of 1916, The (O'Brie
Insanity	Death	"The Century M	Best Short Stories of 1916, The (O'Brie
Dialect	Fiddles	"Scribner's Mag	Best Short Stories of 1916, The (O'Brie
Alabama	Poverty	"The Metropolit:	Best Short Stories of 1916, The (O'Brie

Record: ⏮ ◀ 1 ▶ ⏭ ▶* of 424

⑯ Close the table and the database. Leave Access open for the next lesson.

Lesson 4: Analyzing Database Performance

Performance Analyzer
A tool that looks at database objects and gives recommendations, suggestions, and ideas for improving their performance.

In Lesson 3, you learned how to use an analysis tool to analyze a table. Access also offers a tool to analyze the performance of a database. This analysis is not restricted to tables, but will work on queries, forms, reports, macros, and modules. It is always a good idea to back up your database before you run any of the analyzers.

In this lesson, you analyze all of the database objects in the Short Stories database and correct one of the problems found.

To Analyze Database Performance

1 **Make a copy the student data file Proj0302.**

2 **Rename the copy** Checking Performance.

3 **Open the Checking Performance database.**

The database window should now be open to the Tables area, although it does not matter what area you are in. The analyzers work from anywhere in the database.

4 **Choose Tools, Analyze from the menu, then select Performance.**

The first Performance Analyzer dialog box appears (see Figure 3.18). This dialog box has several tabs that enable you to choose the database object type on which you want to work.

Figure 3.18
The first Performance Analyzer dialog box enables you to choose a table to analyze.

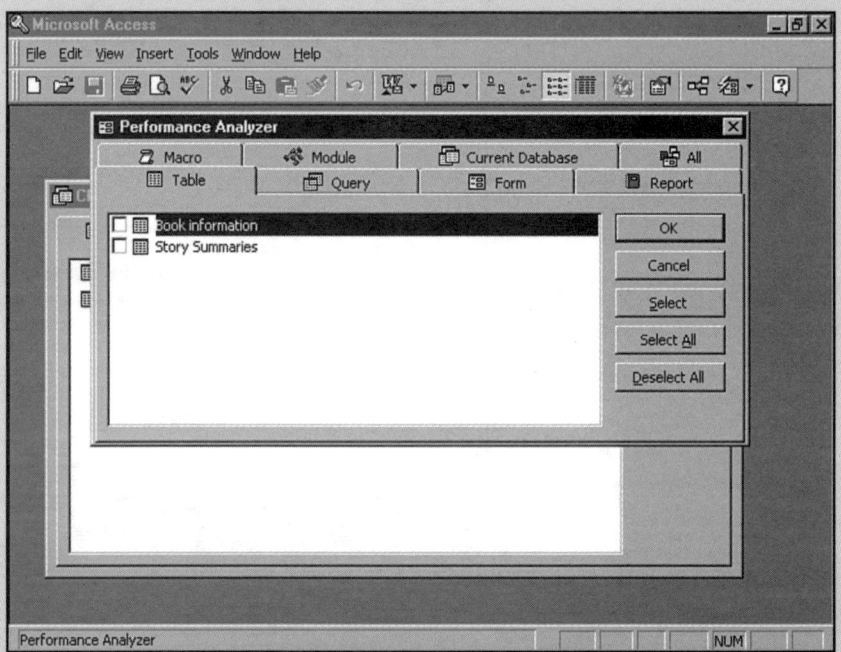

5 **Choose the Table tab, if necessary.**

Both of the tables in the database are shown.

6 **Choose the Story Summaries table and click OK.**

The second Performance Analyzer dialog box appears. This dialog box shows you the analysis results (see Figure 3.19).

Figure 3.19
The second Performance Analyzer dialog box shows you the analysis results.

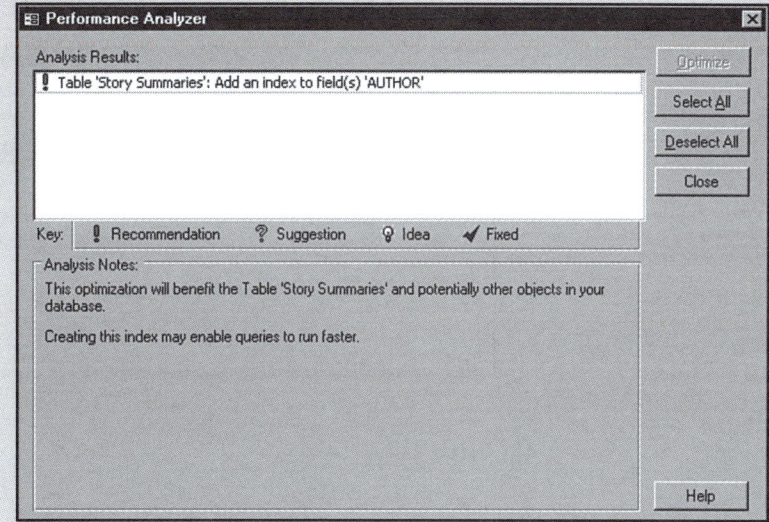

The Performance Analyzer gives you three types of information that can be used to improve performance—Recommendations, Suggestions, and Ideas.

7 Click the recommendation that appears in the Analysis Results box.

The Recommendation in this case is that you index the Author field. Indexing will speed up searches if the field is ever used in a sort routine (you used an index when you added Primary Key fields). This can be done in the properties section of the Table Design area, or can be done automatically at this time. Notice that the Optimize button has become active.

8 Click the Optimize button.

The program turns the index on for the Author field, then places a check mark to the left of the item, showing that the problem has been fixed.

9 Close the Performance Analyzer dialog box.

In the first part of this lesson, you analyzed the performance of just one database object. It is possible to analyze all of the database objects at once.

10 Choose Tools, Analyze from the menu, then select Performance.

The first Performance Analyzer dialog box again appears.

11 Choose the All tab, then click Select All.

All of the objects in the database are shown, and all of them have been selected (see Figure 3.20).

continues

To Analyze Database Performance   (continued)

Figure 3.20
The Performance
Analyzer dialog box
now shows all of the
database objects.

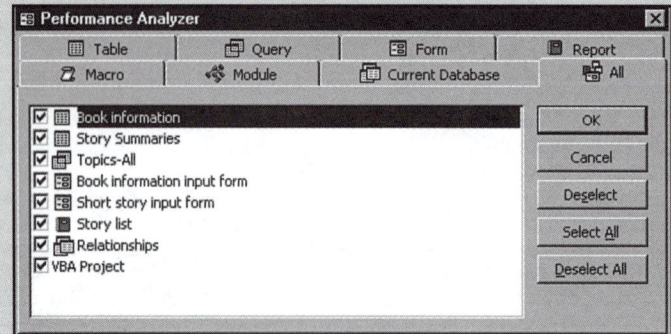

⑫ **Click OK.**

The Performance Analyzer now analyzes each object in the database. This procedure can take a long time in a complex database, particularly if you are using a slow machine or are operating on a network version of the software.

The Recommendations, Suggestions, and Ideas are shown, along with the database object they refer to. The Analysis Notes at the bottom of the dialog box refer to the item that is highlighted (see Figure 3.21).

Figure 3.21
The Performance
Analyzer gives
Recommendations,
Suggestions, and Ideas
on how to improve
database performance.

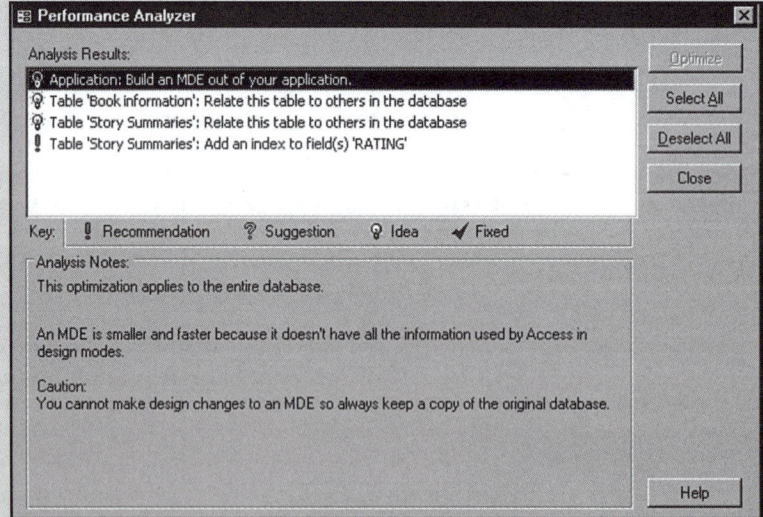

⑬ **Look through the Analysis Results, then close the window.**

Some of the suggestions deal with the use of Visual Basic code and compressed (MDE) files that are beyond the scope of this lesson. We will not make any further changes at this time.

⑭ **Leave the database open for the next lesson.**

Some of the Recommendations, Suggestions, and Ideas make great sense, while others seem to make no sense at all. Be careful when you make changes based on the analyzers, particularly those of which you are not sure. Back up your database before you run the Performance Analyzer.

Lesson 5: Determining Database Characteristics Using the Documenter

Documenter
A tool that looks at database objects and gives information on each object and control.

The more complex a database becomes, the harder it is to remember the properties of each control or database object. The third of the analysis tools is the *Documenter*. The Documenter has several levels of detail, and you can choose how much information you want Access to provide.

To Determine Database Characteristics Using the Documenter

❶ Make sure the Checking Performance database is open.

It does not matter what area you are in. The analyzers work from anywhere in the database.

❷ Choose Tools, Analyze from the menu, then select Documenter.

The first Database Documenter dialog box appears. This dialog box has tabs that enable you to choose the database Object **T**ype you want to work on, and displays all of the objects of that type.

❸ Choose the Tables tab, if necessary.

Both of the tables in the database are shown (see Figure 3.22).

Figure 3.22
The Documenter dialog box enables you to choose the database object you want to analyze.

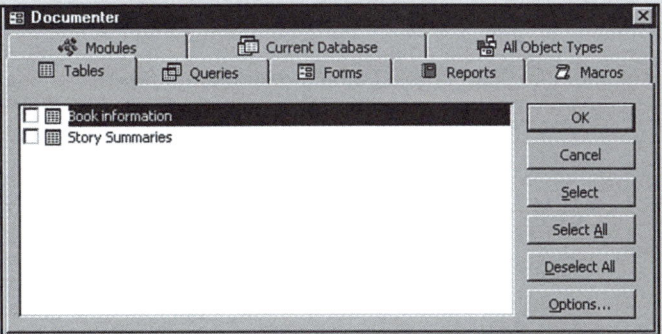

❹ Choose the Book Information table and click _O_ptions.

The Print Table Definition dialog box appears. This dialog box enables you to control the amount of detail you want (see Figure 3.23).

continues

To Determine Database Characteristics Using the Documenter (continued)

Figure 3.23
The Print Table Definition dialog box enables you to control how much detail you want in the report.

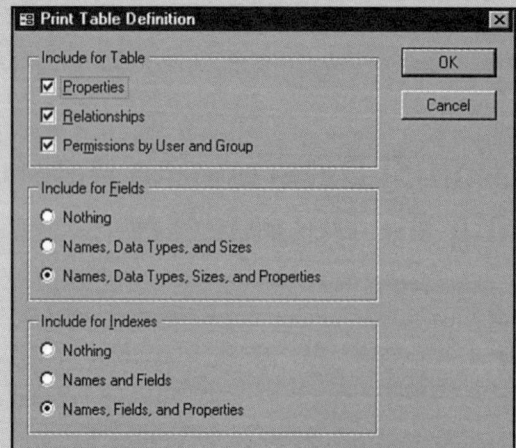

⑤ **Make sure your Print Table Definition dialog box matches the one shown in Figure 3.23. This will produce the maximum information for each of the categories. Click OK to close the Print Table Definition dialog box.**

⑥ **Click OK to close the Documenter dialog box.**

Access runs the Documenter and prepares a report (see Figure 3.24). The procedure will take a while.

Figure 3.24
The Documenter creates a report on the table's characteristics.

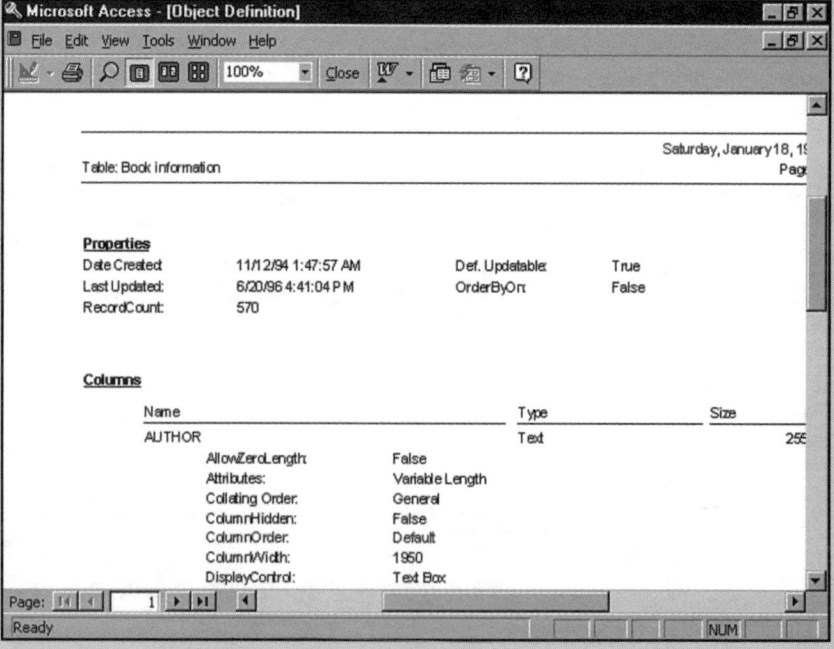

This report is two pages long. If you had selected both tables, the process might have taken a couple of minutes, and the report would have been more than twice as long, since the Story Summaries table is much more complex than the Book Information table.

7 Print the report, then Close the Print Preview window.

You can run the Database Documenter on any database object.

8 Close the database. Leave Access open for use in the next lesson.

  You may want to keep an electronic version of the Documenter information. You can use the Publish It with MS Word button to export the report to Microsoft Word.

Lesson 6: Using OfficeLinks to Analyze Data Using Excel and Create Reports Using Word

In many cases you will want to perform calculations using the fields in your database. While Access has many capabilities, such as calculated fields and summaries on reports, it is usually far easier to perform calculations in an Excel spreadsheet. You can send the contents of a table to Excel, but in many cases it is better to send a query that contains only the data you want to use. You can also send data to Excel from forms and reports.

In this lesson, you use two queries from the census database you used in Project 1. The first query looks at women who have children, as reported in the 1900 census. This query will be transferred to Excel for analysis. The second query identifies those persons listed as farmers in the 1900 census, and will be used in the second part of this lesson.

This first part of this lesson requires that you have Microsoft Excel available. If it is not, please move to step 9. If you do not have Microsoft Word available, please skip this lesson.

To Use OfficeLinks to Analyze Data Using Excel and Create Reports Using Word

1 Make a copy the student data file Proj0303.

2 Rename the copy Haynes Township Census.

Add the .mdb extension only if you can see the extension on the Proj0303 file.

3 Open the Haynes Township Census database.

4 Click on the Queries tab if necessary.

The two queries in this database will be displayed.

5 Select and Open the Alcona County (Haynes Township) Women: Number of Children query.

Notice that the query contains only seven of the 38 fields in the 1900 Alcona County (Haynes Township) Census table (see Figure 3.25).

continues

To Use OfficeLinks to Analyze Data Using Excel and Create Reports Using Word   (continued)

Figure 3.25
The query contains only seven fields.

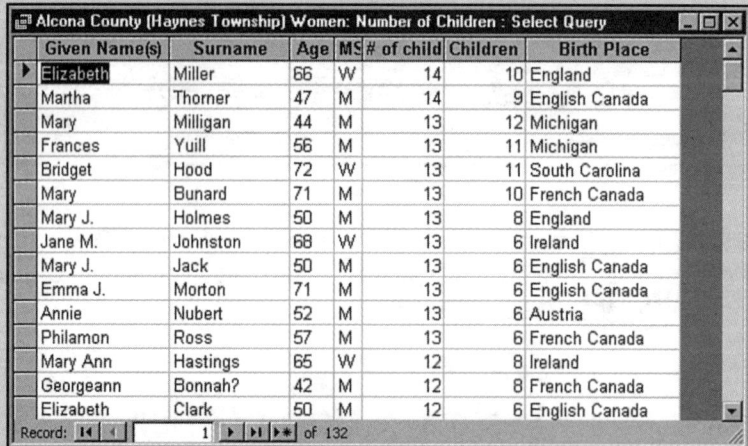

6 Choose **Tools, OfficeLinks** from the menu, then select **Analyze It with MS Excel.**

The program opens Excel and transfers the data from the query to the Excel program. This is now an Excel file, and can be edited, modified, and saved in the same way you would work on any other Excel file (see Figure 3.26).

Figure 3.26
The Analyze It with MS Excel option creates a new Excel file and transfers data from Access.

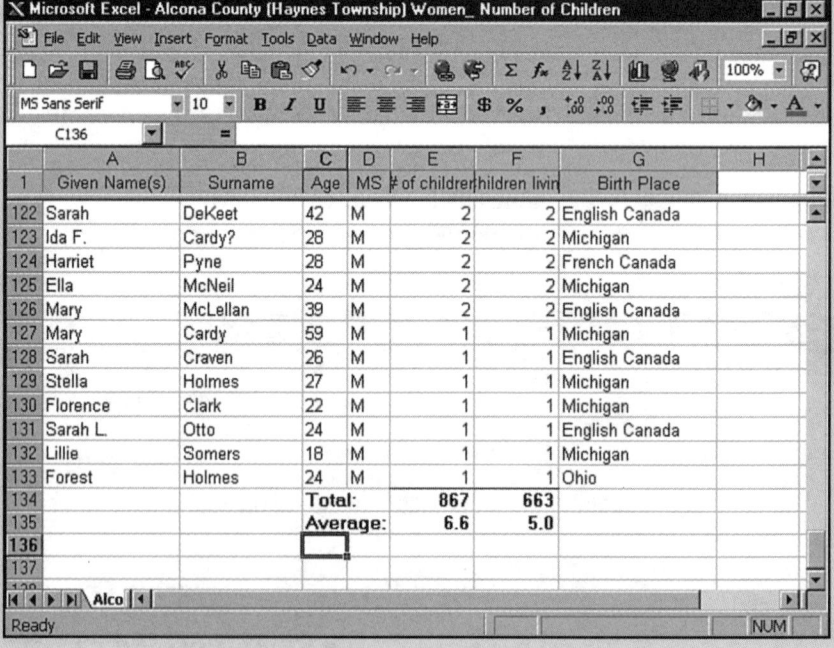

The Excel file created in this way is in its final form; updates that you make to the data in Access will not be transferred to the new Excel file.

7 **Close Excel and move back to Access.**

8 **Close the Alcona County (Haynes Township) Women: Number of Children query.**

You can also send information from an Access database to Microsoft Word.

9 **Select and Open the Alcona County (Haynes Township) Farmers query.**

A list of all of the farmers identified in the 1900 census appears (see Figure 3.27). Only seven of the fields have been requested for this query.

Figure 3.27
The query contains only those who have a farm number.

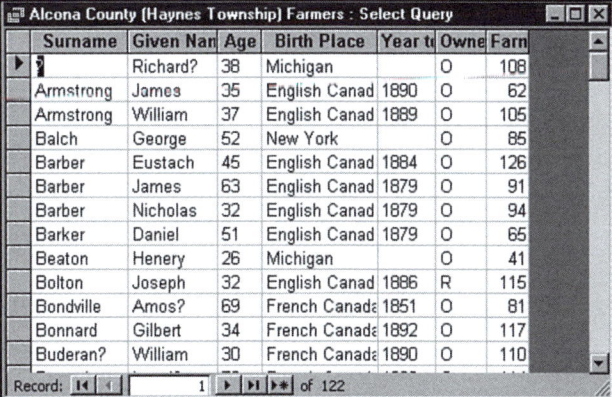

10 **Choose Tools, OfficeLinks from the menu, then select Publish It with MS Word.**

The program opens Word and transfers the data from the query to a Word document (see Figure 3.28). This is now a Word file, and can be edited, formatted, and saved in the same way you would work on any other Word file.

continues

To Use OfficeLinks to Analyze Data Using Excel and Create Reports Using Word (continued)

Figure 3.28
The Publish It with MS Word option creates a new Word file and transfers information from Access.

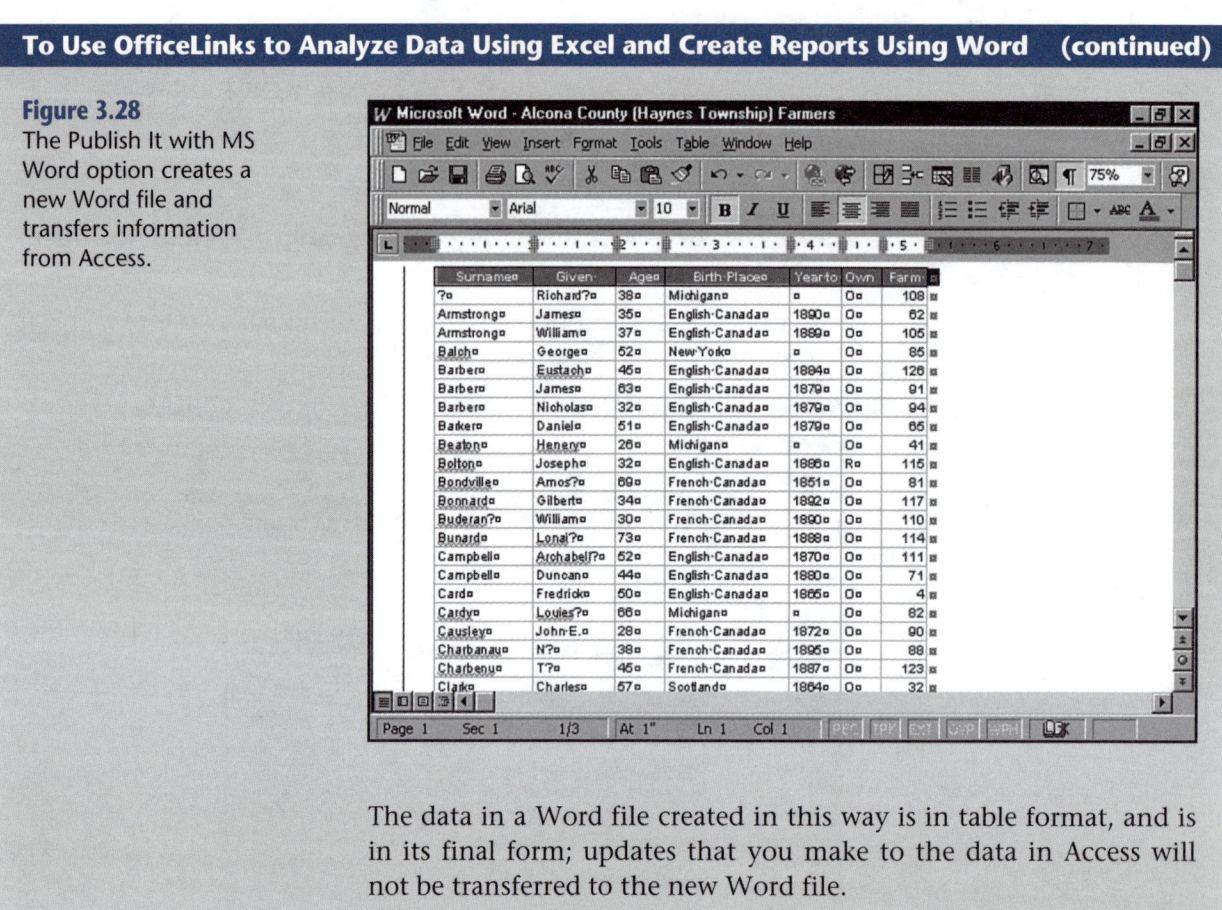

The data in a Word file created in this way is in table format, and is in its final form; updates that you make to the data in Access will not be transferred to the new Word file.

⑪ Close Word and Access, saving files as necessary.

Project Summary

To	Do This
Correct spelling with the Spell Checker	Go to the Tables tab and open the table you want to check. Select the column (field) or columns to check, then choose **T**ools, **S**pelling or click the Spelling button. Make any necessary changes.
Customize data entry using AutoCorrect	Choose **T**ools, **A**utoCorrect. Type a shortcut in the **R**eplace box, then type the replacement in the **W**ith box. Click **A**dd to add your shortcut to the AutoCorrect list.
Analyze a table	Choose **T**ools, Anal**y**ze, then select **T**able. Select the table or tables you want to analyze. Choose whether to let the wizard decide how to split the table(s). Rename the new tables. Correct any typos, then decide whether to create a query to duplicate the original table.
Analyze database performance	Choose **T**ools, Anal**y**ze, then select the Analyze tool. Choose the Object Type you want to work with. Choose the object(s) you want to analyze. Consider the ideas, recommendations, and suggestions, and make the appropriate changes.

To	Do This
Determine database characteristics using the Documenter	Choose **T**ools, Anal**y**ze, then select **Documenter**. Choose the object type you want to document, then select one or more of the objects. Click Options to set the level of detail, then run the analysis. Print out the results.
Use Office**L**inks to analyze data using Excel and create reports using Word	Open the object you want to link, then choose either **T**ools, Office**L**inks, **A**nalyze It with MS Excel, or **T**ools, Office**L**inks, **P**ublish It with MS Word. Use Excel or Word to edit, modify, or reformat the information.

Checking Your Skills

True/False

For each of the following statements, check *T* or *F* to indicate whether the statement is true or false.

__T __F **1.** If you add a new word to your Custom dictionary in Access, it will not automatically be included in the Custom dictionary in Microsoft Word.

__T __F **2.** An AutoCorrect shortcut added in Access will also be available in Excel.

__T __F **3.** You can run the Analyze tool from anywhere in the database.

__T __F **4.** Choose Optimize to accept a Performance Analyzer recommendation.

__T __F **5.** The Documenter works only on tables.

Multiple Choice

Circle the letter of the correct answer for each of the following questions.

1. The _____ tool enables you to enter shortcuts for longer words or phrases.

    a. AutoCorrect

    b. Documenter

    c. Table Analyzer

    d. Performance Analyzer

2. In order to activate the shortcut feature in AutoCorrect, type the shortcut, followed by _____.

    a. a   only

    b. a punctuation mark only

    c. the Tab⇄ key

    d. all of the above

3. The _____ is a tool that looks at database objects and gives information on each object and control.

    a. Performance Analyzer

    b. Documenter

    c. Table Analyzer

    d. AutoCorrect

4. It is usually a good idea to accept a Performance Analyzer recommendation to index a field if you ever plan to _____ on that field.

    a. run a Spelling Checker

    b. do a Performance Analysis

    c. sort

    d. create a Crosstab

5. When you send a query to Excel using OfficeLinks:

    a. the file is in its final form and won't be updated as you update information in the database

    b. the file is automatically updated as you update the database

    c. you can change information in the spreadsheet and the changes will also be made in the database

    d. the query will look at the spreadsheet and import the information to your database

Completion

In the blank provided, write the correct answer for each of the following statements.

1. To run the Spelling Checker on only one field, click the _____ header to select the field.

2. The _____ is a tool that looks for duplications in fields and splits tables to make them more efficient.

3. When you split a table into two or more tables, it is a good idea to _____ the tables so you'll know what they contain.

4. The _____ Analyzer is a tool that looks at database objects and gives recommendations, suggestions, and ideas for improving their performance.

5. You would use _____ to send information directly from Access to Word or Excel.

Applying Your Skills

At the end of each project in *Access 97 Essentials Level III*, you learn how to apply your Access skills to various situations. The following exercises help you practice the skills you have learned in this project. Take a few minutes to work through these exercises now.

Exploring the Documenter

The Documenter can give you a great deal of information about a table. In Lesson 5, you looked at the characteristics of a small table. In the following exercise, you will look at a much larger table. Notice how much longer the Documenter takes to run, and how much longer the report is.

To Explore the Documenter

1. Open the Proj0304 database and rename it `Exploring the Documenter`.

2. Use the Documenter and choose the 1900 Alcona County (Haynes Township) Census table.

3. Select the **O**ptions choice.

4. Select everything but the Properties in the Include for **F**ields and Include for **I**ndexes areas.

5. Run the Documenter.

6. Scan the results to see what information is included.

7. Print out your results.

Exploring the Table Analyzer

You used the Table Analyzer in Lesson 3, but let Access make all the decisions. In this exercise, you will take control of the analyzer and make your own choices.

To Explore the Table Analyzer

1. Open the Proj0305 database and rename it `Exploring the Table Analyzer`.

2. Use the Table Analyzer tool and choose the 1900 Alcona County (Haynes Township) Census table.

3. Choose to identify the fields yourself.

4. Follow the on-screen instructions to drag and drop the Place field to create a new table (there is only one entry in the Place field, but more will follow).

5. Call the first table `Census Information`, and rename the new table as `Place`.

6. Follow the on-screen instructions to drag and drop the Year field to create a new table.

7. Call the new table **Year**.

8. Finish the wizard, which will take you to the Query window.

9. In the Query design, turn off the Show button for the Year_ID and Place_ID.

10. Move to the Census Information table to make sure the Lookup to Place and Lookup to Year appear (they should be on the far right-hand side of the table).

Exploring the AutoCorrect Feature

The AutoCorrect feature, when used in combination with Combo and List boxes, makes data entry far easier. In this exercise, you will continue to add AutoCorrect entries for Short Stories data entry form.

To Explore the AutoCorrect Feature

1. Open the Proj0306 database and rename it **Exploring AutoCorrect**.

2. Open the Book Information table.

3. Create a shortcut called **rr** for Review of Reviews.

4. Create a shortcut called **hm** for Houghton Mifflin

5. Deselect the Correct TWo INitial CApitals option.

Project

4

Using Advanced Reports

In this Project, you learn how to:

➤ Create Simple Crosstab Queries and Reports

➤ Create Crosstab Queries with Conditions and Total Columns

➤ Review Linked Tables Simultaneously

➤ Insert Subreports into Reports Using the Subform/Report Wizard

➤ Create Reports Using the Chart Wizard

Why Would I Do This?

T he best database is of little use unless its data can be communicated and turned into information. A crosstab query and its report are very useful in analyzing data. You will learn how to produce a table that will count, average, or sum the data by groupings that you choose.

If you are using tables that are joined, it is very useful to view both tables at the same time. You learn how to do this using subforms and subreports.

The best way to communicate some types of data is to represent the data as a chart. You learn how to create a chart using the Chart Wizard, and how to edit the chart in Microsoft Graph.

Lesson 1: Creating Crosstab Queries and Reports

A crosstab query produces a dynaset where the contents of one field provide the column headings and the contents of another field are used as row headings. The cells of the query are calculated based on the fields that match the values of both the row and column fields.

The first thing you need to do is make a copy of a database file that is included with this book. Once you copy and rename the file, you are ready to complete the first lesson.

To Open the Census Database

❶ **Make a copy of the student data file Proj0401.**

❷ **Rename the copy Orders.**

Include the .mdb extension only if you can see the extension on the Proj0401 file.

❸ **Launch Access 97.**

❹ **Open the Orders database.**

The database window should now be open to the Tables area (see Figure 4.1). Keep the database open for the next exercise.

Figure 4.1
The database window displays the Tables area of the Orders database.

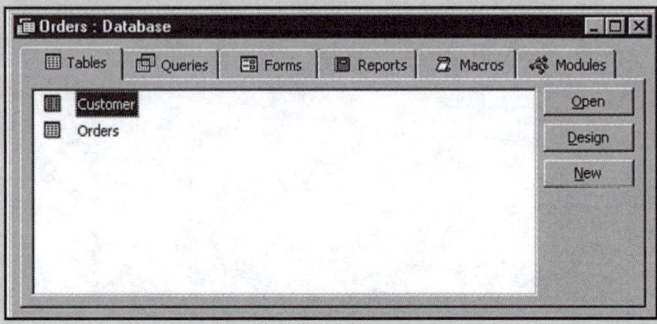

In this example, you learn how to create a crosstab query based on two tables that show customer information and orders placed by those customers for various types of cleaning supplies. The crosstab query calculates the total quantity of each item sold to each customer.

To Create a Crosstab Query Based on Two Tables

1 Click the Queries tab.

2 Click the New button.

The New Query dialog box appears.

3 Click Design View and then click OK.

The Show Table dialog box appears (see Figure 4.2).

Figure 4.2
The Query design and Show Table windows are displayed.

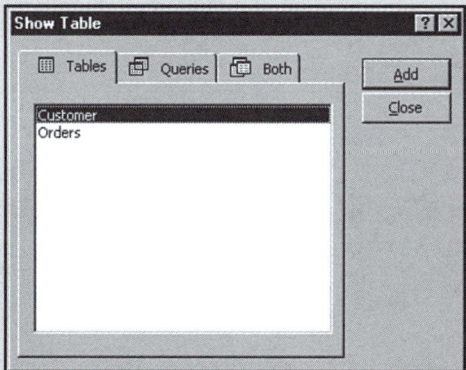

4 Click the Customer table name and then click Add.

The Customer table is added to the query design window.

5 Click the Orders table name and then click Add.

6 Click Close.

The Show Table dialog box closes and the query design window appears with the Customer and Orders tables (see Figure 4.3).

Figure 4.3
The Query design window shows that the Customer and Orders tables have been added.

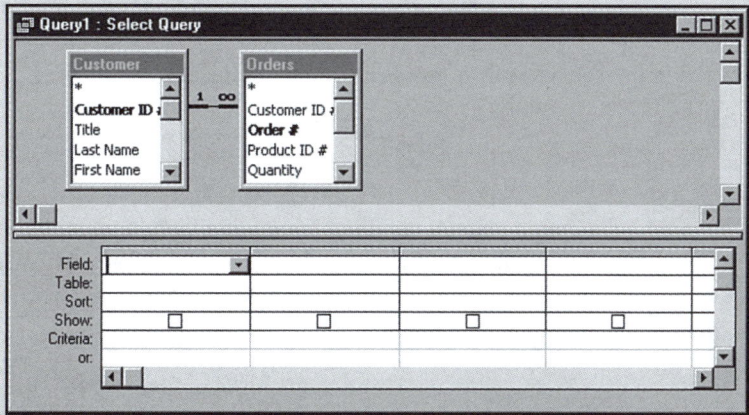

continues

To Create a Crosstab Query Based on Two Tables   (continued)

7 Click the Query Type button.

A menu of query types will be displayed (see Figure 4.4).

Figure 4.4
The Query Type menu displays the various Query options.

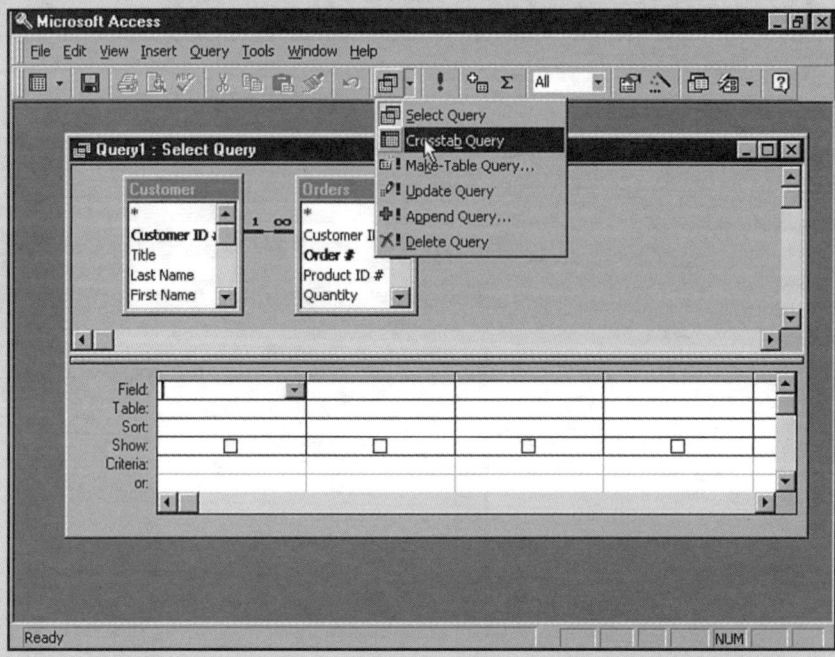

8 Click the Crosstab Query option.

Notice that the Query by Example (QBE) table now has two new rows named Crosstab and Total (see Figure 4.5).

Figure 4.5
The Crosstab Query has Crosstab and Total rows added to the QBE table.

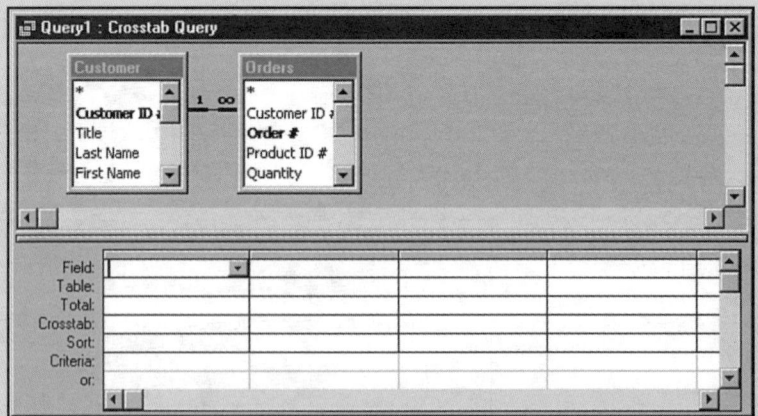

9 Scroll down the list of fields in the Customer table to the Company name. Drag this field name to the first column of the query table.

The first column shows the Company field and fills in the next two boxes with the table name and the default setting of Group By in the Total box.

Use the company names as row headings on the left side of the Crosstab table that will be produced.

⑩ Click the Crosstab box in the Company column then click the down arrow at the right side of the box to reveal a menu of choices.

A menu of options for the Crosstab box appears (see Figure 4.6).

Figure 4.6
The options for the Crosstab box in the Company column.

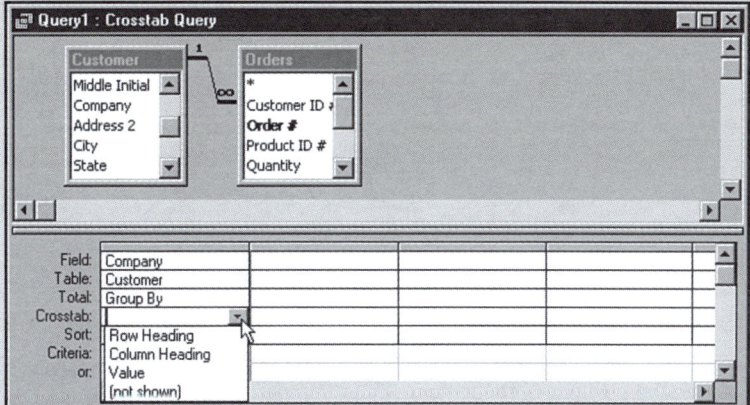

⑪ Click the Row Heading option.

⑫ Scroll down the list of fields in the Orders table. Drag the Product Description field into the second column.

The name of each type of product is used as the column headings in the resulting Crosstab table.

⑬ Click the Crosstab box in the Product Description column and the down arrow in that box. Select Column Heading from the list of options.

⑭ Drag the Quantity field from the Orders table into the third column.

Add up the quantity of each type of product sold to each customer and display it in the cells of the resulting Crosstab table.

⑮ Click the Crosstab box in the Quantity column and click the down arrow in that box. Select Value from the list of options.

This will specify that the program will calculate a numeric result to be placed in the table. The Total box must be changed from Group By to a mathematical operation.

⑯ Click the Total box in the Quantity column and then click the down arrow to reveal a menu of mathematical operations.

A drop-down menu appears (see Figure 4.7).

continues

To Create a Crosstab Query Based on Two Tables   (continued)

Figure 4.7
The Total drop-
down menu displays
several mathematical
operators.

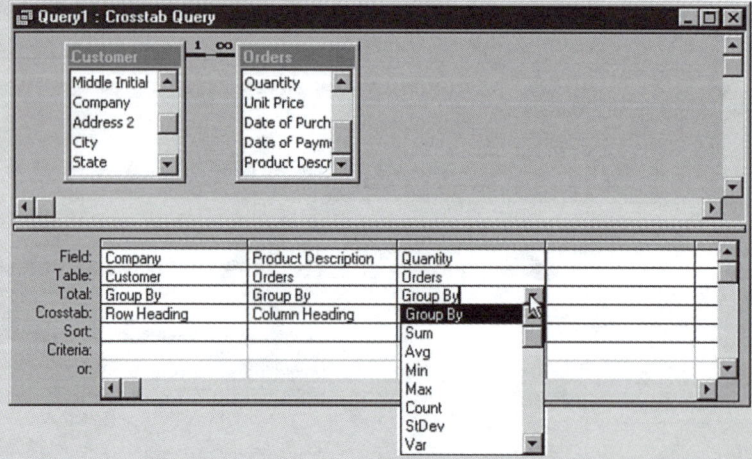

17 **Click the Sum option.**

This adds up the quantity sold for each product to each customer.
Check to see if your settings in the three columns match those in
the following figure (see Figure 4.8).

Figure 4.8
The Crosstab Query
design window displays
the necessary settings.

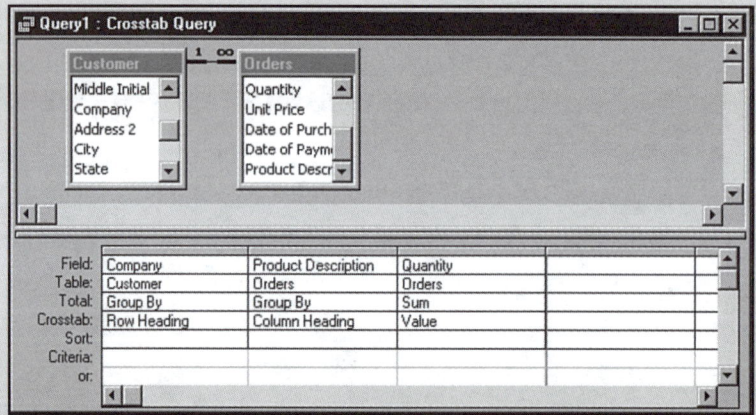

18 **Click the View button to view the resulting Crosstab query
table.**

The Crosstab Query table is displayed (see Figure 4.9).

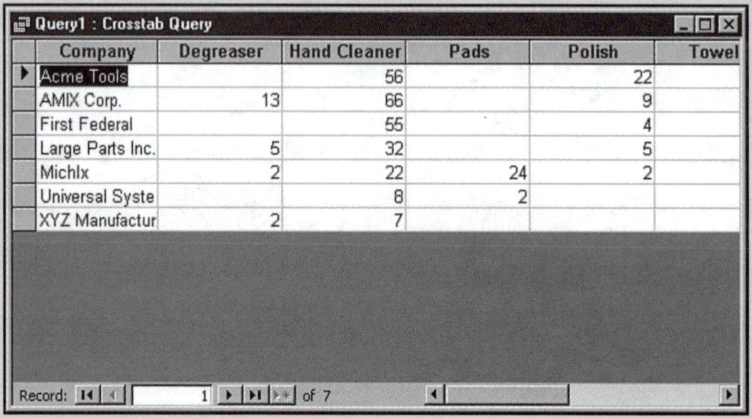

Figure 4.9
The Crosstab Query
table shows the
quantity of each
product sold for each
customer.

Company	Degreaser	Hand Cleaner	Pads	Polish	Towel
Acme Tools		56		22	
AMIX Corp.	13	66		9	
First Federal		55		4	
Large Parts Inc.	5	32		5	
Michlx	2	22	24	2	
Universal Syste		8	2		
XYZ Manufactur	2	7			

Record: 14 4   1 ▶ ▶I ▶* of 7

19 Click the Save button on the toolbar and save the query with the name `Products Sold by Customer`.

20 Click the View button to return to Design View.

Leave the Design View open for the next lesson.

Lesson 2: Creating Crosstab Queries with Conditions and Total Columns

It is possible to use criteria to limit the crosstab query calculations. You can also include additional columns of summary data.

In this lesson, you learn how to limit the orders in the crosstab query to those sold between two given dates. You also learn how to add a column to the table to calculate the total bill for each customer.

To Use a Criteria Based Upon Another Field in a Crosstab Query

1 In the Design View of the Crosstab query in the Orders database, drag the Date of Purchase field from the Orders table to the fourth column of the query table.

2 Click the Total box in Date of Purchase column and click the down arrow to reveal the menu of choices. Scroll down and click Expression.

The Total box in the fourth column will contain the word Expression.

3 Enter the following expression in the Criteria box for the Date of Purchase column:

Between 1/1/96 and 1/31/96

If you press the ↵Enter key or click another cell, the program will add # signs on either side of the dates (see Figure 4.10). (The window in the figure has been widened to show the expression. It is not necessary for you to do so.)

Figure 4.10
A criteria expression has been added to the Date of Purchase field.

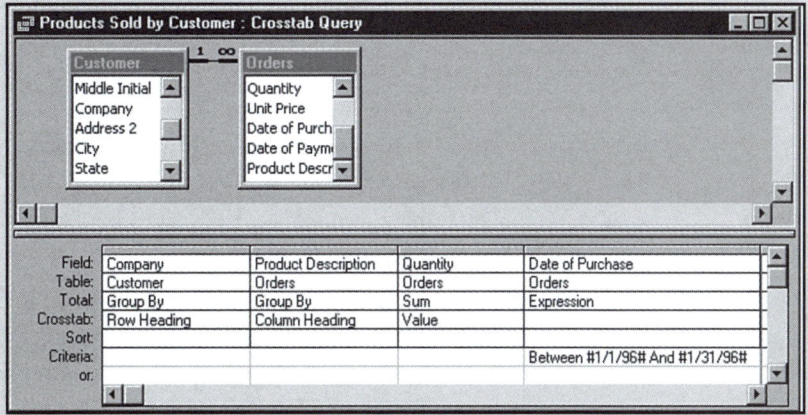

continues

To Use a Criteria Based Upon Another Field in a Crosstab Query (continued)

4 Click the View button to view the Crosstab Query datasheet.

The table only includes those purchases made in January 1996 (see Figure 4.11). The Between expression is inclusive; that is, purchases made on the beginning and end dates will be included in the table.

Figure 4.11
The Crosstab table shows purchases made in January 1996.

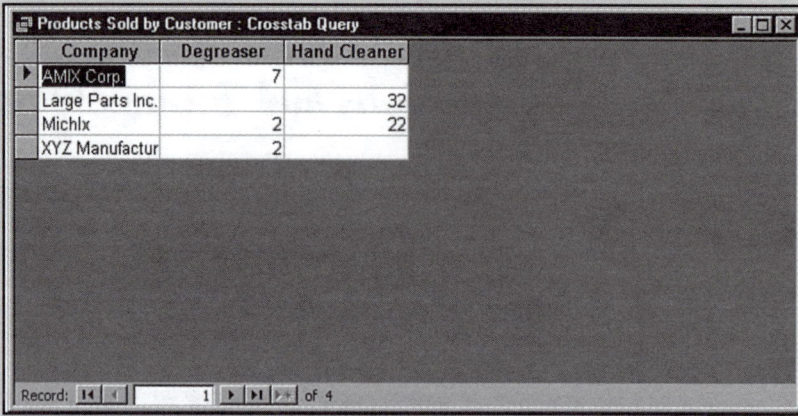

5 Click the View button to return to the Design View.

Leave the Design View open for use in the next section.

In the next section of the lesson, delete the Date of Purchase criteria and add a column to display the total cost to the customer for each type of purchase.

To Include a Column of Totals in a Crosstab Query

1 Click the narrow column selector bar at the top of the Date of Purchase column to select the column.

The Date of Purchase column will be highlighted.

2 Press the `Del` key to delete this column from the Crosstab query design.

3 Enter the following expression in the Field box in the next empty column in the Crosstab query design table:

```
Total Cost: [Quantity]*[Unit Price]
```

The words to the left of the colon will be used as the label for the new column. The expression to the right of the colon will multiply the contents of the Quantity and Unit Price fields for each type of purchase for each customer. Each field in the expression must be enclosed by brackets.

4 Click the Crosstab box in the new column. Click the down arrow and then click Row Heading.

Even though we are seeking to produce a column of totals, these totals are considered by the program to be row headings.

Notice that the Total box has the default entry Group By.

5 Click the View button to go to the Datasheet view.

The Crosstab Query will display the cost for each purchase by customer with a separate row for each purchase (see Figure 4.12).

Products Sold by Customer : Crosstab Query

Company	Total Cost	Degreaser	Hand Cleaner	Pads	Polish
Acme Tools	$253.00				22
Acme Tools	$1,960.00		56		
AMIX Corp.	$103.50				9
AMIX Corp.	$132.00	6			
AMIX Corp.	$154.00	7			
AMIX Corp.	$2,310.00		66		
First Federal	$46.00				4
First Federal	$1,925.00		55		
Large Parts Inc.	$10.00	5			
Large Parts Inc.	$57.50				5
Large Parts Inc.	$1,120.00		32		
Michlx	$23.00				2
Michlx	$44.00	2			

Record: 1 of 20

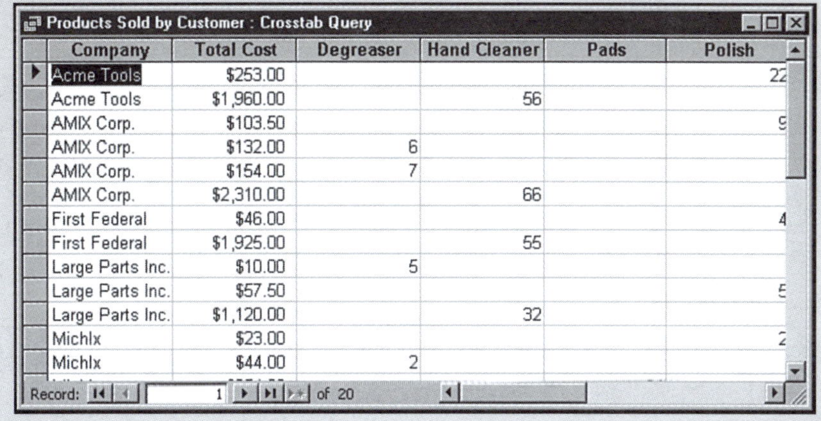

Figure 4.12
The Crosstab Query displaying the cost for each purchase by customer with a separate row for each purchase.

6 Click the View button to return to the Design View.

7 Click the Total box in the column that contains the expression entered in the previous step 3 and click the down arrow to display the menu of choices. Click Sum.

This adds the expressions for each of the purchases to yield a total for each customer.

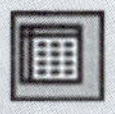

8 Click the View button to view the Crosstab Query datasheet.

The Total Cost expression column now shows a total for each customer for each product. These totals are considered to be row headers (see Figure 4.13).

Products Sold by Customer : Crosstab Query

Company	Total Cost	Degreaser	Hand Cleaner	Pads	Polish
Acme Tools	$2,213.00		56		22
AMIX Corp.	$2,699.50	13	66		9
First Federal	$1,971.00		55		4
Large Parts Inc.	$1,187.50	5	32		5
Michlx	$1,191.00	2	22	24	2
Universal Syste	$309.50		8	2	
XYZ Manufactur	$365.00	2	7		

Record: 1 of 7

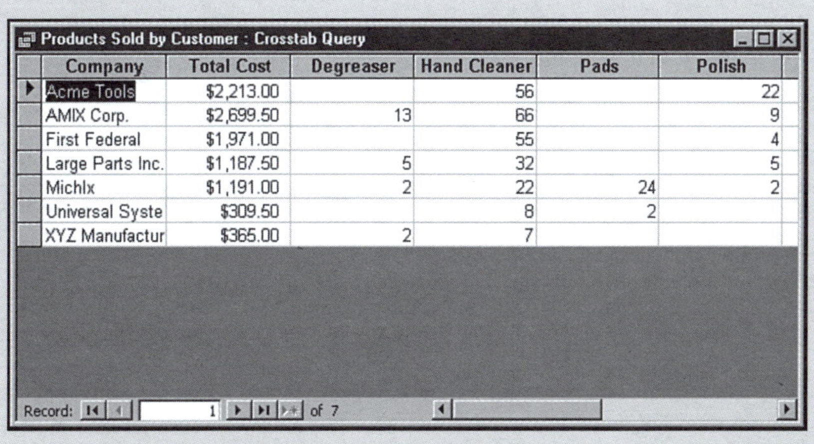

Figure 4.13
The Crosstab Query displaying the total cost for each customer.

continues

To Include a Column of Totals in a Crosstab Query   (continued)

 ⑨ **Click the Save button on the toolbar to save the query design.**

⑩ **Close the query and leave the database open for use in the next lesson.**

 Crosstab queries can be confusing if you jump into the design of one without a clear objective in mind. Decide ahead of time which field should be used as a row header or column header. Determine which field should be used to calculate the value in each cell and what mathematical expression to use.

The Crosstab Query Wizard creates simple crosstab queries for you. You must have at least one choice for row, column, and value fields. You have an option of adding a totals column. If you want to use a calculated expression, you can use the wizard to create most of the query and then modify the design according to the directions in the latter section in this lesson.

Lesson 3: Reviewing Linked Tables Simultaneously

If you have two linked tables, it is often useful to be able to review the data in both tables simultaneously.

In this lesson, you learn how to review two linked tables. A form based on a customer orders table (the subform) is placed within another form based on a table of general customer information. The navigation buttons are automatically synchronized so that the records shown in the orders form are those that match the customer shown in the general information form.

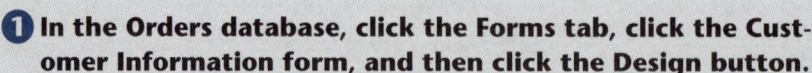

To Review Two Tables Simultaneously Using a Form and Subform

❶ **In the Orders database, click the Forms tab, click the Customer Information form, and then click the Design button.**

First, you open the form based on the table that has the primary key field. In this case, the Customer table contains the primary key field, Customer ID #.

The Customer Information form will open in the Design View.

❷ **Maximize the size of the design window.**

 ❸ **Click the Toolbox button on the toolbar if the Toolbox is not already displayed on the screen.**

Make sure the Control Wizards button is selected on the toolbox.

 ❹ **Click the Subform/Subreport button on the toolbox. Draw a rectangle that fits in the lower portion of the currently open form.**

When you draw the rectangle, it appears as a thin line. This marks the boundary of the subform (see Figure 4.14).

Figure 4.14
The Customer
Information form dis-
plays the designated
area for the subform.

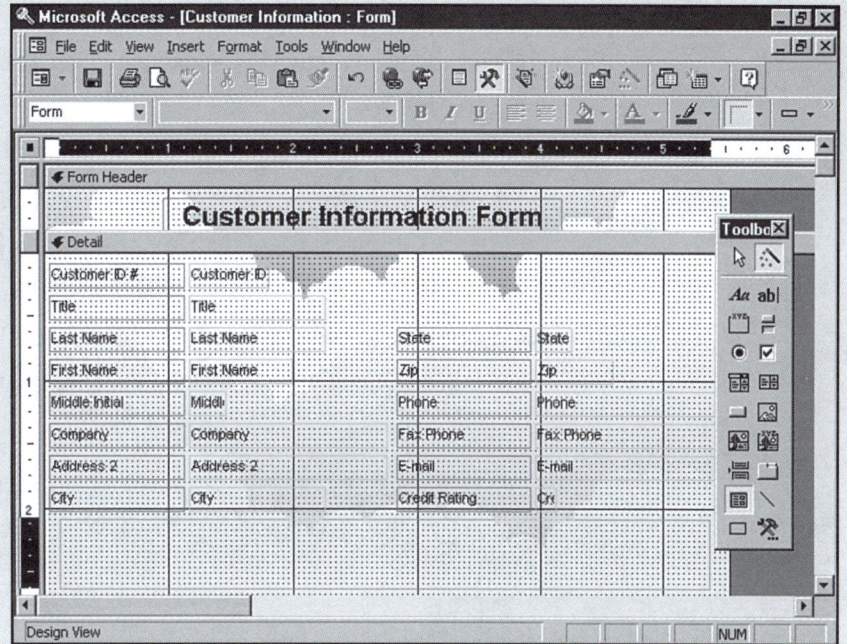

When you release the mouse button, the Subform/Subreport wizard is activated. After a minute or so, the Subform/Subreport Wizard dialog box appears.

⑤ Click the Forms option. Click the down arrow to show a menu of available forms, then select Orders.

You can use the wizard to create a subform or use an existing form. Usually the subform is a tabular form like the Orders form used in this example (see Figure 4.15).

Figure 4.15
The second Subform/
Subreport Wizard
dialog box asks for a
source.

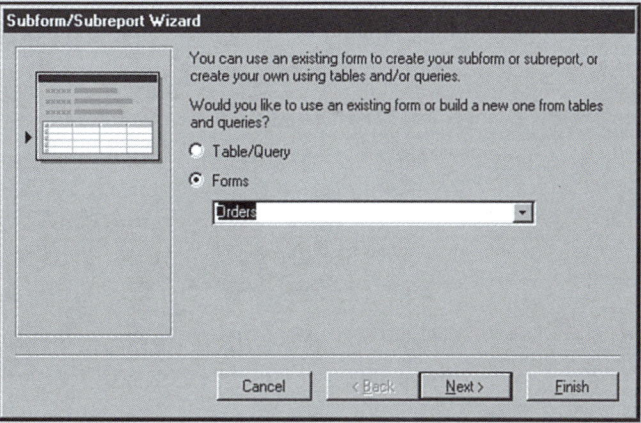

⑥ Click Next.

The next Subform/Subreport Wizard dialog box appears. It identifies the field that links the two tables and gives you the option of linking the two forms using that field or leaving the two forms unlinked.

continues

To Review Two Tables Simultaneously Using a Form and Subform   (continued)

7 **Click the option named Show orders for each record in Customer using Customer ID #. Then, click Next.**

The next wizard dialog box appears and asks for a form name.

8 **Click the Finish button to accept the default name, Orders.**

The wizard finishes the design and returns you to the design of the Customer Information form.

9 **Click the View button to switch to the Form View.**

The Customer Information form is shown with the subform Orders embedded in it (see Figure 4.16).

Figure 4.16
The Customer Information form is shown with the Orders form embedded in it.

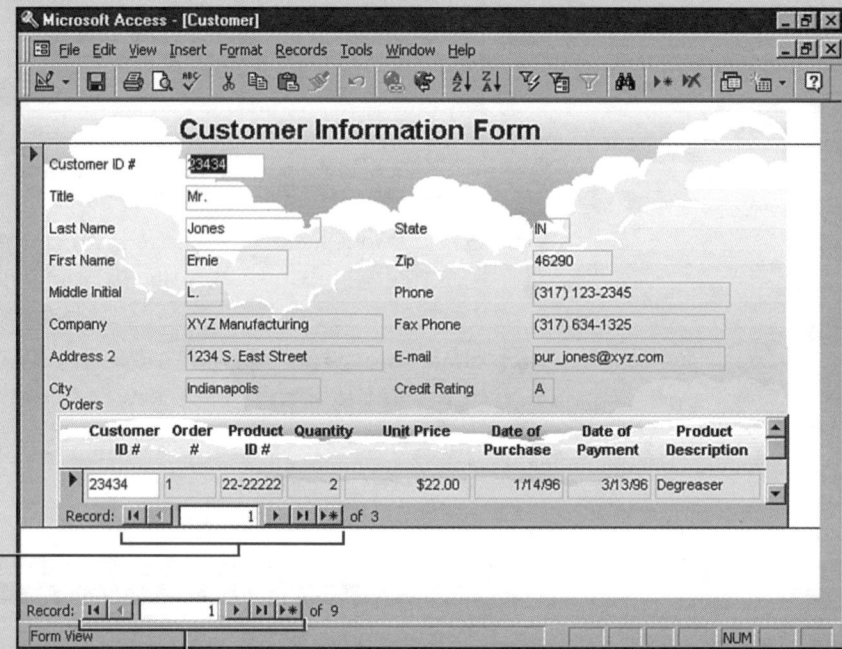

Navigation buttons for the Orders form

Navigation buttons for the Customer Information form

10 **Click the next record navigation button for the Orders form to navigate through the records that match the currently displayed customer in the Customer Information form.**

Notice that the Orders form only shows the records that match the customer in the Customer Information form.

11 **Click the next record navigation button at the bottom of the screen to look at the information for the next customer.**

Notice that the available orders change when you change customer names.

This design still needs a few refinements. The area for the subform is too small to show more than one record at a time.

⑫ **Click the View button to return to the Design View.**

⑬ **Scroll down to show the bottom part of the form. Click in the gray area at the bottom of the screen to deselect the subform.**

The form footer and subform area are moved to the middle of the screen, and the subform is no longer selected (see Figure 4.17).

Figure 4.17
The bottom portion of the Customer Information form displays a blank area where the subform will go.

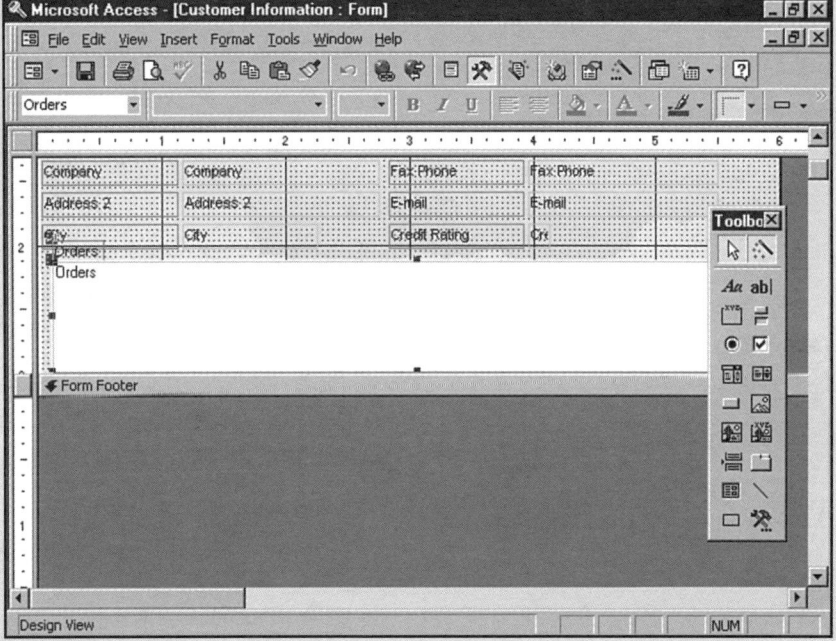

Notice that the Orders subform has a title box that was automatically created when you inserted the subform. It is unnecessary in this example, and it may overlap the label of the City field depending on where you drew the box.

⑭ **Carefully move your pointer to a portion of the Orders title that does not also include a portion of the City label. Click to select the title.**

Handles appears around the Orders title (see Figure 4.18).

continues

To Review Two Tables Simultaneously Using a Form and Subform   (continued)

Figure 4.18
Click carefully on the
Orders title to select it.

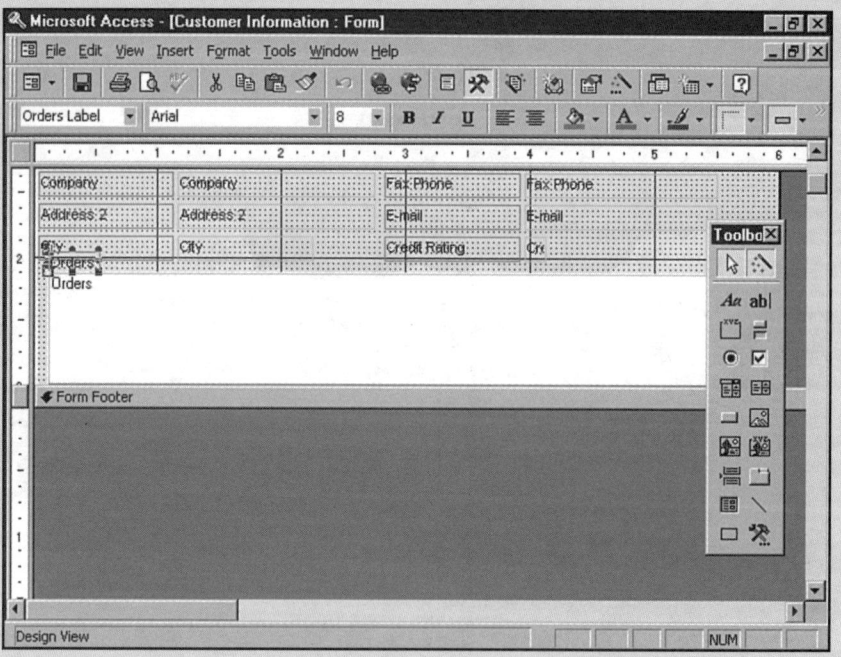

15 **Press the** Del **key to delete the Orders title.**

If you accidentally delete something else, use the Undo button
on the toolbar. If the title completely overlaps the field above it,
drag the entire orders subform downward to eliminate the overlap,
delete the title, and then move the subform back.

16 **Place the pointer on the top edge of the Form Footer bar and
drag it down to increase the detail area of the form.**

The pointer will turn into a double-headed arrow. Make sure you
place it at the top edge of the footer bar (see Figure 4.19).

Figure 4.19
The pointer on the top
edge of the footer bar is
shown after it has been
dragged downward to
increase the detail area.

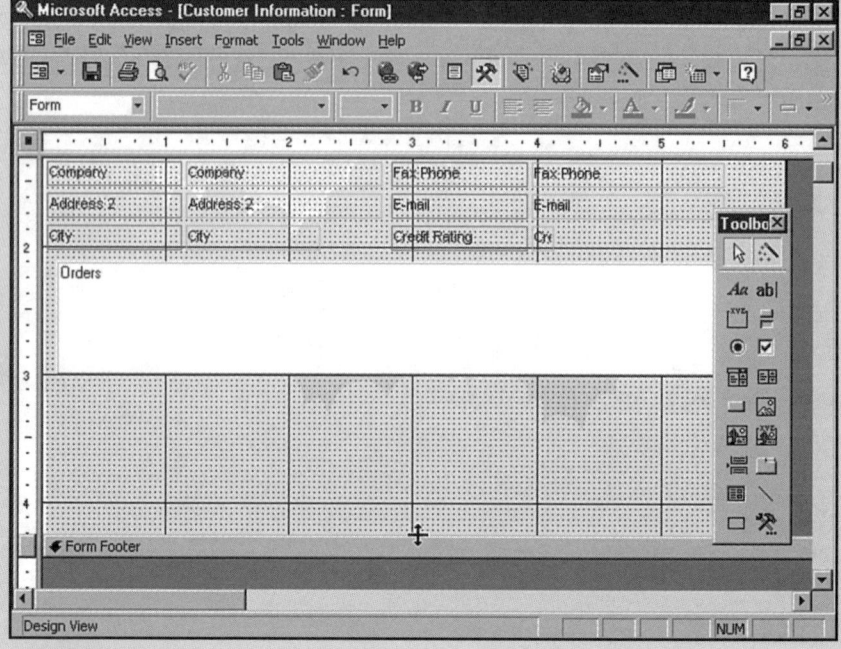

17 Click the Orders subform area to select it. Click and drag down the handle in the middle of the bottom side of the area to increase its size by about a half inch.

18 Click the View button on the toolbar to switch to the Form View.

The form should show both forms and their navigation bars (see Figure 4.20).

Figure 4.20
The two forms have been adjusted for size so that they both fit on one screen with both sets of navigation buttons.

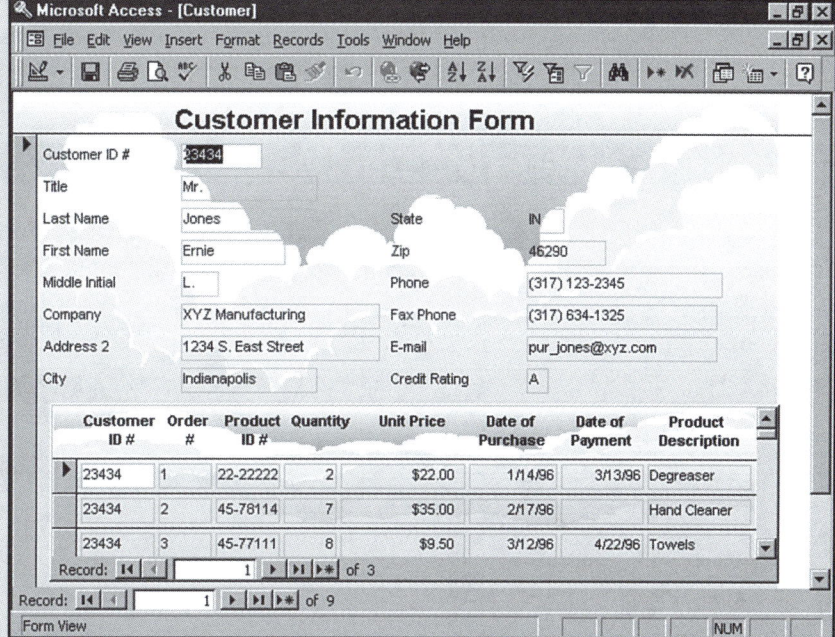

19 Compare your design with the one shown in Figure 4.20.

You will probably need to adjust the size of the subform and detail area. Switch back to the Design View if necessary and make those adjustments.

20 Close the form and save the changes.

Leave the database open for the next lesson.

If you have problems...

The Subform/Subreport feature may not be installed on your computer. It is not installed if the "Typical" option was used when Office 97 was installed. If you are working on your own computer, you can run the Setup program on your Office 97 master disk and add the advanced wizards.

Lesson 4: Inserting Subreports into Reports Using the Subform/Report Wizard

It is also possible to combine two reports that are based on joined tables. In this lesson you learn how to combine a report that shows the customer information from the Customer table in columnar format with the individual orders by that customer shown in a tabular format report.

First, we will preview the two reports that will be joined. These reports are already provided, for your convenience. The Customer report is based on the Customer table and was created with a columnar AutoReport and then modified by rearranging the fields. The Orders report is based on the Orders table and was created with a tabular AutoReport.

To Preview the Two Reports

1 In the Orders database, click the Reports tab. Click the Customer report, and then click the **P**review button.

The preview of the Customer report appears (see Figure 4.21).

Figure 4.21
The Preview button displays the Customer report.

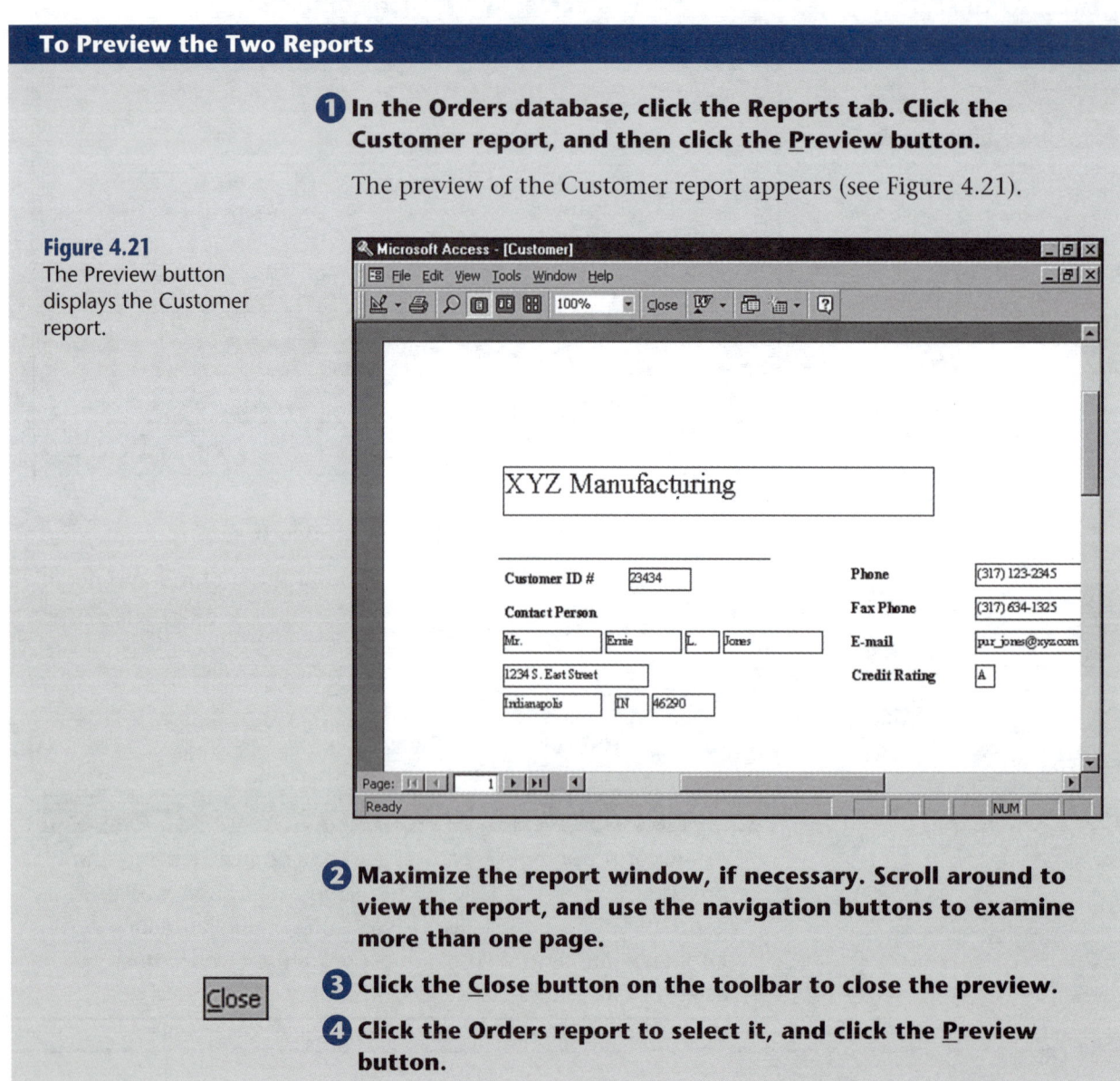

2 Maximize the report window, if necessary. Scroll around to view the report, and use the navigation buttons to examine more than one page.

3 Click the **C**lose button on the toolbar to close the preview.

4 Click the Orders report to select it, and click the **P**review button.

The preview of the Orders report appears (see Figure 4.22).

Figure 4.22
The Preview button displays the Orders report.

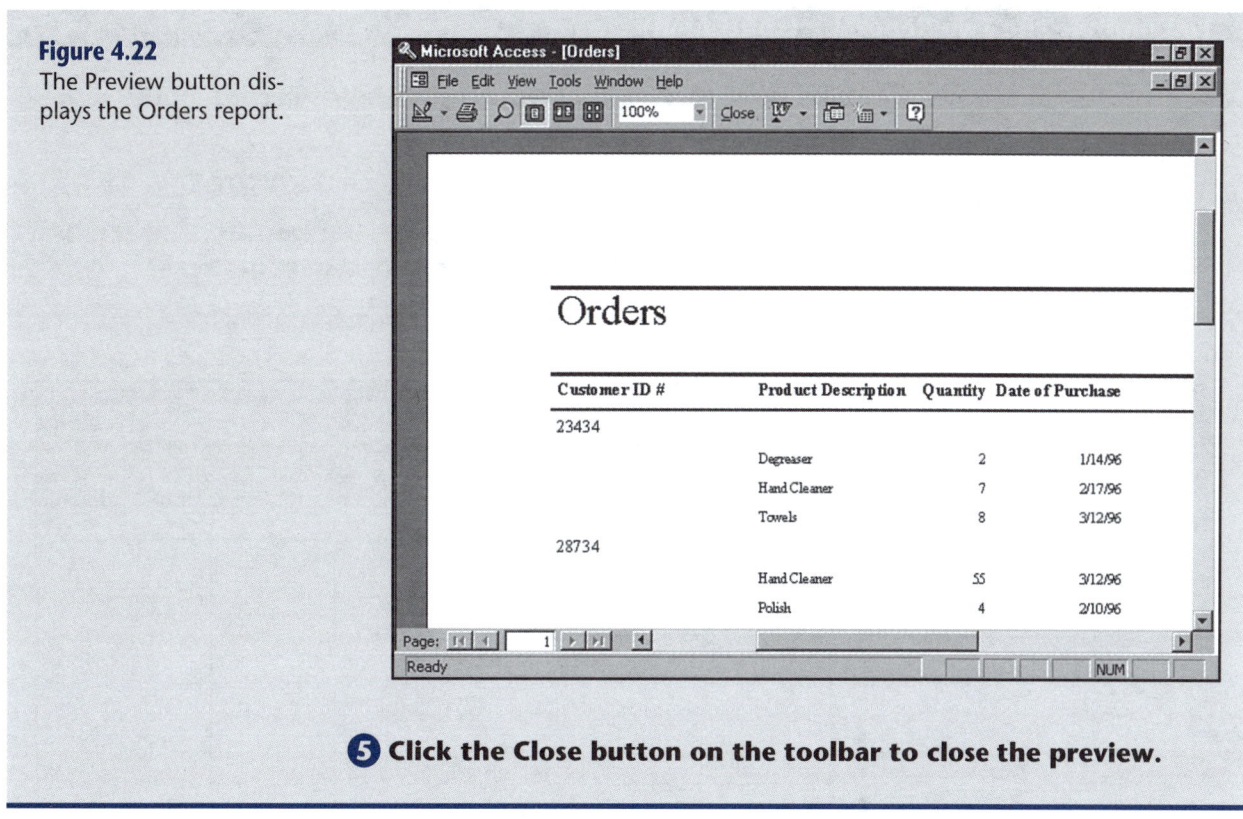

⑤ Click the Close button on the toolbar to close the preview.

In the next section, you learn how to make the Orders report a subreport of the Customer report.

To Combine the Two Reports

❶ Click the Customer report to select it, and then click Design.

The Customer report opens in the Design View (see Figure 4.23).

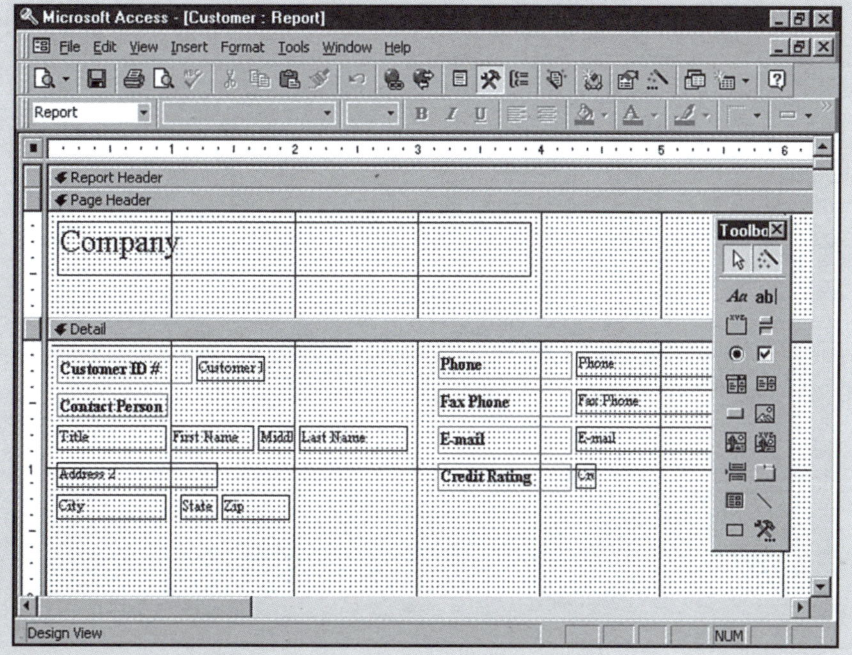

Figure 4.23
The Design View of the Customer report shows the report layout.

continues

To Combine the Two Reports (continued)

2 **Make sure the Control Wizards button is selected on the toolbox.**

The wizard helps establish the link between the two reports.

3 **Maximize the Report Design window, if necessary, and scroll down to show the bottom part of the report design.**

The bottom portion of the Detail area appears (see Figure 4.24).

Figure 4.24
The Design View of the Customers report is shown after it has been scrolled.

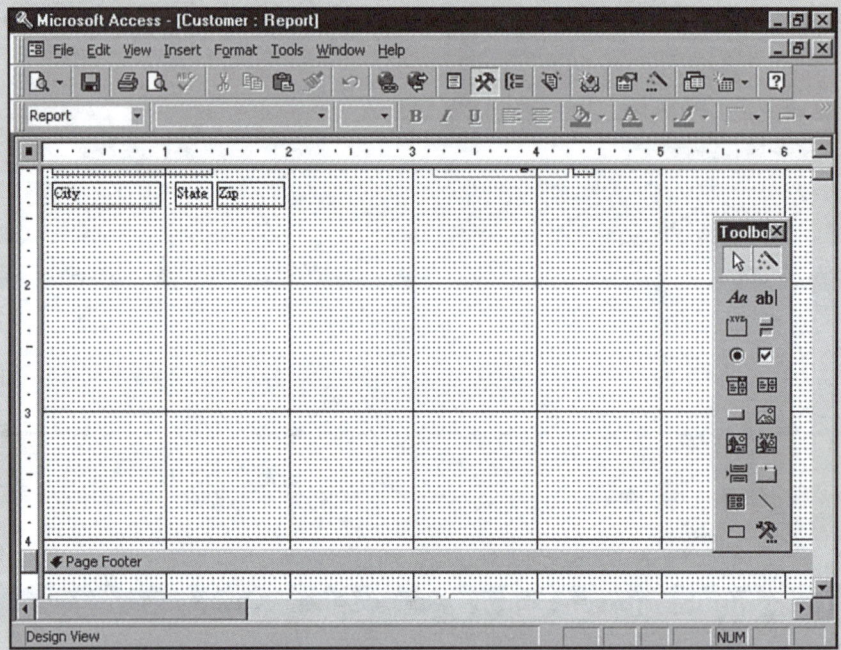

4 **Click the Subform/Subreport button in the toolbox and draw a rectangle in the empty portion of the report design.**

Draw a rectangle to indicate the location of the subform (see Figure 4.25).

Figure 4.25
The Customer report with the area for the subreport drawn.

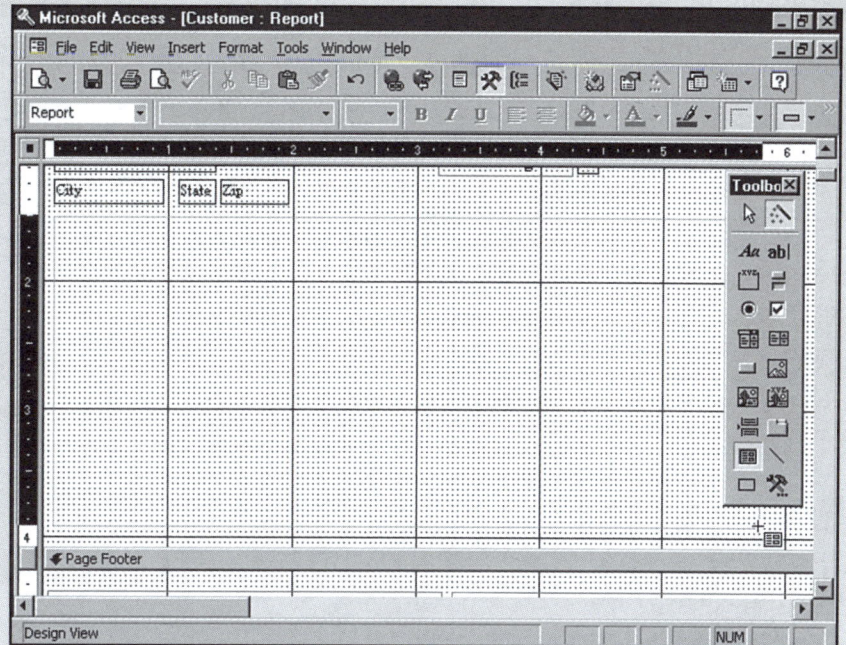

When you release the mouse button, the first Subform/Subreport Wizard dialog box appears.

5 Click the Reports and forms option button. Click the down arrow next to the text box and click the Orders report.

This dialog box enables you to select an existing report or to create a new report from a table or query. In this case, you will choose an existing report.

6 Click Next.

The second dialog box appears. If the reports you have selected are based on tables that are joined in a one-to-many relationship, you will see a choice that will link the reports in the same way (see Figure 4.26).

Figure 4.26
The Subform/Subreport Wizard dialog box that shows a choice that links the two reports.

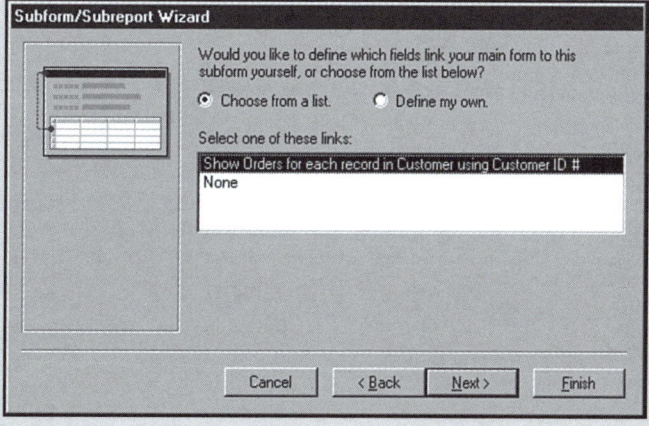

continues

To Combine the Two Reports   (continued)

7 Click the option Choose from a list, if necessary. Select the first link, Show Orders for each record in Customer using Customer ID #, and then click Next.

The final dialog box appears that asks for a name for the subreport.

8 Type Orders (if necessary), and then click Finish.

The wizard places the subreport in the report design. Notice that the title of the subreport may overlap the City label and that the size of the subreport may not match the rectangle you drew.

9 Drag the subreport down about a half-inch, if necessary, so its title does not overlap the City label.

The subreport should not overlap the other fields (see Figure 4.27).

Figure 4.27
The report design needs to be adjusted to avoid overlap.

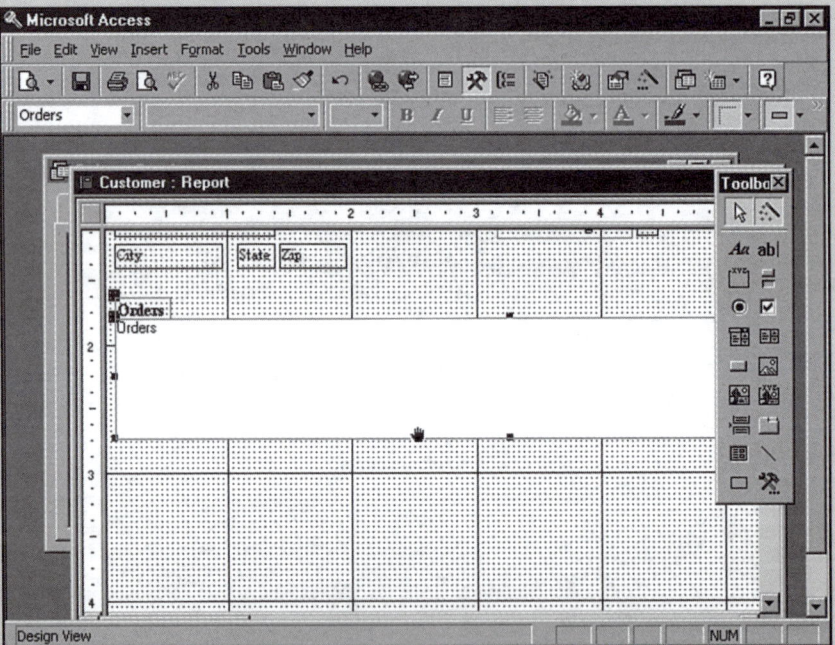

10 Click the View button on the toolbar to preview the report.

You may get a warning message that the report does not fit the page. This problem will be dealt with in following steps.

11 Maximize the window. Scroll the window so that you can see the subreport and most of the main report.

Notice that the list of orders is restricted to those that match the customer information above. Also, there is an extra "Orders" title the program automatically included (see Figure 4.28).

Figure 4.28
A preview of the final report that shows orders for one customer.

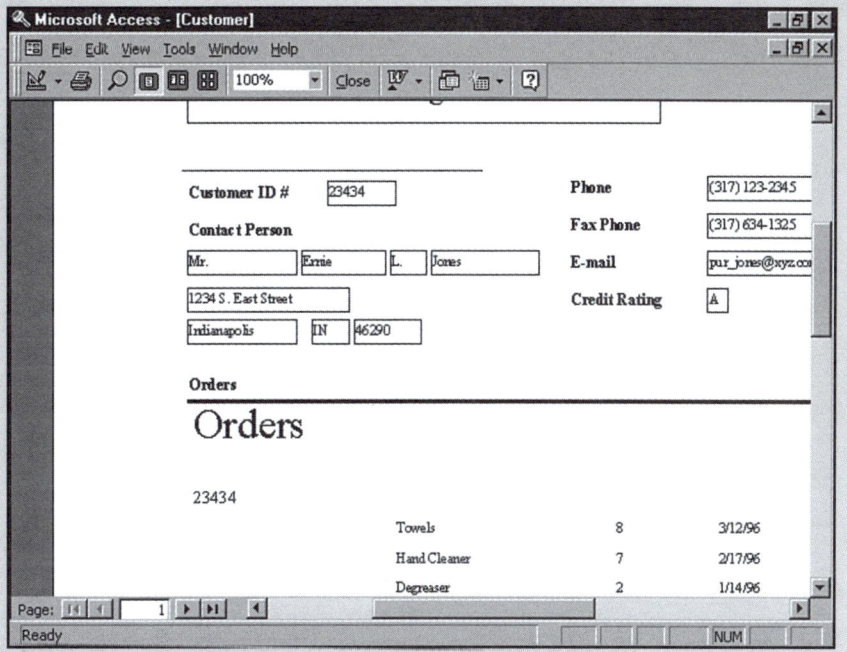

🔢**12** **Close the preview to return to Design View.**

🔢**13** **Click the Orders title above the subreport to select it and then delete it.**

🔢**14** **Close the report and save the changes.**

Leave the database open for use in the next lesson.

Lesson 5: Creating Reports Using the Chart Wizard

Some types of information are best presented using charts instead of numbers. Access has a built-in Chart Wizard that uses an application called Microsoft Graph to help you create a chart. Charts created in Access are somewhat difficult to edit, however, and the chart module has only limited charting capabilities. If you have Excel, you should export or copy your data to a spreadsheet and create your charts there.

In this lesson, you create a chart to show the relative frequency with which products are ordered.

To Create Reports Using the Chart Wizard

1 **In the Orders database, click on the Report tab, if necessary.**

2 **Click New.**

The New Report dialog box appears.

3 **Select the Chart Wizard. Select Orders from the drop-down list, then click OK.**

continues

To Create Reports Using the Chart Wizard   (continued)

After a brief delay, the first of the Chart Wizard dialog boxes appears, asking which field contains the data you want to chart (see Figure 4.29).

Figure 4.29
The Chart Wizard enables you to select the field to chart.

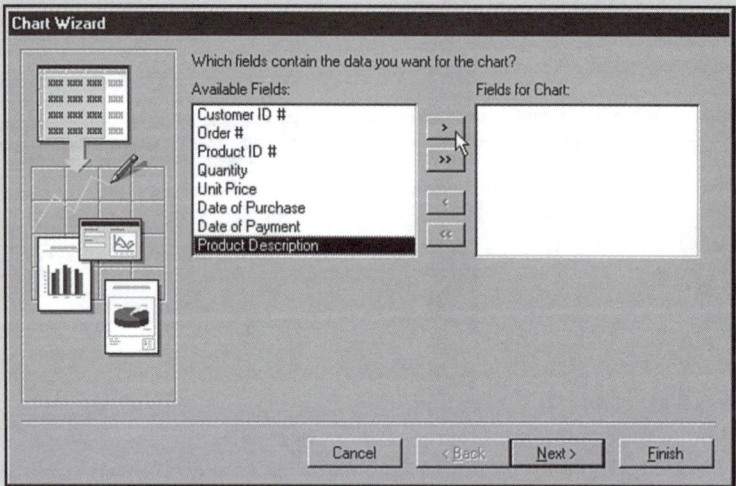

④ **Select the Product Description field, then click the right arrow button to move it to the Fields for Chart list box. Click Next.**

The second Chart Wizard dialog box appears, asking what type of chart you want to use (see Figure 4.30). When you click a chart type, a description of that type appears in a box on the right-hand side of the dialog box.

Figure 4.30
The second Chart Wizard dialog box asks you to choose a chart type.

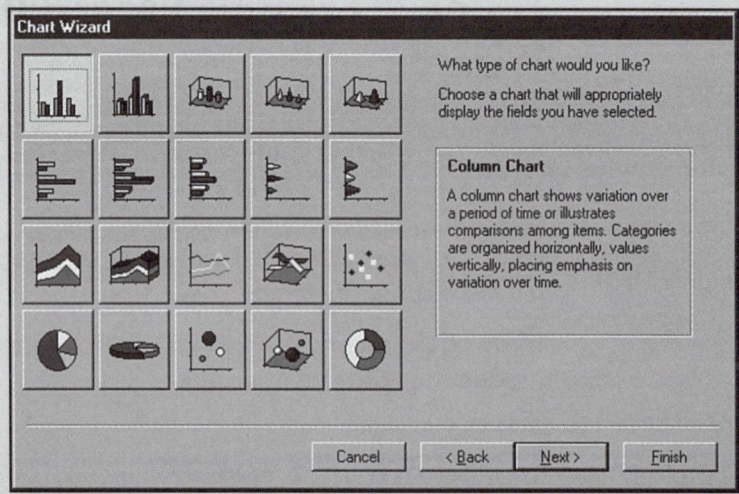

⑤ **Select the Column Chart, then click Next.**

The third Chart Wizard dialog box appears, giving you a preview of the final chart (see Figure 4.31). The Pie Chart would also be a good selection for this type of data, but is probably the most difficult to format properly in Access.

Figure 4.31
The third Chart Wizard dialog box shows a preview of the final chart.

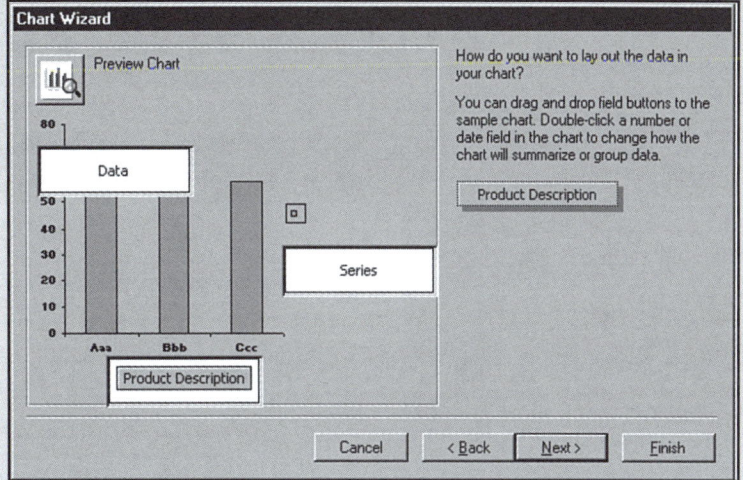

6 **Click Next.**

The fourth Chart Wizard dialog box appears, giving you several additional options (see Figure 4.32).

Figure 4.32
The fourth Chart Wizard dialog box includes several formatting options.

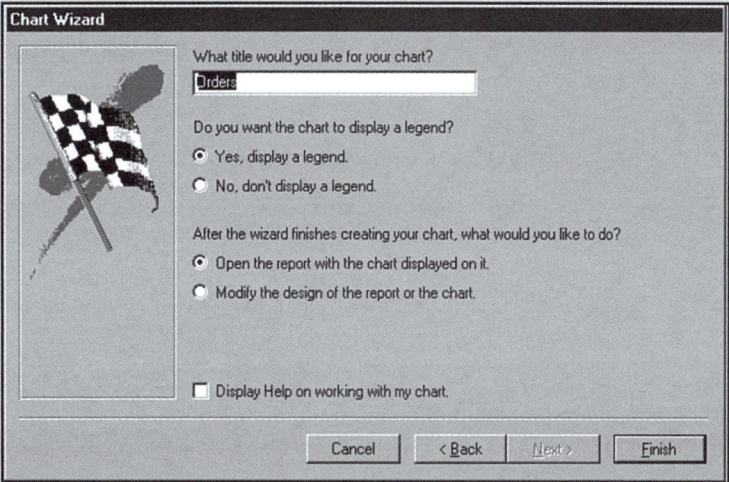

7 **Change the title of the chart to** Orders for Each Product.

8 **Click the option button for No, don't display a legend.**

Because there is only one data set in this chart, a legend is unnecessary. If you had two or more data sets, a legend would be necessary.

9 **Click Finish.**

The final report is shown in Preview mode. There are problems with the chart, particularly the data labels on the x-axis (see Figure 4.33). The Chart Wizard has automatically chosen to display every other label on the x-axis.

continues

To Create Reports Using the Chart Wizard   (continued)

Figure 4.33
The x-axis labels only display every other label on the initial chart produced by the wizard.

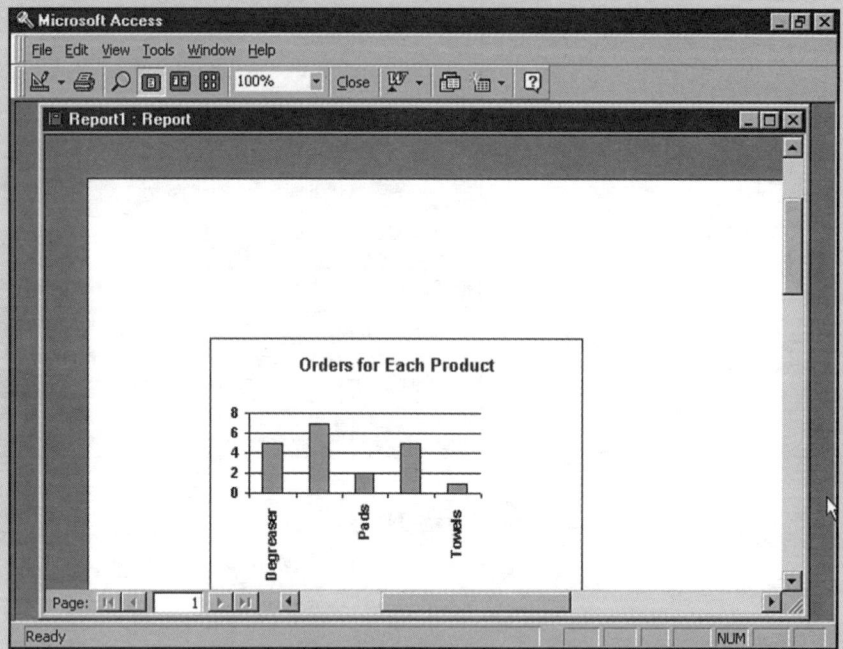

10 **Click the Close button in the toolbar.**

You are now in the Report Design View.

11 **Double-click the chart to launch Microsoft Graph.**

The Microsoft Graph window appears, showing both the datasheet for the graph and the graph itself (see Figure 4.34). Notice that the graph and numbers are not those you requested. Instead, they are the default values from Microsoft Graph.

Figure 4.34
Chart editing is done in the Microsoft Graph window.

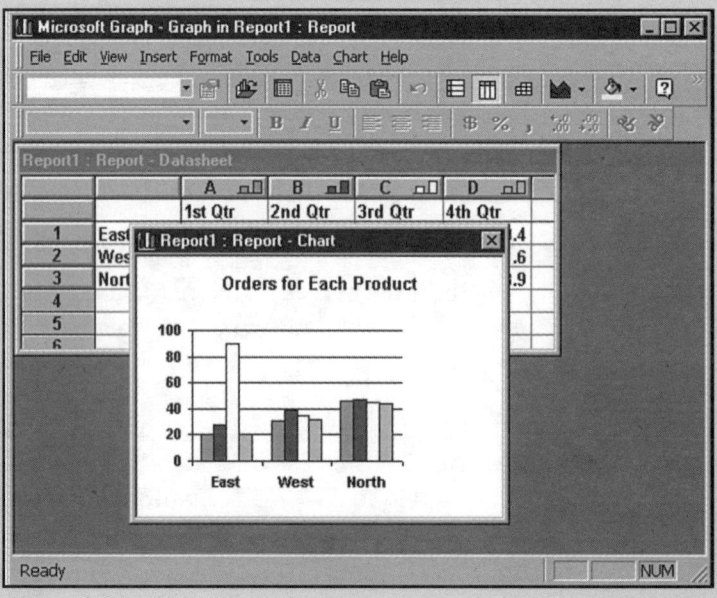

⑫ **Maximize the Microsoft Graph window, if necessary.**

⑬ **Move the pointer to the lower right corner of the chart window.**

The pointer turns into a two-sided arrow.

⑭ **Click the corner of the chart window and drag it down and to the right to increase the width and height by about 50%.**

The size of the chart window increases (see Figure 4.35).

Figure 4.35
Increase the size of the chart window to make enough room for all of the x-axis labels.

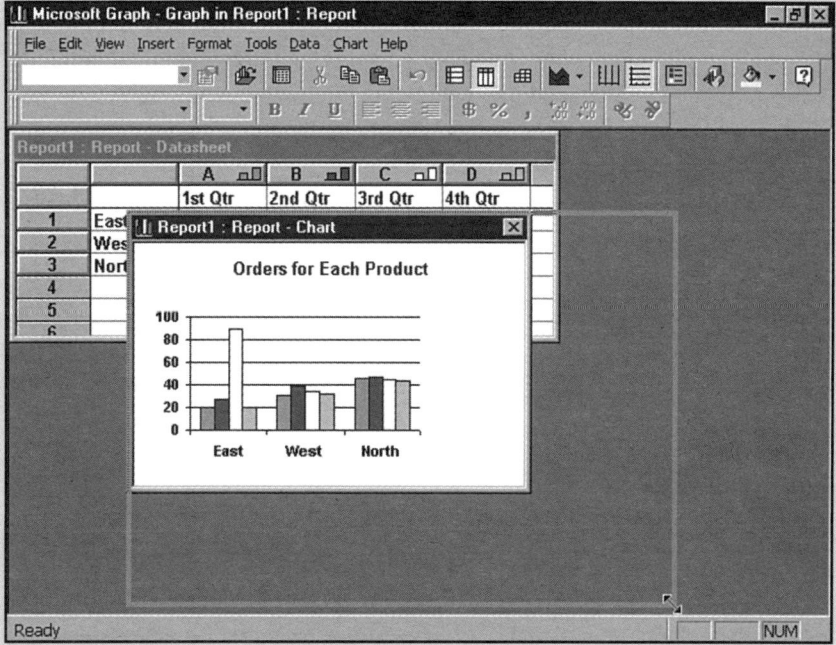

⑮ **Choose File and Exit & Return to Report1.**

The Microsoft Graph program will close, and the view will return to the design view of the report. Notice that the chart no longer fits in the object placeholder (see Figure 4.36).

continues

To Create Reports Using the Chart Wizard   (continued)

Figure 4.36
Changing the size of
the chart in Microsoft
Graph causes problems
in the Access Report
Design.

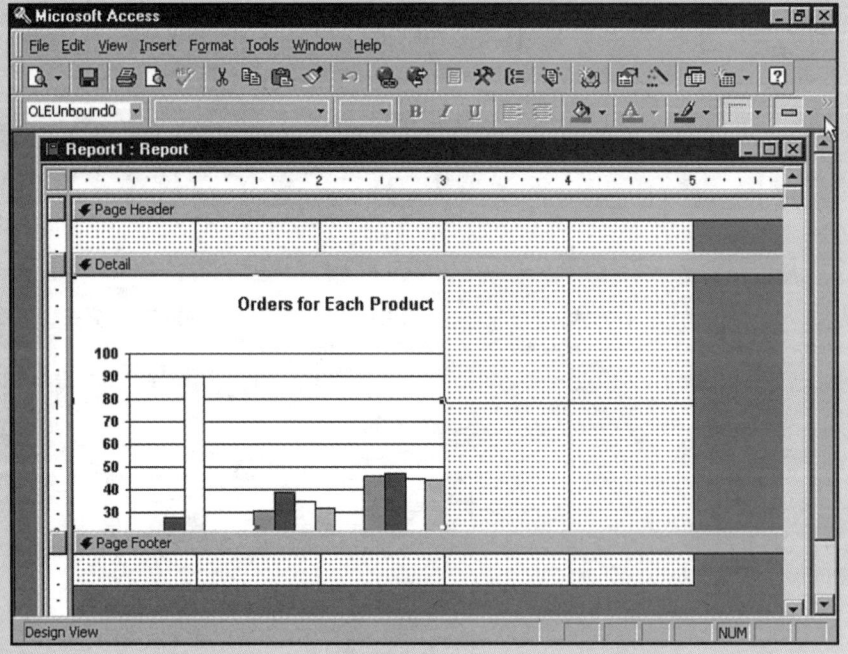

🔟6️⃣ **Click the handle on the lower-right corner of the chart and drag to the right and down until the chart is about one inch larger in both directions.**

1️⃣7️⃣ **Click the Preview button.**

Your chart should appear with all five data labels (see Figure 4.37). If you have cut off any of the chart, or have too much room on the right edge, adjust the size again.

Figure 4.37
The chart displays all
the product labels after
it has been resized and
reformatted.

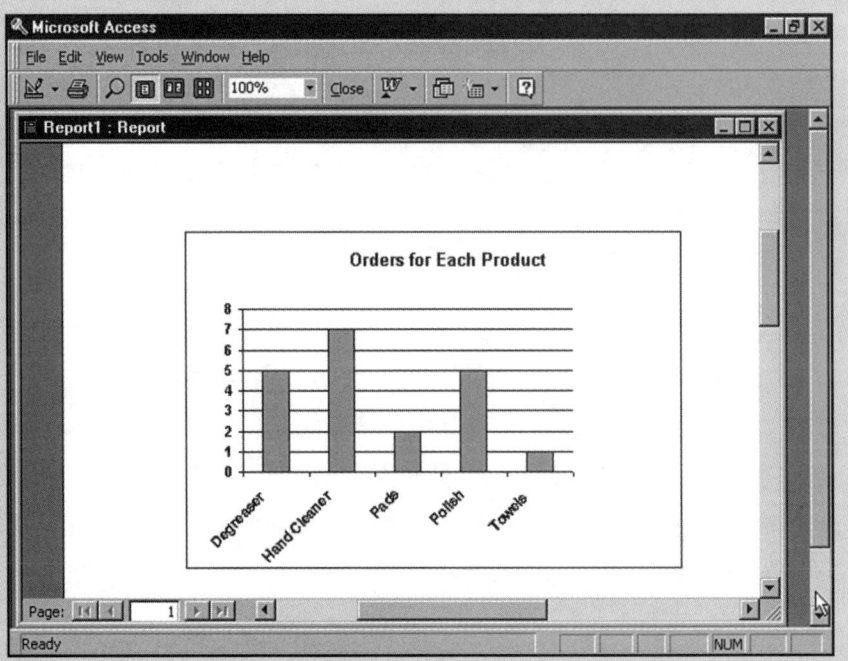

18 **Close the Preview window and close the Design View.**

19 **Save your changes, and give the new report the name** Orders for Each Product.

20 **Close the database and close Access.**

Project Summary

To	Do This
Create a simple crosstab query	Create a select query based on the desired table or tables. Use the Query Type button to change the type of query to Crosstab. Drag the necessary fields to the query design grid. Use the Crosstab box to choose which fields will be used as row header, column header, and cell value. Click the Total box in the column that will be used as the cell value and pick the type of mathematical operation desired. Click View to see the Crosstab Query.
Create crosstab queries with conditions	Follow the previous directions to create a crosstab query. Drag any additional fields that may be necessary for setting conditions. Change the Total box in those fields to Expression. Enter the condition(s) in the criteria box(es).
Create crosstab queries with a column of simple totals	Create a query as previously described. Drag a field to the next empty column in the query design grid. Change the contents of the Crosstab box in that column to Row Heading. Change the contents of the Total box to Sum.
Create crosstab queries with a column of calculated totals	Create a query as prevously described. Enter an expression in the field box of the next empty column in the query design grid. Change the contents of the Crosstab box in that column to Row Heading. Change the contents of the Total box to Sum.
Insert Subforms into forms	Open an existing form in the Design View. Open the Toolbox and make sure the Wizard button on the toolbox is selected. Click the Subform/Subreport button on the toolbox and draw a rectangle in the Form Design window where the subform will go. Select the subform from a list of existing forms, or create it using the wizard. The two forms must be based on tables that are joined one-to-many.
Insert Subreports into reports	Open a report in the Design View. Open the Toolbox and make sure the Wizard button on the toolbox is selected. Click the Subform/Subreport button on the toolbox and draw a rectangle in the Report Design window where the subreport will go. Select the subreport from a list of existing reports or create it using the wizard. The two reports must be based on tables that are joined one-to-many.

continues

continued

To	Do This
Create a report using the Chart Wizard	Create a new report. Choose a table or query, then select the Chart Wizard. Choose the chart type, then add a title and decide whether to include a legend. Alternate between the Chart Wizard and the report design view to adjust the final appearance of the chart.

Checking Your Skills

True/False

For each of the following statements, check *T* or *F* to indicate whether the statement is true or false.

__T __F **1.** The design for a crosstab query must have at least one row header, column header, and value.

__T __F **2.** In a crosstab query design, the field that has been chosen to provide the values in the cells must have its Totals box changed to "Group By."

__T __F **3.** If the records in a subform are going to be linked to the records in the main form, the tables on which they are based must be joined in a one-to-many relationship.

__T __F **4.** In Access, you can use the Chart Wizard to create a chart and then use Microsoft Chart to edit the chart.

__T __F **5.** If you want to display data in chart form, you must export the table to Excel and use the Excel charting option.

Multiple Choice

Circle the letter of the correct answer for each of the following questions.

1. If a field name is used in an expression, it must be enclosed by:

   a. []

   b. ()

   c. {}

   d. <>

2. To add an additional set of values such as totals on the left side of a crosstab query, the Crosstab box must be set to:

   a. Column Header

   b. Row Header

   c. Value

   d. Expression

3. If a form and its subform are based on tables that are joined in a one-to-many relationship, _____.

    a. the records shown in the subform are limited to those that match the record shown in the main form

    b. they use the same navigation buttons

    c. they cannot both show a record with the same key field value

    d. you cannot change the contents of a field in the subform

4. To add a subreport to a report, you can:

    a. choose from a list of existing reports

    b. create a report based on a table

    c. create a report based on a query

    d. all of the above

5. Charts can be created in Access as a type of:

    a. Report

    b. Form

    c. Query

    d. Table

Completion

In the blank provided, write the correct answer for each of the following statements.

1. In a crosstab query design, the Row Header setting goes in the _____ box.

2. In a crosstab query, the Totals box must be set to _____ to show totals in the cells of the query.

3. The subreport must be based on a table that is the _____ (choose **one** or **many**) of a one-to-many relationship.

4. To scroll through the records in a subform, you use the _____ buttons at the bottom of the subform.

5. In a chart, a _____ is necessary if there is more than one data set.

Applying Your Skills

At the end of each project in *Access 97 Essentials Level III*, you learn how to apply your Access skills to various situations. The following exercises enable you to practice the skills you have learned in this project. Take a few minutes to work through these exercises now.

Creating a Crosstab Query

In the following exercise you will create a crosstab query to display the total quantity purchased by item for each month. The rows will consist of the product descriptions, the columns will be the months of the year, and the cells will contain the total of the quantity field.

To Create a Crosstab Query

Create a crosstab query that shows the total quantity of each item purchased in each month.

1. Copy Proj0401 and name the copy **Orders2**. Create a new query based on the Orders table.

2. Change its type to Crosstab.

3. Drag the Quantity, Product Description, and Data of Purchase fields to the query design grid.

4. In the Crosstab box, select Row Heading for Product description, Column Heading for Date of Purchase, and Value for Quantity.

5. Change the contents of the Total box for the Quantity field to Sum.

6. Switch to the datasheet view to see how it worked.

7. Close and save the query. Name it **Products sold by date**.

Adding a Subform to Another Form

In this exercise you will create two forms using the Autoform wizard. These forms will be based on two linked tables. You will then place one form inside the other as a subform.

To Add a Subform to Another Form

1. Open the **Orders2** database created in the previous exercise or copy Proj0401 and rename it Orders2. Create a form based on the Orders table. Use the Autoform: Tabular wizard.

2. Close the form and name it **Orders2**.

3. Create a form based on the Customer table. Use the Autoform: Columnar option. Save it and name it **Customers2**.

4. Open the Customers2 form in the Design View. Move some of the fields to make the two columns of fields approximately the same length.

5. Open the toolbox and make sure the Wizard button is selected. Click the Subform/Subreport button and draw a rectangle across the bottom of the form where the subform will go.

6. Select the Orders2 form from the list.

7. Edit the placement of the fields and the subform. Switch to datasheet view to check your work. Save the resulting form.

Creating a Report with the Chart Wizard

Create a chart based on the Orders table to display the number of items ordered by product. In this case you will select two fields to be charted. The text field Product description will be used as the x-axis label and the Quantity field will be totaled for each product.

To Create a Report with the Chart Wizard

1. Create a new report using the Chart Wizard.

2. Use the Orders table as the data source.

3. Select the product description and the quantity as the fields to be charted.

4. Use a column chart format.

5. Make the chart title `Number of Items Ordered by Product`.

6. Increase the size of the chart to approximately six inches wide and four inches high.

7. Save the report as `Items Ordered` and print a copy.

Project 5

Filtering Data Using Parameters, Custom Dialog Boxes, and Form Filters

Use queries, filters, and dialog boxes to add database flexibility

In this Project, you learn how to:

➤ Use Parameters as Criteria in a Query

➤ Use Parameters in Calculations in a Query

➤ Create a Dialog Box to Define Filter Conditions

➤ Create a Macro to Open a Report or Form and Apply the Filter

➤ Modify the Dialog Box to Link It to the Macro

➤ Remove Scroll Bars and Navigation Buttons and Test Your Filter

➤ Filter a Form by Selection of a Field

Why Would I Do This?

Parameter
An entry that can be used as a filter or an argument in a formula.

In this project, you learn how to modify queries so that they are even more flexible. A *parameter* query will ask you for input whenever the query is used, and use your input as the criteria for the query. In this way, you can use the same query structure repeatedly without having to open up the design of the query and make changes.

The parameter query does not allow the user to answer several questions at the same time, or go back and change an input before it is acted upon. The last three lessons of this project work together to produce a customized dialog box in which the user can specify one or more criteria and then preview or print a report based upon those conditions.

Lesson 1: Using Parameters as Criteria in a Query

The database used in this lesson contains a table of information about the customers of an industrial cleaning supplies distributor. In this lesson, you add a parameter to the City criteria to enable the user to pick a different city each time he or she wants a list of customers.

To Open the Customer Records Database

1 **Make a copy of the student data file Proj0501.**

2 **Rename the copy** Customer Records.

Include the .mdb extension only if you can see the extension on the Proj0501 file.

3 **Launch Access 97.**

4 **Open the Customer Records database.**

The database window should now be open to the Tables area (see Figure 5.1). Keep the database open for the next exercise.

Figure 5.1
The database window displays the Tables area of the Customer Records database.

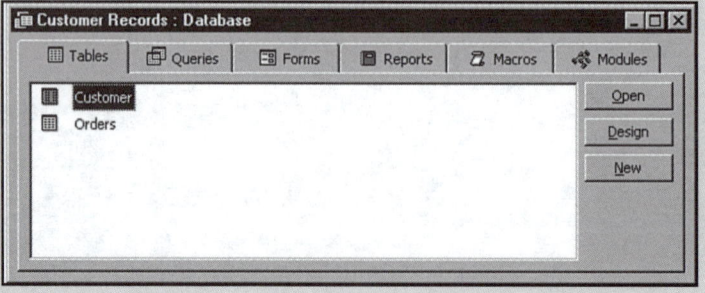

To Create a Parameter Query

① **Click the Queries tab.**

The name of the existing query is displayed (see Figure 5.2).

Figure 5.2
The database window displays the Queries area of the Customer Records database.

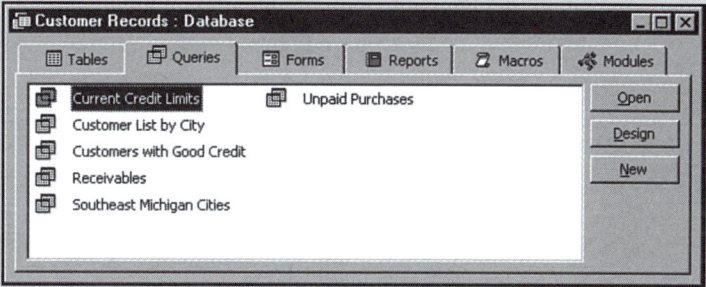

② **Click the Customer List by City query and then click the Design button.**

The design of the Customer List by City query appears (see Figure 5.3).

Figure 5.3
The design of the Customer List by City query is displayed.

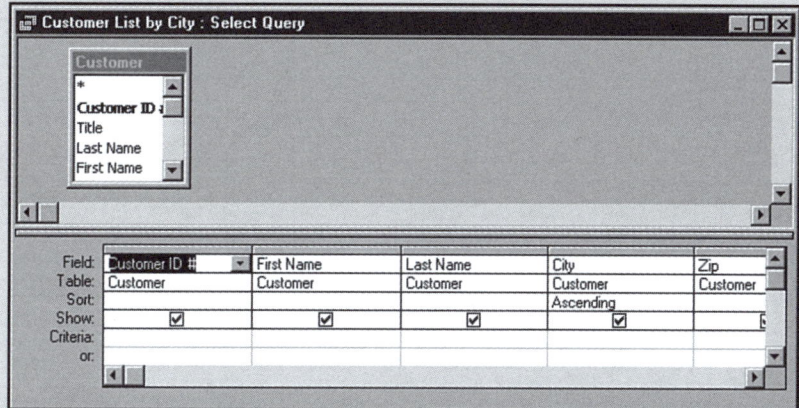

③ **Click the criteria box in the City column and enter the following:**

    [Enter the name of the city below:]

See Figure 5.4. (The column has been widened in the figure shown. You may only see part of the prompt.)

continues

To Create a Parameter Query   (continued)

Figure 5.4
The prompt for the criteria is placed within brackets in the criteria box.

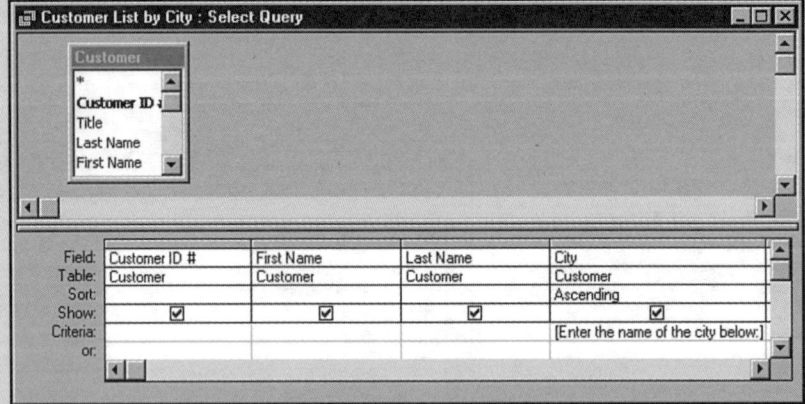

In this case, you did not enter an actual city name or the name of a field. The message you enter inside the square brackets will be displayed as a message.

 4 Click the View button to switch to Datasheet View.

The Enter Parameter Value dialog box appears and displays the message you entered within square brackets in the criteria box (see Figure 5.5).

Figure 5.5
The Enter Parameter Value dialog box appears with the message you entered in the criteria box.

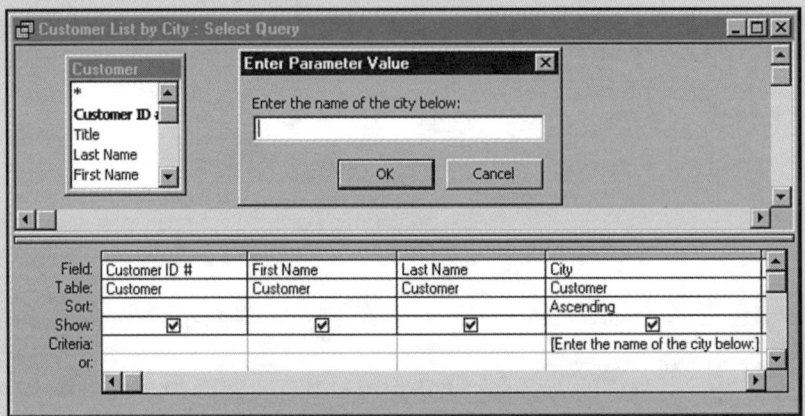

5 Enter the following city name in the text box:

Ann Arbor

Click OK. The list of customers in Ann Arbor appears in the Datasheet View (see Figure 5.6).

Figure 5.6
The Datasheet View of the query only shows the cities that match the parameter value you entered.

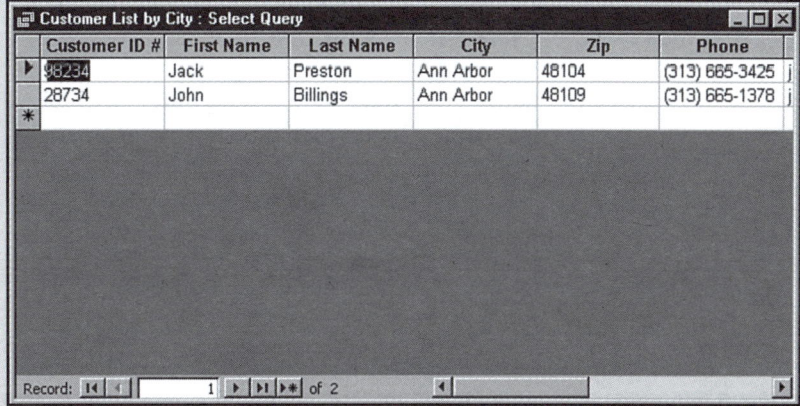

6 **Close the query and save the changes.**

If you open this query or use it as the basis of a report or form, the same Parameter Value dialog box appears and the report or form will be limited to those records that match the criteria entered.

7 **Click the Reports tab to see the available reports.**

8 **Click the Customer List by City report and then click Preview.**

The Enter Parameter Value dialog box appears, displaying the message that you entered in the query.

9 **Enter the following city name in the text box:**

Ypsilanti

Click OK. The report opens in preview mode, displaying records for those customers in Ypsilanti (see Figure 5.7).

Figure 5.7
The Customer List by City report limited to those records that match the parameter.

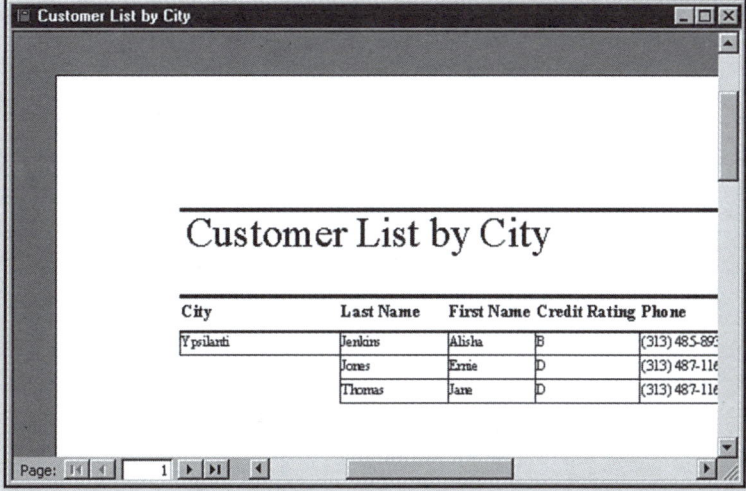

10 **Close the Print Preview.**

Leave the database open for use in the next lesson.

Lesson 2: Using Parameters in Calculations in a Query

Parameters may be used in place of field names in calculated fields as well as criteria boxes. In this lesson, you use a table of customer information that includes a field for credit limit. You can print a report showing current credit limits and also raise or lower these limits each time you print the report.

In this lesson, you learn to use a parameter in an expression in a calculated field.

To Use a Parameter in a Calculation

① **In the Customer Records database, click the Queries tab and click Current Credit Limits to select it.**

② **Click Design.**

The design of the Current Credit Limits query is displayed (see Figure 5.8).

Figure 5.8
The design of the Current Credit Limits query is displayed.

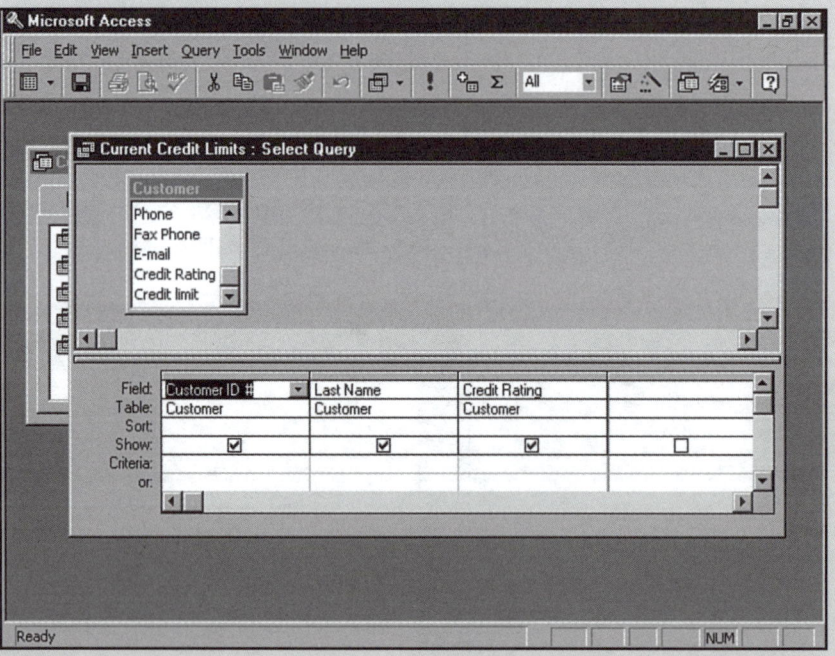

③ **Click the Field box in the next empty column. Enter the following expression:**

```
Current Credit Limit:[Credit limit]*[Enter adjustment
factor:]
```

The term, "Current Credit Limit" will be the name of the new column in the query. The expression to the right of the colon will take the value in the Credit limit field and multiply by whatever the user enters in the parameter values dialog box. The column has been widened to show the entire entry (see Figure 5.9).

Figure 5.9
The query design shows the parameter expression entered in the Field box.

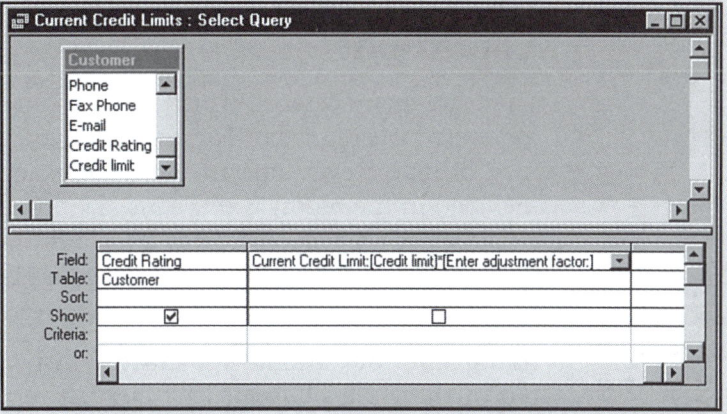

If the words inside the brackets match a field name, the program will use the current contents of that field. If they do not match an existing field, the program will assume you want to enter a value from a parameter value dialog box.

4 **Click the View button to switch to the Datasheet View.**

The Enter Parameter Value dialog box appears (see Figure 5.10).

Figure 5.10
The Enter Parameter Value dialog box showing the parameter message.

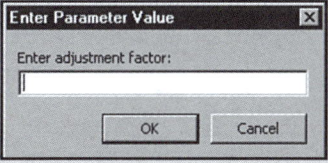

5 **Increase all of the current credit limits by 20%. Enter** 1.2 **in the dialog box and click OK.**

The query will be displayed in Datasheet View with the new values for the Current Credit Limit (see Figure 5.11).

Figure 5.11
The query displaying the adjusted credit limits.

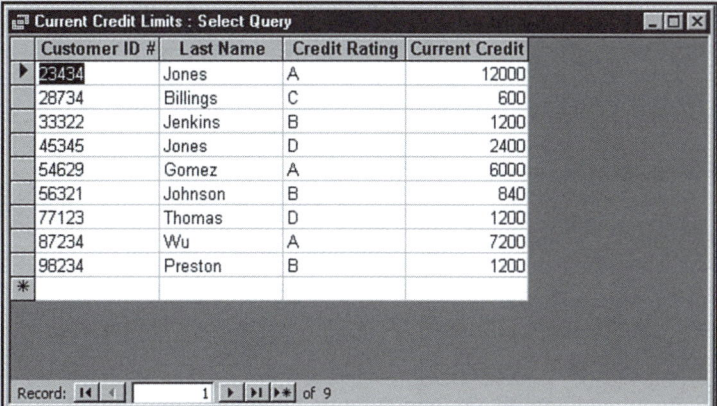

Any report or form based on this query will also display the Enter Parameter Value dialog box and enable you to adjust the credit limits displayed.

6 **Close the query and save the changes.**

Leave the database open for use in the next lesson.

Project 5 Filtering Data Using Parameters, Custom Dialog Boxes, and Form Filters

124

Lesson 3: Creating a Dialog Box to Define Filter Conditions

There are many cases in which it is not practical to create a query or report for every possible need. For example, you may need to produce the same type of report every month, but the exact range of dates that should be included in the report is not consistent. It would be much easier if the user could specify a range of dates and only the records that meet the criteria would be included in the report. It would be even better if the user did not need to change the design of a query for each new report.

In the following section, you create a *user-defined filter* that restricts the output of the Orders Grouped by Product report to a specific range of dates. This process is divided into three parts: creating the form, creating the macro, and linking the form and macro.

User-defined filter

A form and query that work together to enable the user to set the filter conditions that restrict the output of a report or the records shown in a form.

To Create a Dialog Box to Define Filter Conditions

❶ In the Customer Records database, select the Forms tab.

The names of the existing forms will be displayed.

❷ Click New, but do not select a table or query from the drop-down list.

This form is not linked to one particular table or query.

❸ Select Design View and click OK.

The Design View of a form will appear that does not have any field or label controls.

❹ Maximize the form window.

Maximizing the window gives you a wider view of the form.

❺ Click the Toolbox button to open the toolbox (if it doesn't already appear on-screen).

You can move the toolbox to the right side of the form so it does not obscure the working area (see Figure 5.12).

Figure 5.12
The form and toolbox windows are shown with the form window maximized.

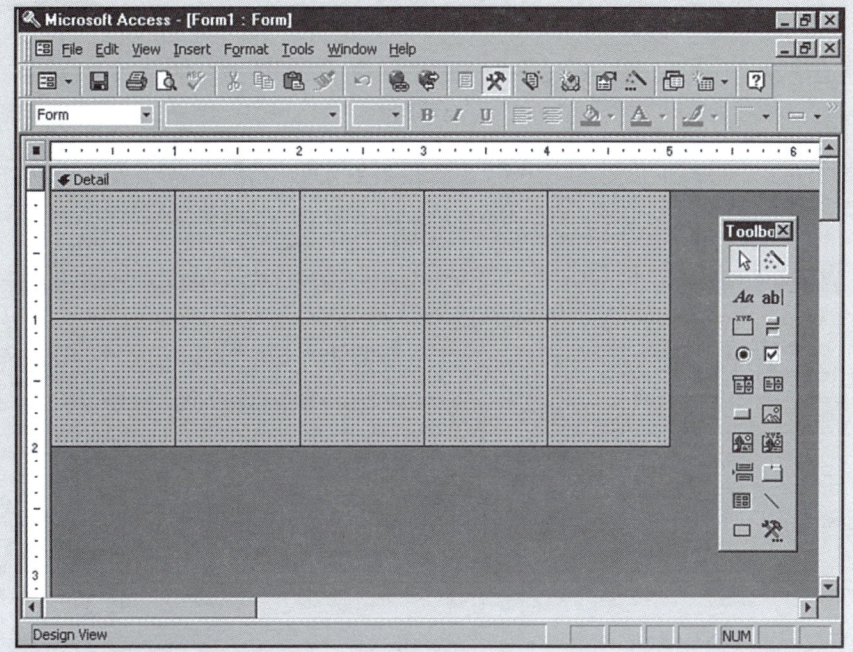

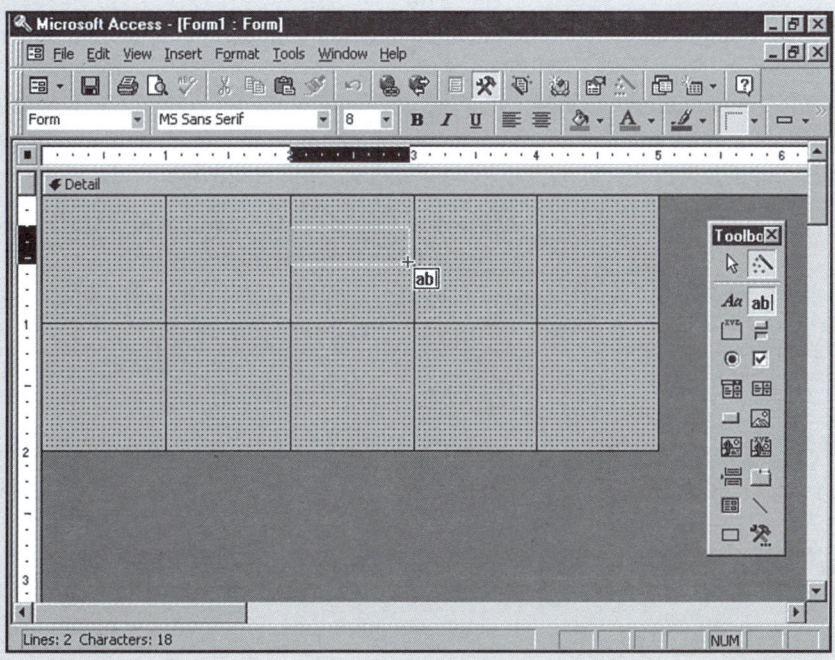

6 Click the Text Box button in the toolbox.

The Text Box tool helps you to add titles, instructions, and explanations to the form.

7 Move the pointer to the blank form. Draw a rectangle in the blank form (see Figure 5.13).

This rectangle will be used to position the first prompt for a user input.

Figure 5.13
The text box outline is shown in the blank form.

continues

To Create a Dialog Box to Define Filter Conditions   (continued)

8 **Release the mouse button.**

An unbound text box and its label are placed on the form.

9 **Repeat steps 6–8 to create a second text box.**

Your screen should look similar to Figure 5.14.

Figure 5.14
Two unbound text boxes are shown in the blank form.

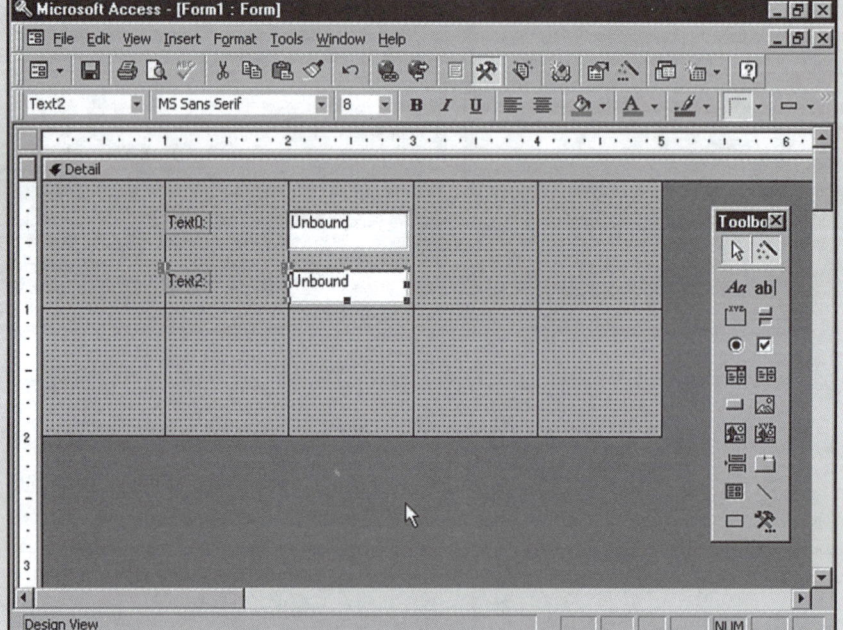

The program picks label numbers based on how many have been created, even though they may have been erased. The label number on your form may differ from those shown in Figure 5.14.

10 **Click the label box for the first text box to select it.**

The text in the label box will be edited to provide the prompt message for the first user input.

11 **Move the pointer onto the label (Text0: in Figure 5.14) and double-click to select it.**

The text in the label box should be highlighted. It will be replaced by whatever you type next.

12 **Type a new caption:** Orders On or After.

This will be the new text in the label box.

13 **Repeat steps 10 and 12 to change the label of the second box to:** Orders On or Before.

The label boxes expand to fit the new labels (see Figure 5.15).

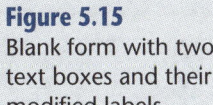

Figure 5.15
Blank form with two text boxes and their modified labels.

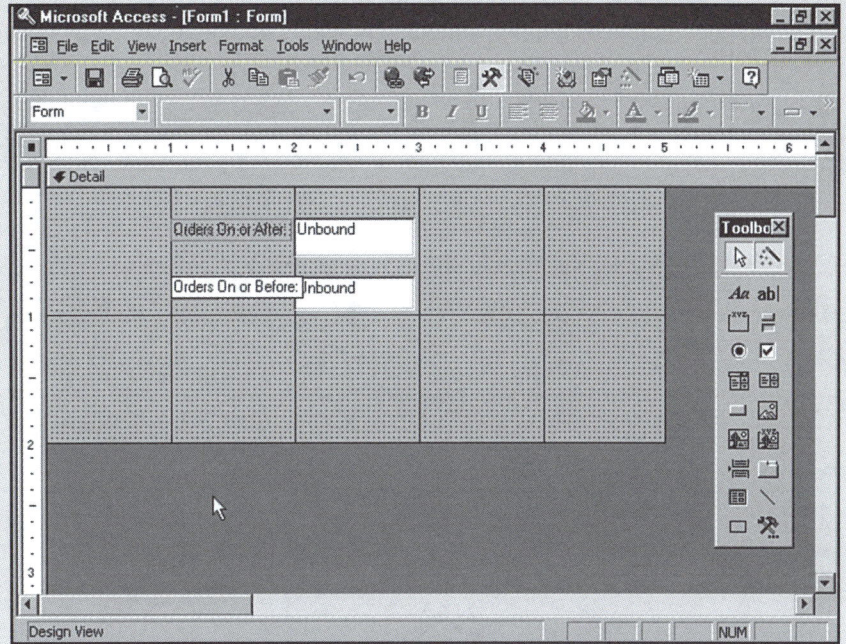

14 **Move the second label box to the left so it does not overlap the text box. Move the label box above it so that they line up.**

To move the label box independently from the text box, select it and drag the handle in the upper-left corner.

15 **Click the first unbound text box in the detail section of the form design to select it.**

Make sure you click the unbound text box and not the label box.

16 **Click the Properties button on the toolbar to open the Properties window.**

The Properties window will display the properties of the currently selected text box.

17 **Click the All tab if necessary, and change the entry in the Name box to Date1 (see Figure 5.16).**

This name can be used in formulas or expressions and the value entered in this box will be used.

continues

To Create a Dialog Box to Define Filter Conditions   (continued)

Figure 5.16
Text box named Date1
in the Properties
window.

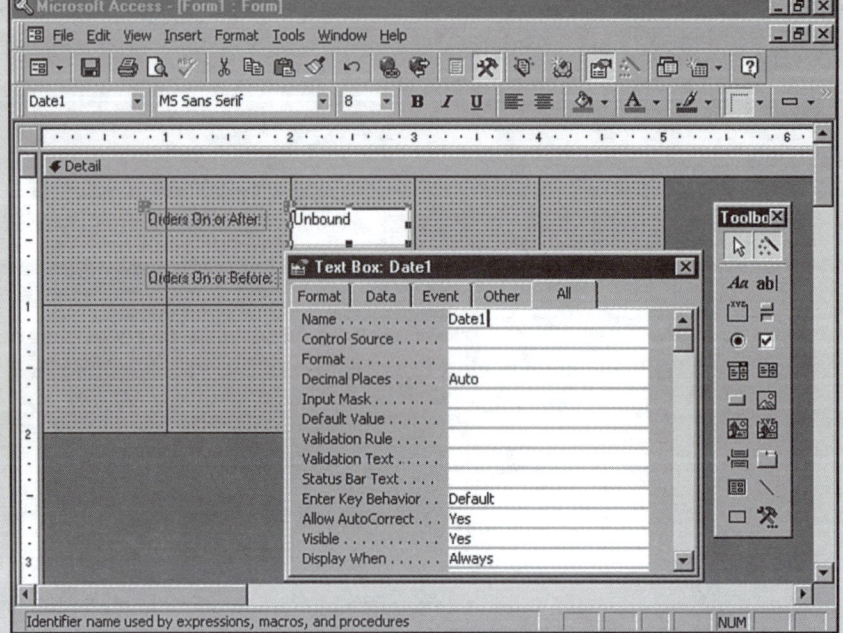

18 **Click the second text box and change its name in the Properties window to** Date2.

The two names can be used in a criteria expression such as "Between Date1 and Date2."

19 **Close the Properties window.**

20 **Close the form and save it with the name** Dates.

Keep the database open for the next procedure.

Lesson 4: Creating a Macro to Open a Report or Form and Apply the Filter

The companion macro that you create in this lesson opens the report you specify and applies a filter. It compares the two dates the user enters in the Date1 and Date2 fields in the companion form with the values in the Purchase Date field in the Orders table. This would be a complex process if you did not have the special wizard called the Expression Builder to help you.

To Create the Companion Macro

1 **In the Customer Records database, select the Macros tab.**

The existing macros will be displayed.

2 **Click** **N**ew.

The macro design window will appear.

3 **Click the drop-down list in the first Action box. Scroll down the list and select OpenReport.**

Notice that the macros are listed alphabetically.

4 **In the Report Name box (in the bottom left corner), select Orders Grouped by Product from the drop-down list.**

This will specify the report that was previously created.

5 **In the View box, select Print Preview (see Figure 5.17).**

When this macro is run the report will be previewed on the screen. The user can then elect to print it.

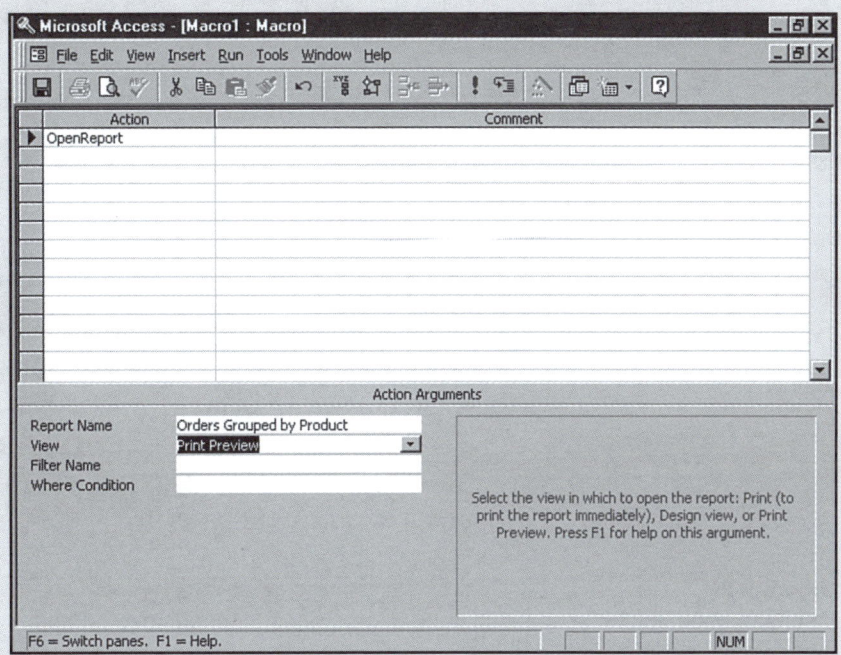

Figure 5.17
The Macro window displays the action and the arguments.

6 **Click the Where Condition box.**

This box can contain a filter condition.

 7 **Click the Build button beside the Where Condition box (the small button with three dots).**

This will launch a wizard to help create complex filter conditions. The Expression Builder dialog box opens (see Figure 5.18).

continues

To Create the Companion Macro   (continued)

Figure 5.18
Expression Builder dialog box can be used to build complex expressions using field names from tables and queries or control names from forms.

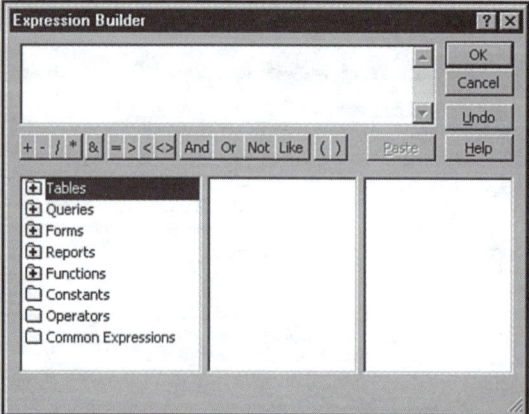

8 **Double-click the Tables folder to display the available tables.**

In this example, two tables are displayed.

9 **Click the Orders table folder to display the available fields in that table.**

The fields contained in the table are made available for selection.

10 **Double-click the Date of Purchase field to add this field to the expression in the window (see Figure 5.19).**

The name of the table is shown within brackets, followed by an exclamation point. The field name follows, enclosed in brackets. This is how fields are identified in this type of expression. The wizard takes care of these details for you.

Figure 5.19
The Expression Builder contains a partially completed expression.

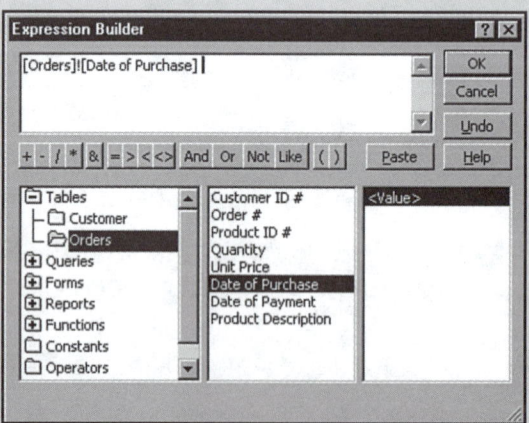

11 **Type the word between in the expression (see Figure 5.20).**

You are going to create a condition that will filter records to match those between two dates.

Figure 5.20
The between condition has been added to the expression.

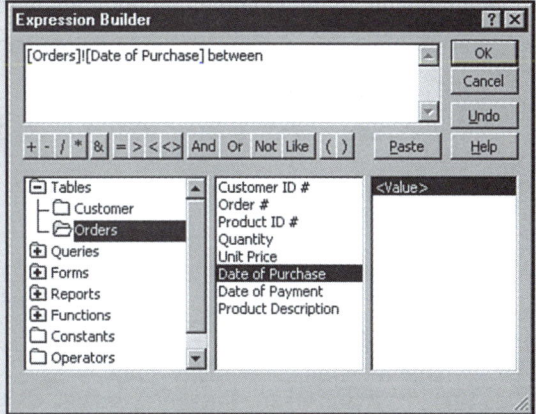

⓲ **Double-click the Forms folder to display the available forms.**

Two folders are displayed that contain the database forms.

⓳ **Double-click the All Forms folder.**

This action will display all of the available forms.

⓴ **Click the Dates form to display the available fields.**

You may have to scroll down to find it.

⑮ **Double-click the Date1 field to add it to the expression (see Figure 5.21).**

This is the name of the unbound text box you added to the Dates form in a previous lesson.

Figure 5.21
The expression shows the Date1 field added.

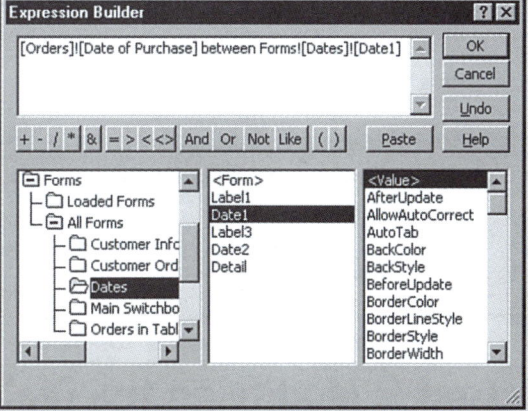

⑯ **Click the button labeled And (or type the word And).**

You always use And with between when building a between expression.

⑰ **Double-click the Date2 field to add it to the expression (see Figure 5.22).**

continues

To Create the Companion Macro   (continued)

The expression will now compare the contents of the Date of Purchase field to the two dates entered in the form to see if the Date of Purchase is between those two dates. This function is inclusive, which means that dates that match either of the two dates entered will also qualify.

Check the expression carefully before you proceed to make sure that it matches the example.

Figure 5.22
The Expression Builder window displays the final expression.

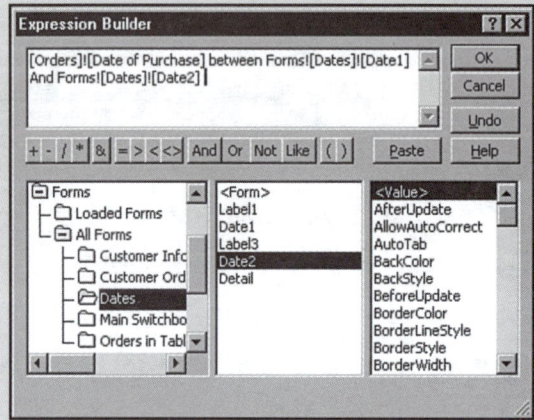

18 **Click OK to close the Expression Builder, and close the Macro design window.**

19 **Save the macro with the name** View Report.

You have now created a macro that will open a report in preview mode that will include only those records that are between or equal to the dates that the user enters on the form. Keep the database open for the next procedure.

If you have problems...

If you have trouble with the expression, look for extra blanks and the use of parentheses ( ) when they should be square brackets [ ].

Lesson 5: Modifying the Dialog Box to Link It to the Macro

In this lesson, you learn how to activate the macro you created in Lesson 4 from the form you created in Lesson 3. This form will look like a dialog box that enables the user to enter two dates, click a button to run the macro, and produce the report.

To Link the Macro and Its Companion Form

① In the Customer Records database, open the Dates form in the Design View.

This will display the Design View of the form you started in the previous lesson that will be used as a dialog box.

② Choose Window, Tile Vertically from the menu to arrange the database window and the form window side-by-side.

This step places both windows side-by-side on the screen so you can drag a macro name from the database window onto the form design. Close the Toolbox, if necessary.

③ Click the Macros tab in the database window to display the available macros (see Figure 5.23).

If the name of a macro is dragged onto a form design, a button will automatically be created that will run the macro if pressed. The button will work once the form is in Form View.

Figure 5.23
The database window and the form window can be displayed together using the **T**ile Vertically command.

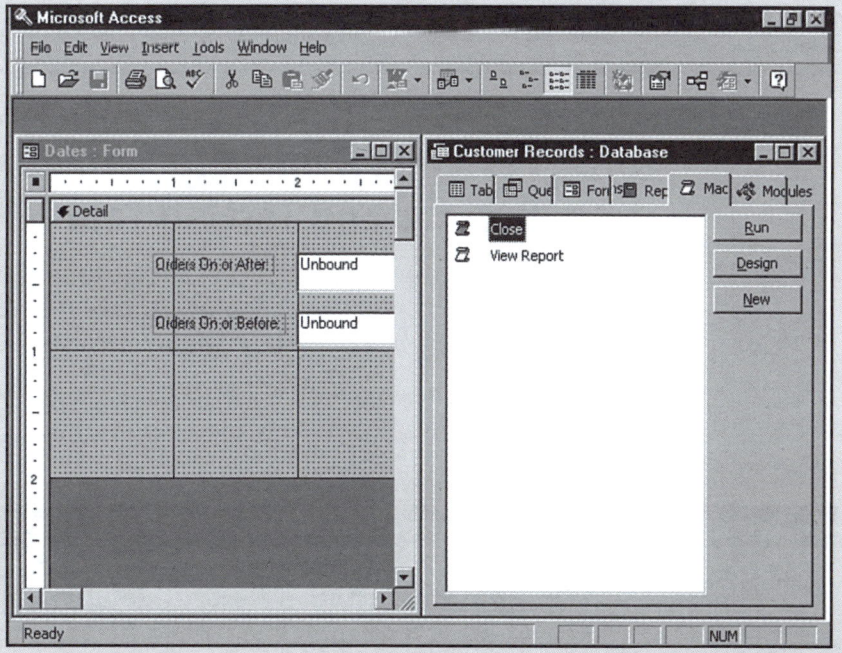

④ Click and drag the View Report macro from the database window to the form design window (see Figure 5.24).

Place the cursor where you intend the upper-right corner of the new button to be placed. This will create a button on the form that will open the report in the preview mode.

⑤ Click and drag the Close macro onto the form (see Figure 5.24).

Adjust the position of the buttons, if necessary. Keep the database open for the next procedure.

continues

To Link the Macro and Its Companion Form   (continued)

Figure 5.24
The Macro buttons appear on the form.

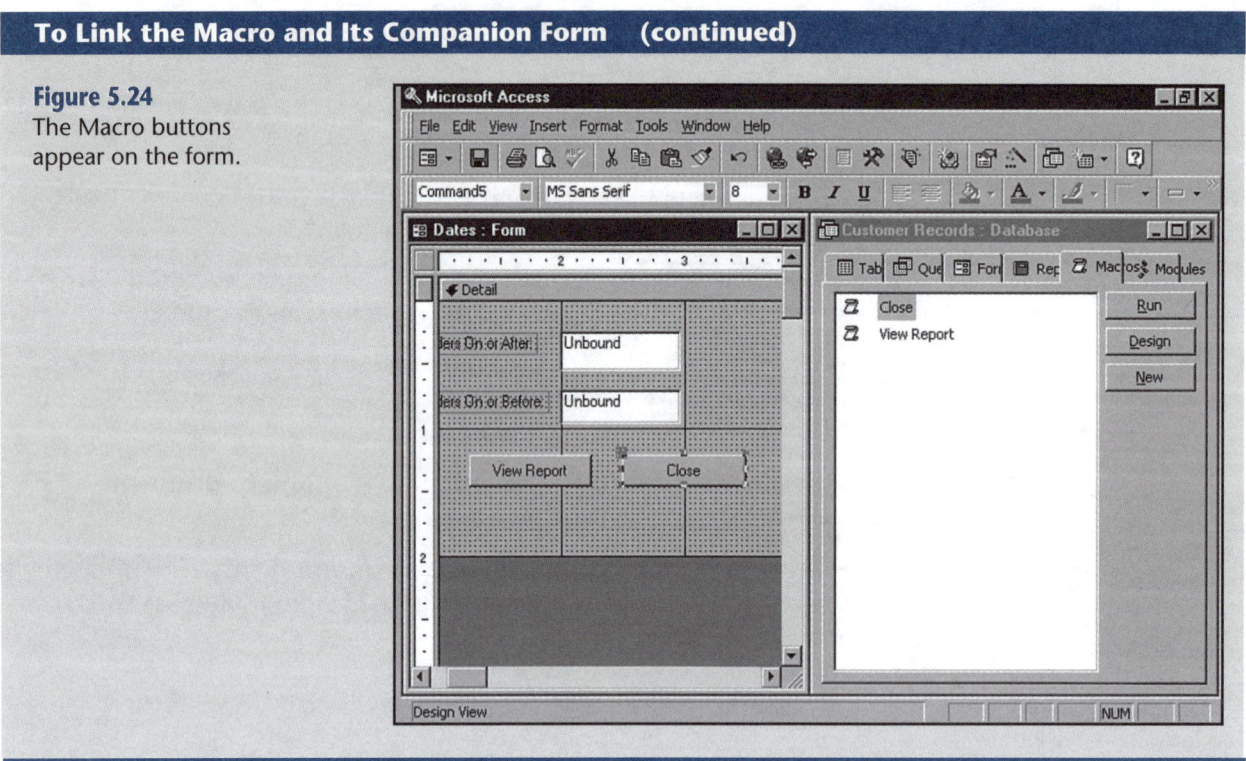

Lesson 6: Removing Scroll Bars and Navigation Buttons and Testing Your Filter

The final steps in the process of creating this filter include removing extraneous features from the form to make it look more like a typical dialog box, testing the macro button, and refining the filter.

This form does not need to have the scroll bars or navigation buttons, which are automatically placed on forms.

To Remove Scroll Bars and Navigation Buttons

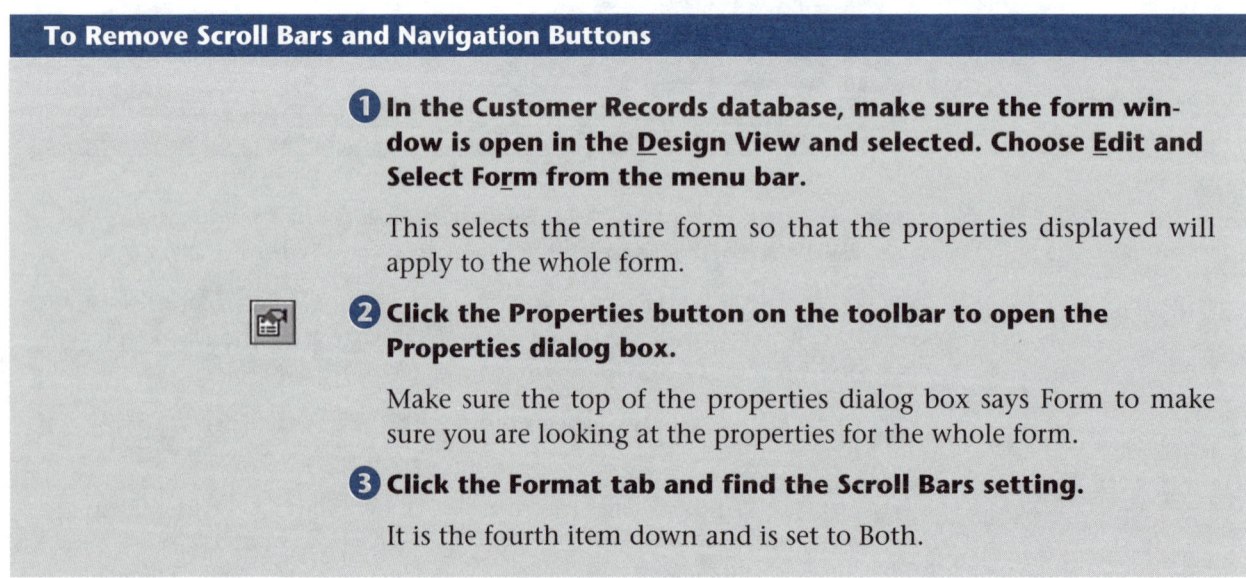

1 **In the Customer Records database, make sure the form window is open in the Design View and selected. Choose Edit and Select Form from the menu bar.**

This selects the entire form so that the properties displayed will apply to the whole form.

2 **Click the Properties button on the toolbar to open the Properties dialog box.**

Make sure the top of the properties dialog box says Form to make sure you are looking at the properties for the whole form.

3 **Click the Format tab and find the Scroll Bars setting.**

It is the fourth item down and is set to Both.

4 Change the Scroll Bars setting to Neither.

You can type the word Neither or select it from the drop-down list.

5 Change the Navigation Buttons setting to No.

Navigation buttons are normally used on forms to move from one record to another. This form is being used as a dialog box and does not need navigation buttons or scroll bars.

6 Close the properties box. Close the form and save the changes.

Keep the database open for the next procedure.

To test the user-defined filter, limit the report to those purchases made during the first month of 1996.

To Test the User-Defined Filter

1 In the Customer Records database, click the Forms tab.

2 Open the Dates form.

The form will open and display two boxes with prompts where the user can enter dates. It will also need buttons that can be used to preview the report or close the form.

3 In the Orders On or After box, enter 1/1/96. Press ⏎Enter or Tab⇆ to move to the next text box.

You could also use January 1, 1996.

4 In the Orders On or Before box, enter 1/31/96.

These entries will filter the report so that it will only show those items purchased in January 1996 (see Figure 5.25).

Figure 5.25
The form has entries that will limit the report to those purchases made in January 1996.

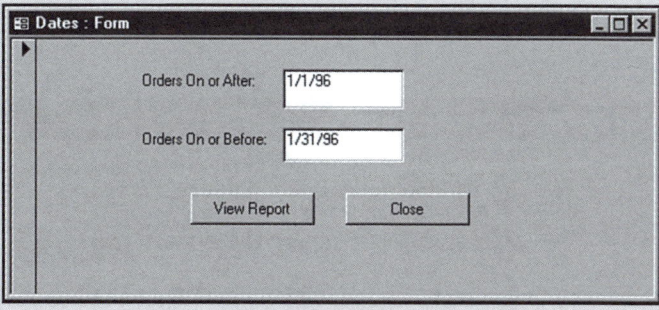

5 Click the button labeled View Report.

The report appears on-screen (see Figure 5.26).

continues

To Test the User-Defined Filter (continued)

Figure 5.26
The Orders Grouped by Product report with only those products purchased in January 1996.

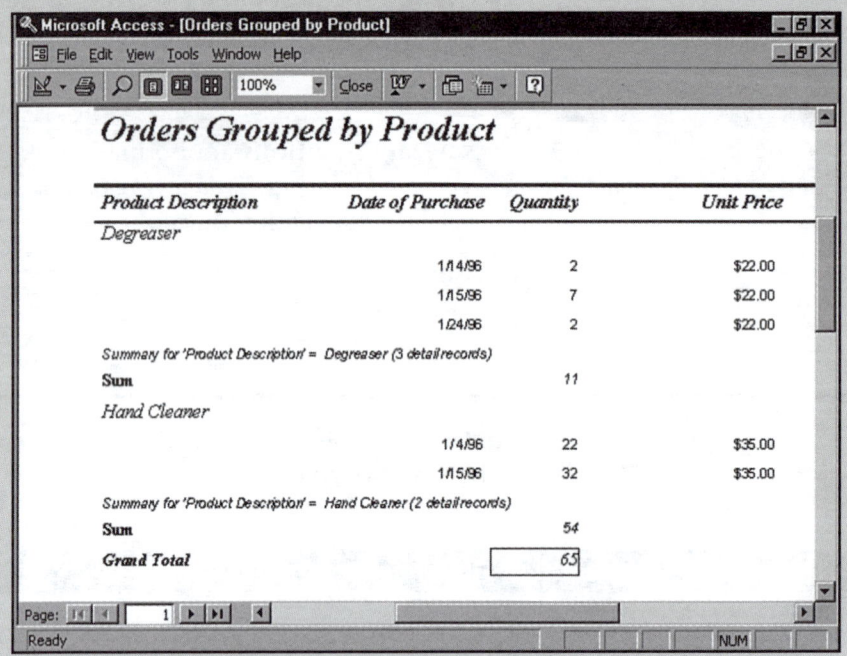

6 **Scroll through the report to make sure that the filter worked and that there are no records with a Date of Purchase other than January 1996.**

If your report does not use the filter as expected, close the report and try it again. Check your entries carefully. If a problem persists, check your macro expression and form properties as described in previous lessons and look for a discrepancy.

7 **Close the report and click the Close button to close the form.**

Keep the database open for the next procedure.

Your final modification will be to create a macro to open this user-defined filter dialog box.

To Create a Macro to Open the User-Defined Filter

1 **In the Customer Records database, click the Macros tab.**

2 **Click New to create a new macro.**

3 **Select OpenForm as the Action.**

This will open the Dates form to enable the user to select a pair of dates and preview the report.

4 **Select the Dates form in the Form Name box (see Figure 5.27).**

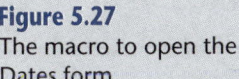

Figure 5.27
The macro to open the
Dates form.

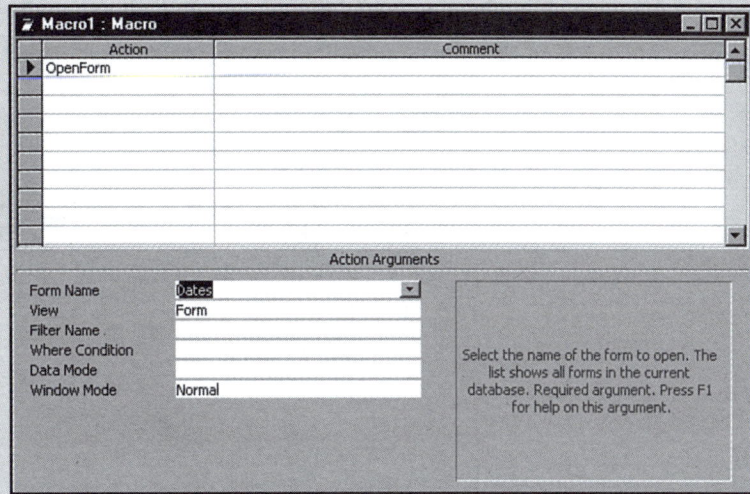

⑤ Close and save the macro with the name Orders Within a Range
of Dates.

This macro can be used as a button on a central switchboard form
or can be run separately.

**⑥ Click the Macros tab, if necessary. Click the Orders Within a
Range of Dates macro to select it. Click Run.**

The form will open.

⑦ Close the form.

Lesson 7: Filtering a Form by Selection of the Contents of a Field

The filters that you created in the previous lessons in this project may be
used with forms or reports. Forms, tables, and queries may be filtered by the
user by using the filter buttons on the toolbar or by clicking the right
mouse button while pointing at a particular field.

In this lesson, you learn how to filter the records shown in a form by selecting one field in the form and specifying the criteria to be used for a filter.

To Filter the Records of a Database by Selecting an Example Value from a Form

**① In the Customer Records database, click the Forms tab. Open
the Customer Information form.**

The Customer Information form is displayed (see Figure 5.28).
Notice that there are nine records that can be viewed with this form.

continues

To Filter the Records of a Database by Selecting an Example Value from a Form (continued)

Figure 5.28
The Customer
Information form
prior to filtering.

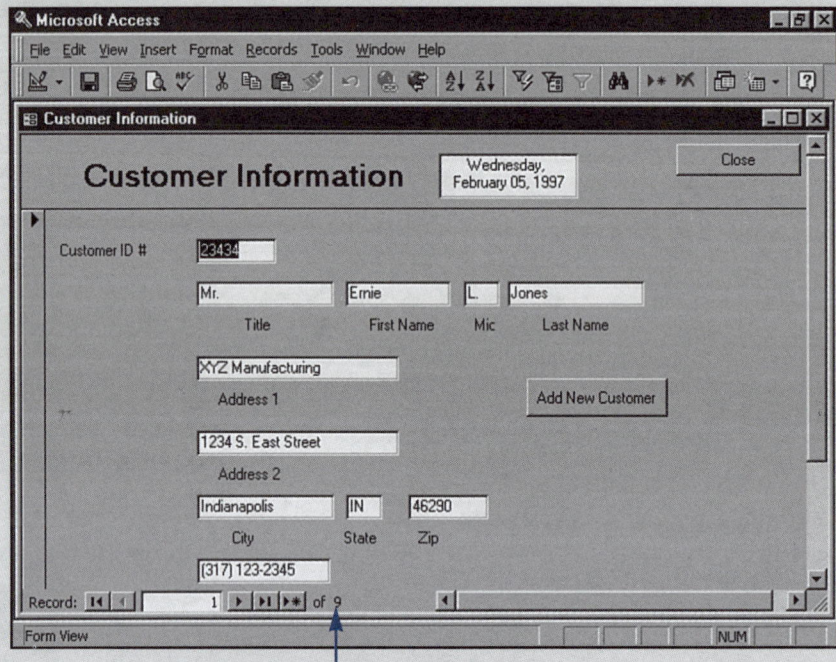

Number of records

 2 Click the Next Record navigation button twice to display a customer with an address in the city of Ypsilanti.

3 Click the City field once to place the cursor in the field.

The entire name of the city does not need to be selected—the cursor just needs to be somewhere in the field.

 4 Click the Filter by Selection button on the toolbar.

A filter will automatically be created that restricts the records shown to those that match the contents of the selected field. A note will be added next to the navigation buttons that indicates that the records shown using the navigation buttons are those that match a filter (see Figure 5.29).

Figure 5.29
The Customer
Information filtered for
customers from the City
of Ypsilanti.

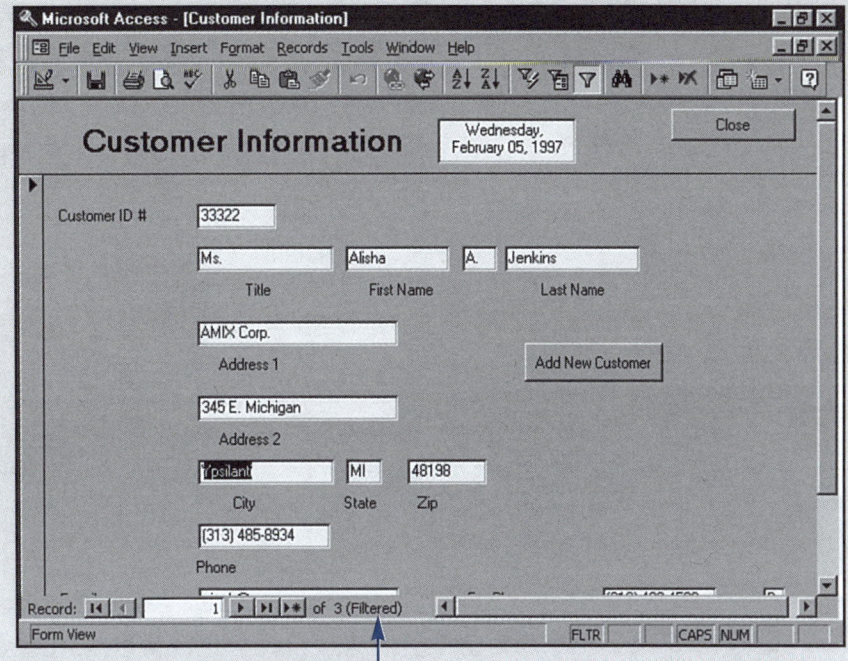

Notification that a filter is in use

5 Click the navigation buttons to scroll through the records to verify that the filter is working.

 6 Click the Remove filter button on the toolbar to disable the filter.

The filter is not deleted and may be applied again. The database will store the most recently used filter for future use even if the database is closed and reopened.

Keep the form open for the next procedure.

There are several options for defining filtering criteria. You may enter a specific word that must be matched, you may use logical expressions such as between and like, or you may exclude matches. These options are available when you click the field with the right mouse button.

To Create a Filter to Exclude Records that Match a Field

1 Click the next record navigation button until you locate a customer from the city of Ypsilanti.

2 Move the pointer to the city field (showing Ypsilanti). Click the right mouse button.

A menu appears with several filtering options (see Figure 5.30).

continues

To Create a Filter to Exclude Records that Match a Field   (continued)

Figure 5.30
A menu of Filter by Selection options may be revealed by pointing at a field and clicking with the right mouse button.

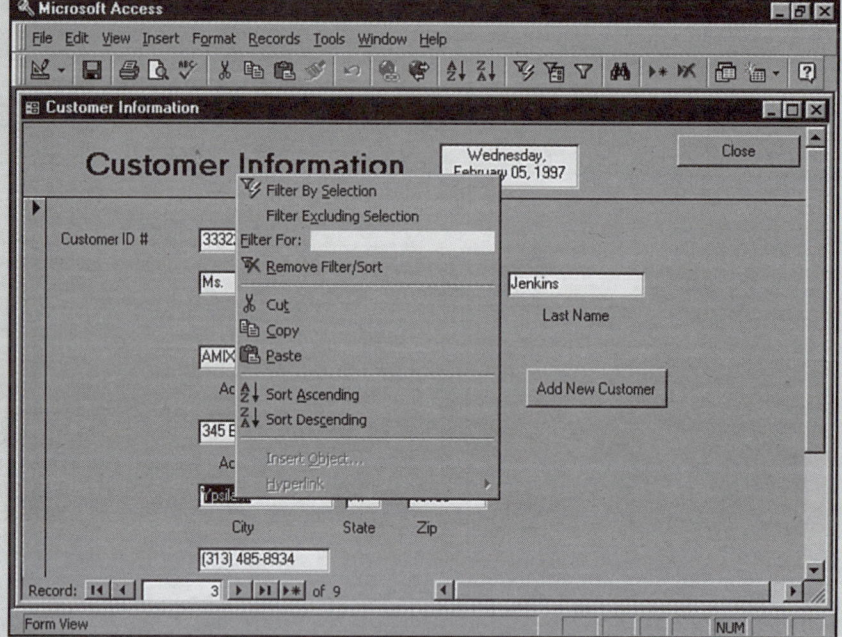

❸ Click the Filter Excluding Selection option.

This will exclude the three records that have Ypsilanti city addresses.

❹ Use the navigation buttons to scroll through the records to confirm that the filter works.

❺ Click the Remove Filter button to disable the filter.

Leave the form open for use in the next section.

You may use this menu to create a filter based on a logical comparison. The same logical comparisons that are used in the criteria field of a query design may be used here. In this section you will filter the records to show the zip codes for the area of Michigan that includes the cities of Ann Arbor and Ypsilanti. All the zip codes in this area are between 48100 and 48200.

To Create a Filter to Match a Range of Values

❶ Move the pointer to the Zip field and click the right mouse button.

The menu appears with a box named **F**ilter For that may be used for entering a logical comparison or exact matches (see Figure 5.31).

Figure 5.31
Pointing at a field and clicking the right mouse button reveals a menu that enables you to enter comparisons or values to be matched.

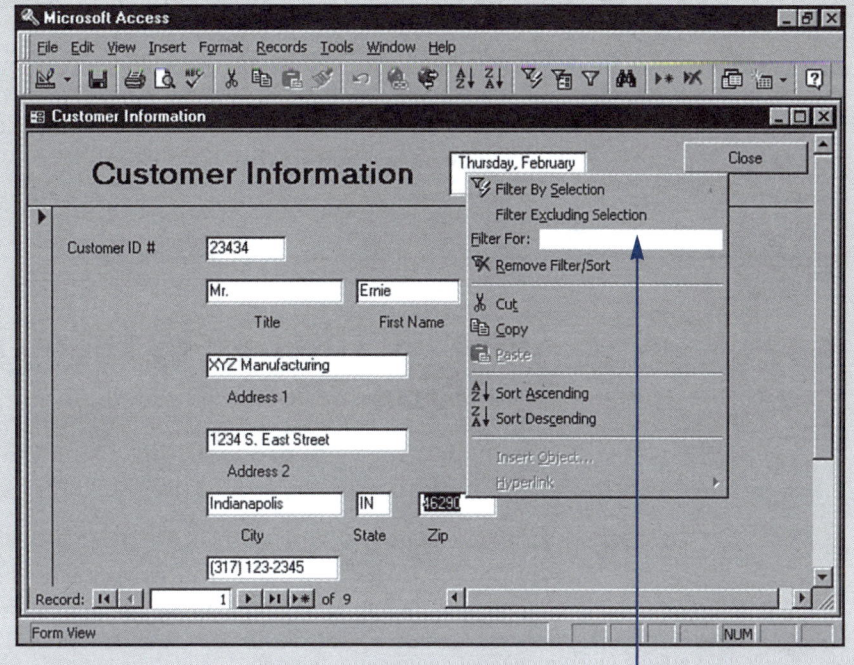

Enter logical comparisons or exact matches

② **Type in the following to filter for zip codes between 48100 and 48200.**

       Between 48100 and 48200

See Figure 5.32.

Figure 5.32
The Between function may be used as a filter.

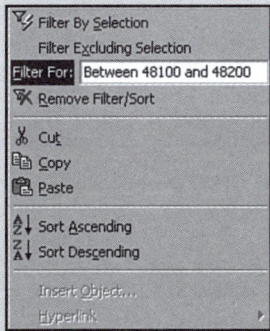

③ **Use the navigation buttons to confirm that the records shown have been restricted to those with zip codes between 48100 and 48200.**

In this example, there are five records that match the filter.

④ **Click the Remove Filter button on the toolbar to disable the filter.**

continues

To Create a Filter to Match a Range of Values   (continued)

This button toggles the filter on and off but does not actually remove the filter from memory. The filter will remain available until it is replaced by another or the conditions are deleted in the form view described in the next lesson.

Leave the form open for use in the next lesson.

Lesson 8: Filtering by Filling in Matching Values in a Form

You may want to filter the records using criteria that affect more than one field. In that case, you would use the Filter by Form button on the toolbar.

In this lesson you will learn how to use criteria in more than one field to filter the records shown. The following example is used to identify the female customers (Mrs. or Ms.) who live in Michigan.

To Use Filter Criteria in More than One Field

 ❶ In the Customer Records database, make sure that the Customer Information form window is open. Click the Filter by Form button on the toolbar.

The form will be displayed with empty fields (see Figure 5.33).

Figure 5.33
The form may be used to enter multiple filtering criteria.

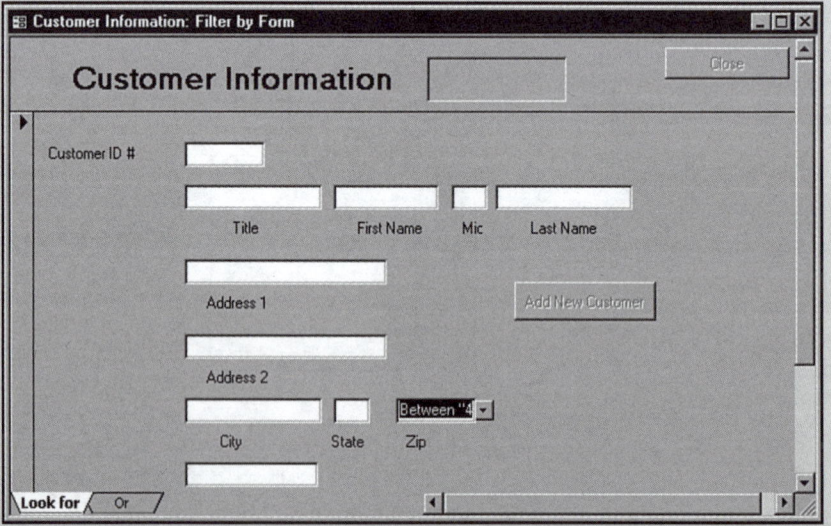

Notice that the condition from the previous lesson is displayed in the Zip field and that it is already selected.

❷ Press the Del key to remove the previous filter criteria.

❸ Click the Title field box.

A list arrow appears at the right side of the box.

④ Click the list arrow to reveal all of the current values for this field.

The titles used in this table were Mr., Mrs., and Ms. (see Figure 5.34).

Figure 5.34
The current contents of the field may be selected from a list to be used for matching criteria.

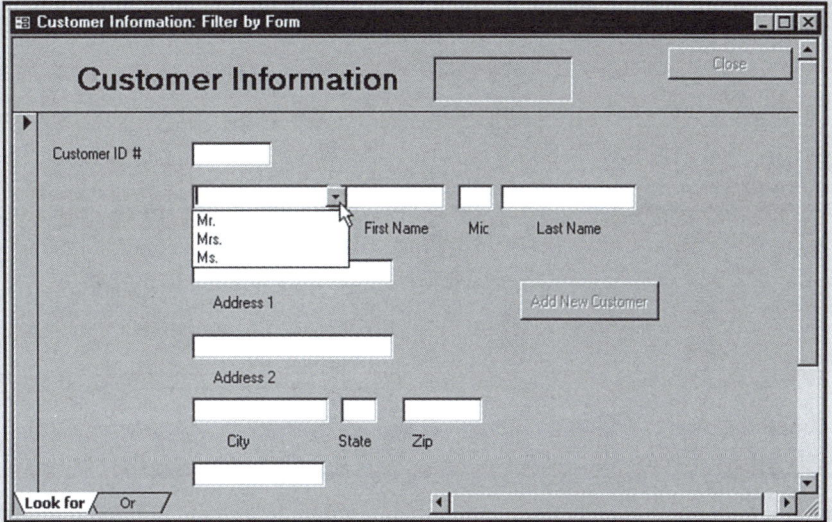

⑤ Select Mrs. from the list.

The selection will be placed in the field box and enclosed by quotation marks.

⑥ Click the State field box. Select MI from the list.

The form should now have two criteria, one for Title and another for State (see Figure 5.35).

Figure 5.35
Values or expressions may be entered into more than one field to be used as a filter.

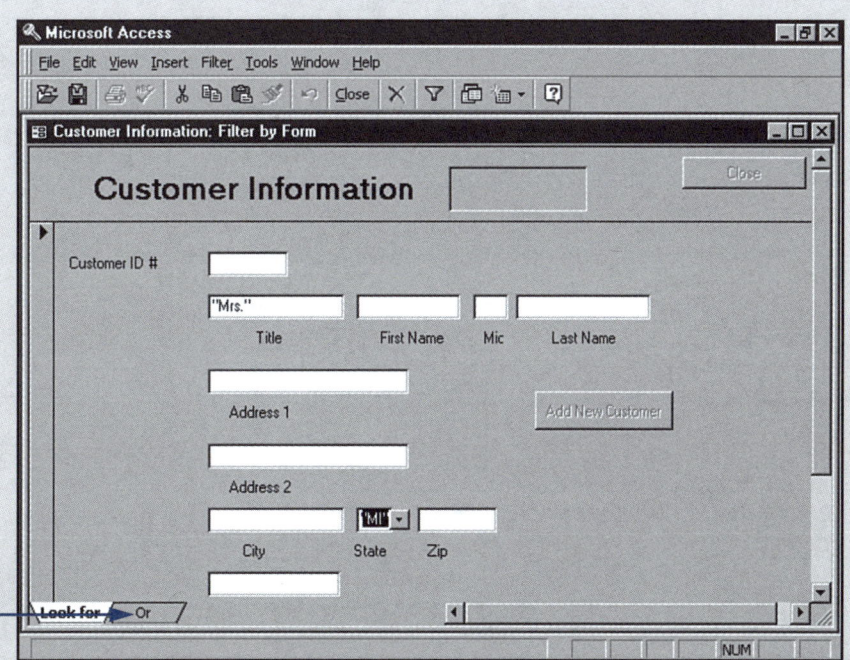

The Or tab is used to display additional criteria using another form

continues

To Use Filter Criteria in More than One Field   (continued)

These two criteria are both required to find matching records. This type of logical condition is called AND.

7 **Click the Or tab at the bottom of the form.**

This will display another empty form where additional criteria may be specified.

8 **Click the Title field and select Ms. from the list.**

9 **Click the State field and select MI from the list.**

Notice that the state had to be specified again. The records that will be displayed must match all of the conditions specified on the first form or all of the conditions on the second form. The two forms are used with the logical Or function to match records.

 10 **Click the Apply Filter button on the toolbar.**

There should be two customer records that match these criteria.

Keep the form open for the next procedure.

The form filter feature is not available for reports; however, it is possible to design an appropriate filter using the form and then save it as a query. A report may be created that is based upon the query that would contain the same records as displayed using the form filter.

In this part of the lesson you will learn how to save the filter design as a query.

To Save the Form Filter Criteria as a Query

 1 **Click the Filter by Form button to reveal the design of the filter.**

The first page of the filter design is displayed.

2 **Move the pointer to an empty space on the form and click the right mouse button.**

A menu will appear that has the Save As Query option (see Figure 5.36).

Figure 5.36
The filter may be saved as a query using a menu that is displayed when you click the right mouse button on an empty area of the filter design.

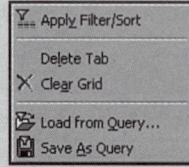

3 **Click the Save As Query option.**

A dialog box appears that may be used to assign a name to the query (see Figure 5.37).

Figure 5.37
The filter may be saved as a query.

4 **Enter** Women in Michigan **as the name of the query and click OK.**

This action creates a new query that may be used as the basis for a report.

5 **Click the** **C**lose **button on the toolbar.**

This will close the filter by form design.

6 **Close the Customer Information form.**

7 **Click the Queries tab of the database to display the available queries.**

Women in Michigan is now one of the queries in the database (see Figure 5.38).

Figure 5.38
The filter has been saved as one of the queries.

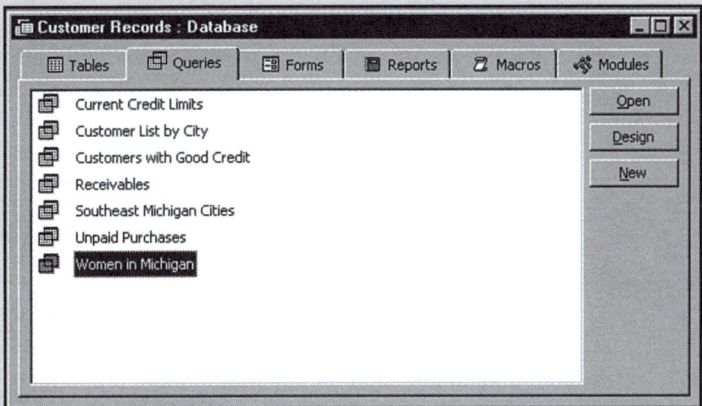

8 **Close the database.**

Project Summary

To	Do This
Use Parameters as Criteria in a Query	Place a message that will prompt the user in the criteria box in the query design grid. Enclose the message within square brackets. Whenever the query is run, a dialog box appears displaying your message as the prompt and a box where the user may enter a value. The query will operate as if you had entered that value in the criteria box.
Use Parameters in Calculations in a Query	If a calculation is used in a criteria box or if a new field is created as a calculated field, you may replace a field name with a prompt message.

continues

continued

To	Do This
	If the query is run, a dialog box appears with your message as the prompt and a box where the user may enter a value. The query will operate as if you had entered that value in the calculation box.
Create a dialog box to define filter conditions	Open a new form in design mode that is not based on any particular table or query. Use the Text box tool from the toolbox to draw boxes on the form that will be used for user input. Edit the labels of the two boxes to provide user prompts. Use the properties button to add a name to each box. Save the form and give it a short name.
Create a macro to open a report or form and apply the filter	Create a new macro. Select the OpenForm or OpenReport actions. Select the desired view. In the Where box, click the Build button. Select a field from a table. Select an operator or type one in such as = or **Between**. Double-click the Forms folder and find the form created in the previous step. Pick the name of the field box(es) that you added to the form. Close the macro and save it with a name that can be used on a button.
Modify the dialog box to link it to the macro	Open the form created previously in the Design View. Arrange the form and database windows so both are visible. Open the toolbox, if necessary, and make sure the Wizard button is selected. Drag the name of the macro from the previous section onto the form design. The wizard will automatically create a button with the macro name on it. Click the form and use the **E**dit, Select Fo**r**m menu options to select the form. Use the Properties button to deselect the navigation buttons and the scroll bars. Close and save.
Remove scroll bars and navigation buttons	Open the form in the Design View. Choose **E**dit and Select Fo**r**m from the menu bar. Click the Properties button on the toolbar and click the Format tab. Set Scroll Bars to Neither and Navigation Buttons to No.
Filter a form by selecting the contents of a field	Open a form and find a record that has a value that you want to use as a filtering criteria for one of the fields. Click the value to place the cursor in that field box. Click the Filter by Selection button on the toolbar.
Remove a filter	Click the Remove Filter button on the toolbar.
Create a filter to exclude records	Find an example of a record that contains the value that you want to use as the criteria for excluding records. Point at the value and click the right mouse button. Choose Filter E**x**cluding Selection.

To	Do This
Create a filter range	Point at the field that will be used to define a range. Click the right mouse button. Enter the logical expression in the Filter For box in the menu that appears. Other logical expressions may be used as well.
Filter by filling in a form	Click the Filter by Form button on the toolbar. Enter the values to be matched in the empty form. The values entered in one form will be used with a logical AND function. Additional forms may be used to specify additional criteria by clicking the Or tab. These criteria will be used with those on the first form with the logical Or function.
Save a form filter as a Query	Click the Filter by Form button, if necessary, to display the filter design form. Point at an empty space on the form and click the right mouse button. Select Save **A**s Query from the menu that appears.

Checking Your Skills

True/False

For each of the following statements, check *T* or *F* to indicate whether the statement is true or false.

__T __F **1.** If you enclose a phrase inside square brackets in a query design, the program will prompt you to enter a value to be used in place of the phrase unless the word or phrase in the brackets is a field name.

__T __F **2.** A parameter is enclosed in parentheses.

__T __F **3.** Using parameters is the only way to get the program to enable user input when restricting the output of a report.

__T __F **4.** If you drag the name of a macro from the database window onto the design of a form, it will be represented by a button on the form.

__T __F **5.** If you click the Remove Filter button it will be erased and you will have to create it again if you need it in the future.

Multiple Choice

Circle the letter of the correct answer for each of the following questions.

1. Which of the following is used to enclose a parameter?

　　a. ( )

　　b. { }

    c. < >

    d. [ ]

2. Which of the following expressions correctly uses a parameter to prompt the user for input? (Assume that Company and Product are field names.)

    a. (Enter the Company Name)

    b. [Enter the Product Name]

    c. [Company]

    d. [Product]

3. Which button on the toolbox is used to draw a box on the form design when you are preparing a user-defined filter?

    a. Label

    b. Text Box

    c. Wizard

    d. Combo Box

4. If you had a database of books that had been loaned out from a library and wanted to create a form-based filter that showed all the books by a certain popular author that had been loaned out during a particular month, you would:

    a. place the cursor in the author field and use filter by selection

    b. place the cursor in the date field and use filter by selection

    c. scroll through the records using the navigation buttons and place a bookmark in each record that met the criteria

    d. use the filter by form button and put the author's name in the author field and a logical criteria such as, Between 1/1/97 and 1/31/97, in the date field.

5. When you create a user-defined filter as described in the previous text, the Where Condition is used to:

    a. tell the macro where to find the report or form that it uses

    b. tell the macro where to send the resulting report

    c. describe a filter condition that may refer to the contents of text boxes in a form

    d. tell the form where the table or query it is based on is located

Completion

In the blank provided, write the correct answer for each of the following statements.

1. One of a set of factors that define a system, determine its behavior, and can be varied is called a(n) _____.

2. A form and query that work together to enable the user to set the filter conditions that restrict the output of a report or the records shown in a form is called a(n) _____.

3. Write an example of a prompt to be used in a parameter query. Enclose your prompt in the correct symbols: _____.

4. If you create a filter using the Filter by Form method and then want to print out a report that lists the same records that were displayed by the filter, you can save the filter as a _____ and then base a report on it.

5. The assistant program that helps you write the complex filter formulas is called a(n) _____.

Applying Your Skills

At the end of each project in *Access 97 Essentials Level III*, you learn how to apply your Access skills to various situations. The following exercises help you practice the skills you have learned in this project. Take a few minutes to work through these exercises now.

Using a Parameter as a Criteria in a Query

Create a parameter query that enables the user to limit the type of books shown based upon what they select.

To Use a Parameter as a Criteria in a Query

1. Copy the file Proj0502 and rename it `Library`.

2. Open the Library database and open the query Mysteries in the design mode.

3. In the Type of Book column, replace the "Mystery" criteria with the following:

    `[Enter the type of book:]`

4. Click the View button to look at the Datasheet View. When the Enter Parameter Value dialog box appears, type any one of the following and click OK.

    `Mystery`, `Fiction`, `Classic`, `Non-Fiction`, `Science Fiction`, or `Humor`

5. Return to the Design View. Add the conditional word Like to the criteria. The new criteria should be:

    `Like [Enter the type of book:]`

6. Switch to Datasheet View. Enter an asterisk to see all of the titles. Asterisks can be used to replace parts of fields you are trying to match when you use the Like operator; for example, **Mys*** would find any book type starting with "Mys".

Using Parameters in Calculations in a Query

Create a query that has a calculated field that enables the user to enter a parameter to be used in the calculation.

To Use Parameters in Calculations in a Query

1. Open the file Proj0503 and rename it **Discount**.

2. Open the Discount database and open the query Discount Prices in the design mode.

3. Scroll to the right to display the last two columns. Adjust the width of the columns so you can see the entire expression in the last two columns of the query design.

   In the Sale Price column, a formula has been used to subtract 0.2 from 1 and then multiply by the Unit Price. This is one way to calculate a discount of 20%.

4. Edit the Sale Price formula so that the discount factor (.2) is replaced by a parameter. The resulting formula should look like the following example:

   ```
   Sale Price: (1-[Enter the discount factor:])*[Unit Price]
   ```

5. Click the View button to change to the Datasheet View. When prompted by the message that was entered in the formula, enter a decimal number between zero and one.

6. Examine the resulting datasheet to determine if the discount was used correctly to determine the new sale price and the resulting Amount Due.

7. Close the query and save the changes. Close the database.

Creating a User-Defined Filter

In this exercise, you create a dialog box that will enable the user to enter the name of the company and the name of a product and then open a report that only contains those records that match the input.

To Create a User-Defined Filter

1. Open the Discount database created in the previous exercise (or copy the Proj0503 database) and rename it **Discount**.

2. Create a new form that is not based on a table.

3. Use the Text Box button on the toolbox to drag two text boxes on the form.

4. Edit the labels for the boxes to read `Company` and `Product`.

5. Use the Properties box to give each text box a name. Name them `Company` and `Product`.

6. Close the form and save it with the name `Filter`.

7. Create a macro to open the Purchases report in preview mode.

8. In the Where Condition box of the macro design, use the builder to create the following condition. (The report is based on the Purchases query. Start the builder by looking for the Company field in the Purchases query.)

   ```
   [Purchases]![Company] = Forms![Filter]![Company] And [Purchases]!
   [Product Description] = Forms![Filter]![Product]
   ```

9. Save the macro with the name `Preview Report`.

10. Open the Filter form in Design View and tile the windows.

11. Drag the Preview Report and Close macros onto the form from the database window.

12. Save the changes to the form.

13. Open the form (Filter) and enter a company name such as `MichIx` and a product name such as `Degreaser` to see how it works.

14. Close the database.

Creating a Filter Based on a Form

In this exercise, you open a form that shows the books that have been borrowed from a library and filter for those that were borrowed in 1997.

To Create a Filter Using a Form

1. Copy the Proj0504 database and rename it `Books`.

2. Open the form Books on Loan.

3. Point at the Borrow Date field and click the right mouse button.

4. Enter the following condition in the Filter For box:

   `Between 1/1/97 and 12/31/97`

5. Use the navigation buttons to scroll through the three records that show descriptions of the books borrowed in 1997.

6. Click on the Remove Filter button to disable the filter.

Project

6

Sharing a Database with Others

Protecting your database with passwords and adding switchboards

In this Project, you learn how to:

➤ Assign a Password to Your Database

➤ Change or Remove a Database Password

➤ Encrypt a Database

➤ Create a Switchboard Using the Switchboard Manager Add-In

➤ Set Startup Parameters

➤ Set Access Defaults

Why Would I Do This?

Many features of Access are designed to allow users to share data and to gain access to data used by others. Problems can arise from sharing data with others, however. Someone may make changes to the tables, forms, reports, or queries you have created, or he or she may enter data into the tables in a non-standard format. In some cases, your database may contain sensitive information that is not for general distribution, or proprietary information that is valuable to the company. In this lesson, you learn some techniques that will provide some protection from accidental changes. You also learn some useful safeguards to protect your database from intentional damage or theft.

Many people need to use databases who do not have the need or the time to learn how to use Access. It is possible to customize a database so that these users are guided through the functions they need to use. This can be done by setting startup and default parameters that will lead these users to custom menus that open forms with customized toolbars.

Lesson 1: Assigning a Password to Your Database

Adding security to your database is like putting a new lock on a door. It provides a measure of protection from some intruders, but it also has several drawbacks:

- ➤ It slows you down every time you want to pass through the door.

- ➤ Other people who need to pass through the door must take up your time by asking you for the key.

- ➤ If you give a duplicate key to someone, you do not always know what he or she has done with it.

- ➤ There are people who have master keys to that type of lock.

- ➤ There are people who understand how the lock works and know how to pick it.

- ➤ If you lose the only key, it can be very inconvenient.

In spite of these disadvantages, most of us still use locks on our doors. You may also want to add a measure of security to your database.

In this lesson, you learn how to require a password to open a database.

To Assign a Password to Your Database

1 **Make a copy of the student data file Proj0601.**

2 **Rename the copy** `Prices`.

Include the .mdb extension only if you can see the extension on the Proj0601 file.

3 **Launch Access 97.**

Close the dialog box that displays previously used files.

4 **Choose File, Open Database from the menu.**

The Open dialog box appears. Use the navigation buttons in this window to locate the folder you are using for your files.

5 **Click the Prices database to select it and click the Exclusive check box.**

This prevents any other users from accessing the database while you are making this change. It is required for the following procedure even if you are not using Access in a network environment. (see Figure 6.1).

Figure 6.1
Use the Open dialog box to open the Prices database for exclusive use.

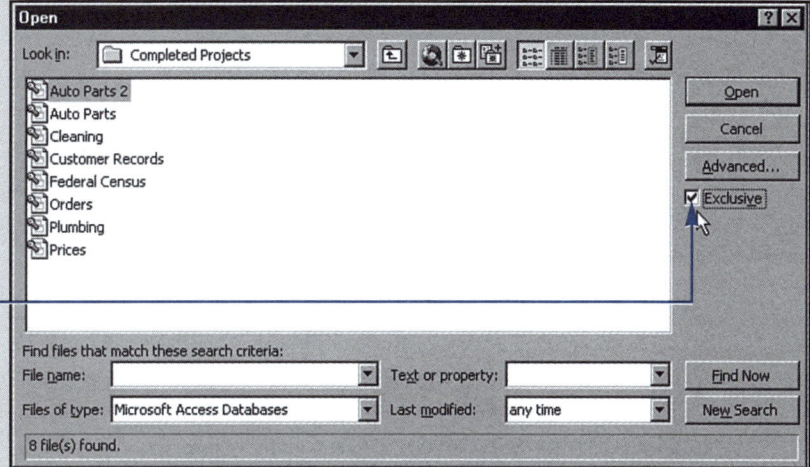

Exclusive Use Check Box

6 **Click Open.**

This action opens the Prices database for your exclusive use. The Prices database appears (see Figure 6.2).

continues

To Assign a Password to Your Database   **(continued)**

Figure 6.2
The Prices database is shown with the database window open.

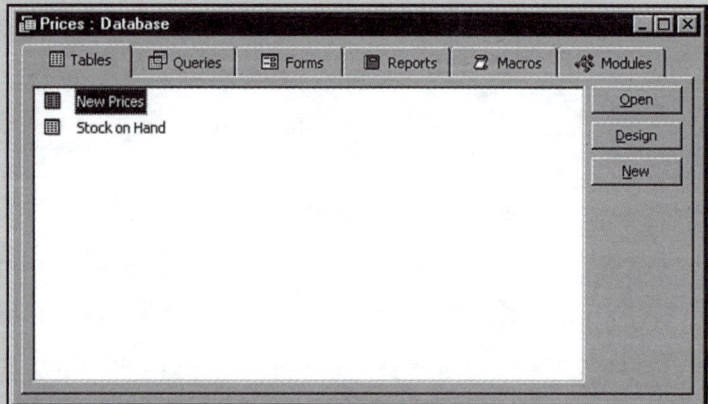

⑦ **Choose _T_ools, Security from the menu; then select Set Database Password.**

The Set Database Password dialog box appears (see Figure 6.3)

Figure 6.3
The Set Database Password dialog box enables you to set a new password.

⑧ **Type the following password in the _P_assword box:**

   ABCabc!

The letters are represented by asterisks (see Figure 6.4). If you are not sure what you typed, press ⨞Backspace and try again carefully.

Figure 6.4
The Set Database Password dialog box is shown after the password has been entered.

⑨ **Type the same password in the _V_erify box. Click OK.**

Be sure to use the same case (uppercase and/or lowercase) that you typed in the **P**assword text box. The Set Database Password dialog box will close and the database window will reappear.

⑩ **Close the database and then open it again.**

You do not have to select the Exclusive option this time. The Password Required dialog box appears (see Figure 6.5).

Figure 6.5
The Password Required dialog box is shown before the password has been entered.

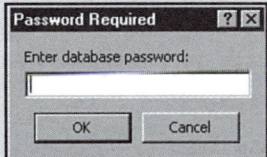

11 Carefully type the password you entered in step 8 and click OK.

The database will open if you correctly matched the password. If you did not match the password exactly, including the proper upper- and lowercase characters, you will see a warning box and then return to the Password Required dialog box to try again.

12 Close the database.

Passwords in Access can be very simple and short or complex and up to 14 characters in length. To get the best security out of your password, do not use a date or a word that would be listed in a dictionary. Do not use passwords others might be able to guess, such as a family member's name, your social security number, or a commonly used phone number. Make the password at least six characters long and include a character that is not a letter. If you do want to use an easily recalled word or date, insert an extra symbol. In the example in this lesson, the password included an exclamation mark for this purpose.

Lesson 2: Changing or Removing a Database Password

Once you have added a password to your database you may need to change or remove it.

In this lesson, you learn how to change or remove the database password.

To Change or Remove a Database Password

1 Choose File, Open Database, and open the Prices database in Exclusive mode.

The Password Required dialog box appears.

2 Enter the password you created in Lesson 1, step 8; then choose OK.

continues

To Change or Remove a Database Password   (continued)

❸ Choose Tools, Security from the menu bar; then choose Unset Database Password.

The Unset Database Password dialog box appears (see Figure 6.6).

Figure 6.6
The Unset Database Password dialog box is used to remove a password.

❹ Type the original password you created in Lesson 1.

ABCabc!

❺ Click OK.

The password has been removed. The database may now be opened without a password.

If you want to change the password, follow the above procedure, then choose **T**ools, Securi**t**y, Set **D**atabase Password and type a new password.

❻ Close the database.

Leave Access open for use in the following lesson.

Lesson 3: Encrypting a Database

Encryption
Data scrambled and stored in coded form that is not easily read by someone who does not have the code.

Even though the database program is protected by a password, it is possible to view the data in a table by opening the database with a word processing program. Most of the screen of the word processing program would be filled with unrecognizable characters, but some of the data in the tables would still be readable (see Figure 6.7).

Figure 6.7
The Prices database (with a password) as displayed by the WordPad program.

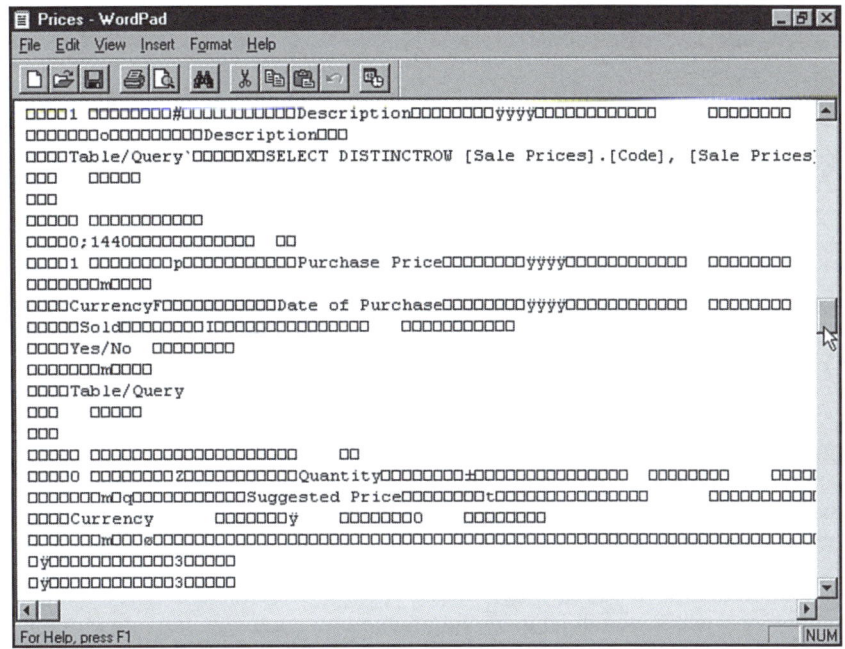

In this lesson, you learn how to save the database in an encrypted mode that will prevent someone from reading the data with a text editor, such as a word processing program.

To Store a Database In Encrypted Form

1 **In Access, without a database open, choose Tools, Security from the menu bar; then choose Encrypt/Decrypt Database.**

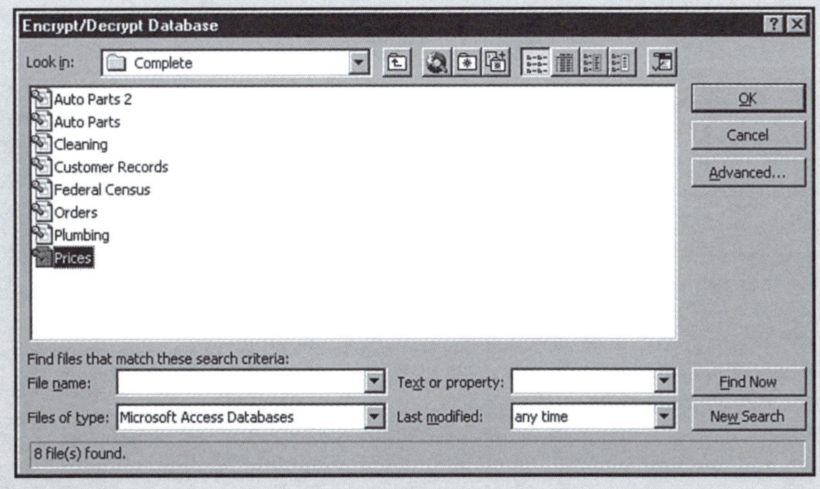

Figure 6.8
The Encrypt/Decrypt Database dialog box is used to locate the database you want to encrypt.

2 **Use the navigation buttons to locate the folder that contains the Prices database, if necessary.**

3 **Click the Prices database, and then click OK.**

The Encrypt Database As dialog box appears.

continues

To Store a Database In Encrypted Form   (continued)

4 **In the File Name text box, enter the following name to be used for the new database:**

    Prices-Encrypted

The dialog box should appear as shown in Figure 6.09.

Figure 6.9
The Encrypt Database As dialog window is displayed with the new name.

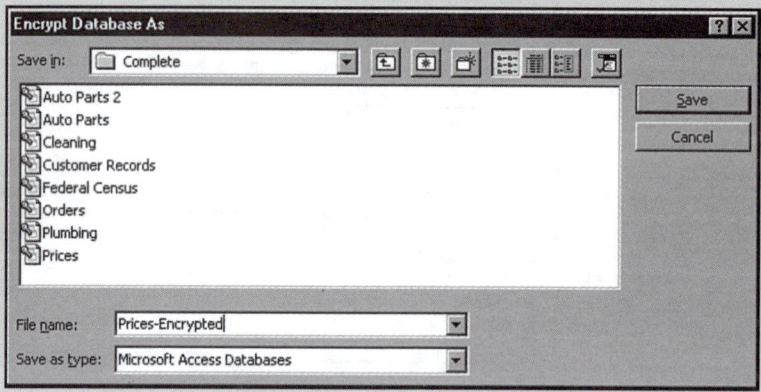

5 **Click the Save button.**

The data is now encrypted so that the text cannot be read. Figure 6.10 displays the database as it would now appear if it were opened using a word processor such as WordPad.

Leave the Access open for the next lesson.

Figure 6.10
The Prices-Encrypted database viewed by WordPad.

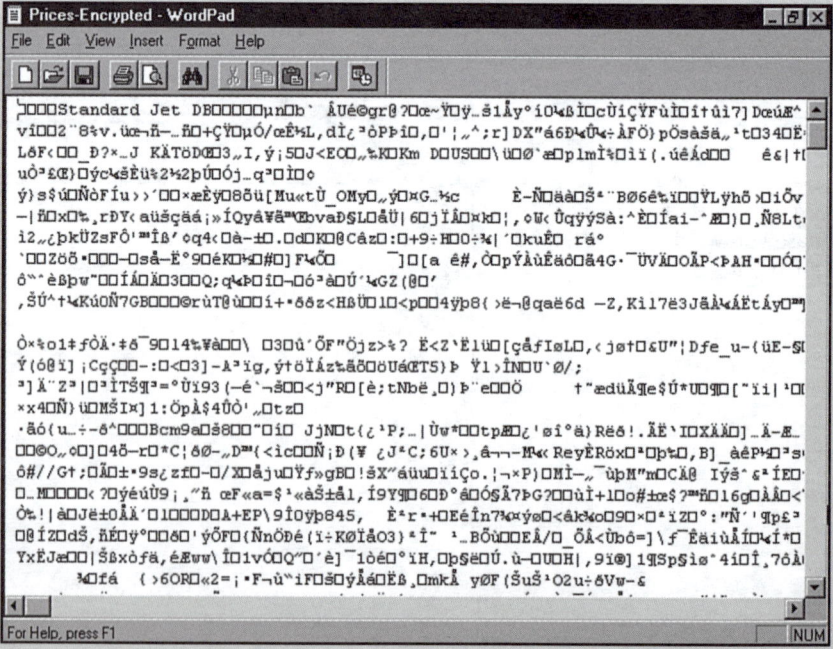

You may now use the encrypted database instead of the original. The original may be deleted after you have tested the encrypted version.

The security measures mentioned in these lessons are useful in providing a first line of defense. Access provides a more sophisticated level of security that is particularly useful in a network environment. It is called user-level security. To find out more about security, use the Help menu and search for help on the word Security. Make copies of any databases that are important. You could lock yourself out!

Lesson 4: Creating a Switchboard

It is also useful to create a switchboard to guide someone else through a set of common tasks, such as entering data and producing standard reports.

In this lesson, you learn how to create a switchboard using the Switchboard Manager. The sample database you will use already includes tables, forms, and reports that can be used in a switchboard.

To Create a Switchboard

Switchboard
The term Access uses for a menu of choices represented by buttons on a form. Clicking a button on a switchboard runs an associated macro to perform functions such as opening forms or printing reports.

① **Make a copy of the student data file Proj0602.**

② **Rename the copy** Customer-Switchboard.

Include the .mdb extension only if you can see the extension on the Proj0602 file.

③ **Open the Customer-Switchboard database.**

④ **Choose Tools, Add-ins from the menu bar; then choose Switchboard Manager.**

Since there is no switchboard to manage yet, a dialog box appears that asks if you would like to create one (see Figure 6.11).

Figure 6.11
This dialog box appears if a switchboard does not already exist.

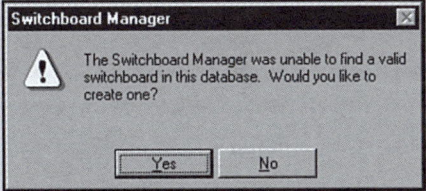

⑤ **Choose Yes.**

After a brief delay, another Switchboard Manager dialog box appears that displays the default switchboard (see Figure 6.12).

continues

To Create a Switchboard   (continued)

Figure 6.12
The switchboard dialog box displays the default switchboard option.

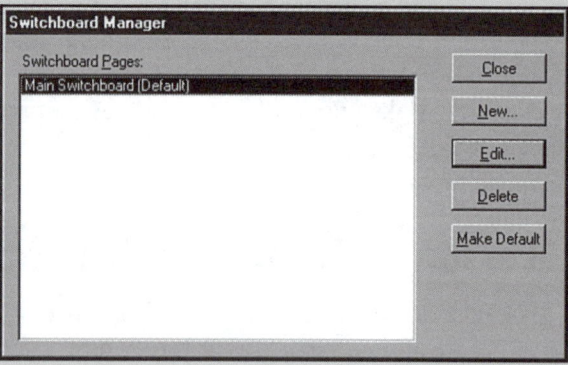

It is possible to link several switchboards together. In this case we will only use one.

6 Click Edit.

This will allow you to add action buttons to the switchboard. The Edit Switchboard Page dialog box appears (see Figure 6.13).

Figure 6.13
The Edit Switchboard Page dialog box may be used to add action buttons to the switchboard.

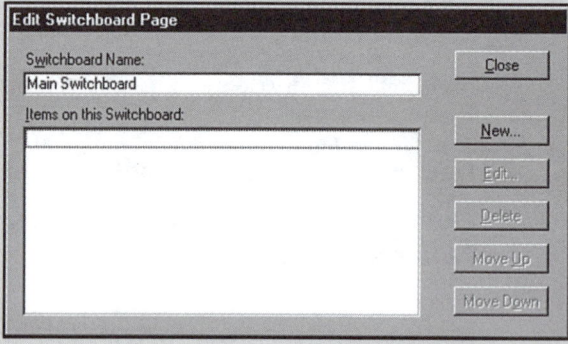

7 Click New.

This action will open the Edit Switchboard Item dialog box (see Figure 6.14). This box contains a **T**ext box that can be used to create a label for the action button. The **C**ommand box can be used to specify commands to do things like open forms or preview reports.

Figure 6.14
The Edit Switchboard Item dialog box is used to specify actions.

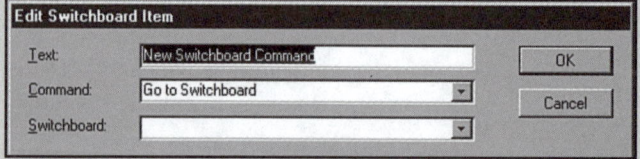

8 Change the text in the Text box to the following:

   Add New Customers

9 Use the down-arrow at the right of the Command box to select the Open Form in Add Mode option.

Notice that the title of the third box changes depending on your choice in the **C**ommand box (see Figure 6.15).

Figure 6.15
The Edit Switchboard Item dialog box changes the third choice in response to the contents of the **C**ommand box.

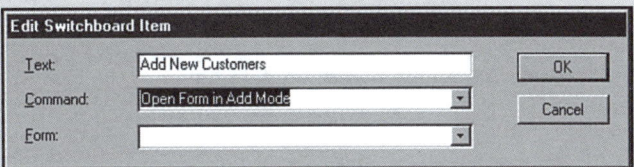

10 **Use the down-arrow at the right of the Form box to select the Customer Information form. Click OK.**

The Edit Switchboard Page dialog box reappears showing the Add New Customers item on its list of switchboard items (see Figure 6.16).

Figure 6.16
The Edit Switchboard Page dialog box displays the items that have been added to the switchboard.

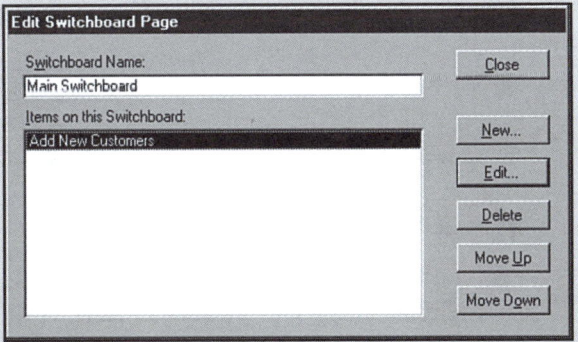

11 **Repeat steps 7-10 to create another switchboard item to open the Customer Orders form in add mode. Use the text** Add New Orders.

The next switchboard item is defined as shown in Figure 6.17.

Figure 6.17
The Edit Switchboard Item dialog box defined to add the next item.

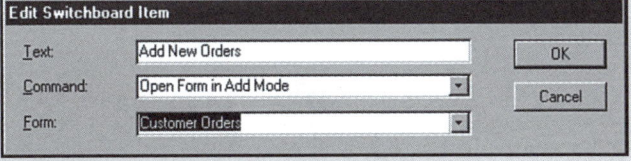

12 **Repeat steps 7-10 to create the next switchboard step, except this time, select the Open Report command and pick the Orders Grouped by Customer report. Use the text** Preview the Report on Orders Grouped by Customer.

The last item is defined to open a report (see Figure 6.18).

continues

To Create a Switchboard (continued)

Figure 6.18
The Edit Switchboard Item dialog box set up to open a report.

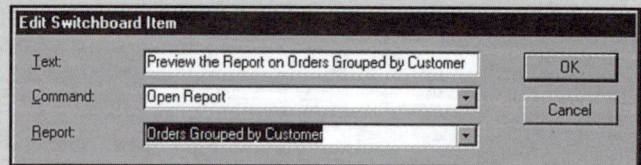

⑬ Click OK.

The Edit Switchboard Page dialog box displays the three action items (see Figure 6.19).

Figure 6.19
The Edit Switchboard Page dialog box displays the three action items.

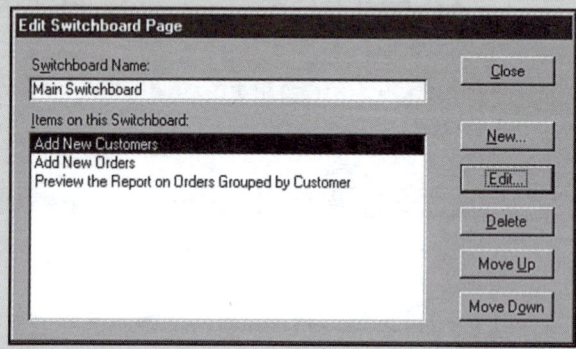

⑭ Click Close.

The Switchboard Manager dialog box appears, displaying the single switchboard that has been created to this point.

⑮ Click Close.

The Switchboard Manager dialog box closes, and the database window is displayed. The database now has an extra table named Switchboard Items and a new form named Switchboard.

⑯ Click the Forms tab to display the available forms. Click Switchboard to select it and then click Open.

The new switchboard appears (see Figure 6.20).

Figure 6.20
The new switchboard form opens.

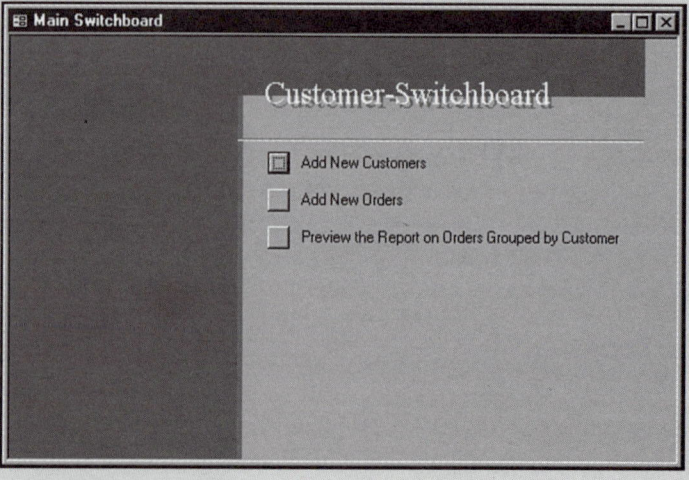

⑰ Test the switchboard by clicking on one of the buttons.

It should automatically open the appropriate form or report.

⑱ Close the form or report and then close the switchboard form.

Leave the database open for the next lesson.

If you have more options than will fit on one switchboard or you would like to have multiple levels of switchboards, one of the commands available in the Command box is Go to Switchboard. You can use this to string together several switchboards and to branch from one to another.

When you use the Startup settings to remove the design options from the menus and toolbars, it is hard to make subsequent changes. To restore full menus and toolbars, close Access and re-open it. Hold down the ⬆Shift key while you open the database.

Lesson 5: Setting Startup Parameters

It is possible to control the way the database appears when it is opened. You can decide which toolbars are available to the user and you can open a switchboard form automatically. In this lesson, you learn how to open the switchboard automatically whenever the database is opened. You can also disable several features that are very useful while the database is being designed but that are not necessary while it is being used by someone else.

To Set Startup Parameters

❶ Open the Customer-Switchboard database, if necessary, and choose Tools, Startup from the menu.

The Startup dialog box appears (see Figure 6.21).

Figure 6.21
The Startup dialog box allows the designer to control the toolbars and menus to simplify them or to restrict the user's ability to change the design.

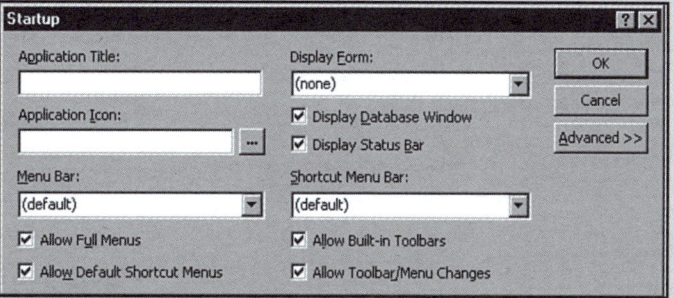

❷ Click the down-arrow at the right end of the Display Form box and select Switchboard.

This causes the Switchboard form to open automatically when the database is opened.

continues

To Set Startup Parameters   (continued)

3 **Check the Display Status Bar check box to make sure it is selected.**

This option could remove the status bar from the bottom of the screen to increase the available window space and simplify the screen. We will leave it turned on in this example.

4 **Click Allow Built-in Toolbars to deselect it.**

This option removes the toolbar from the top of the screen to increase the available window space and simplify the screen.

5 **Click Allow Toolbar/Menu Changes to deselect it.**

This prevents a user from adding the toolbars back to the screen.

6 **Click Allow Full Menus to deselect it.**

This changes the menu options from a full list of editing choices to a short list of choices that are appropriate to using the database rather than designing it.

7 **Click Allow Default Shortcut Menus to deselect it.**

This disables the shortcut menus options that are normally available by clicking with the right mouse button.

8 **Click Display Database Window to deselect it.**

When you close the switchboard form, the database window will not be available to the user so he or she cannot get into the design of the database.

The Startup dialog box can also help you design your own menu bars and shortcut menus. You can also use this dialog box to create a special icon on the desktop that will run this version of the database. We will not use these options at this time.

Check to make sure that your dialog box looks like Figure 6.22.

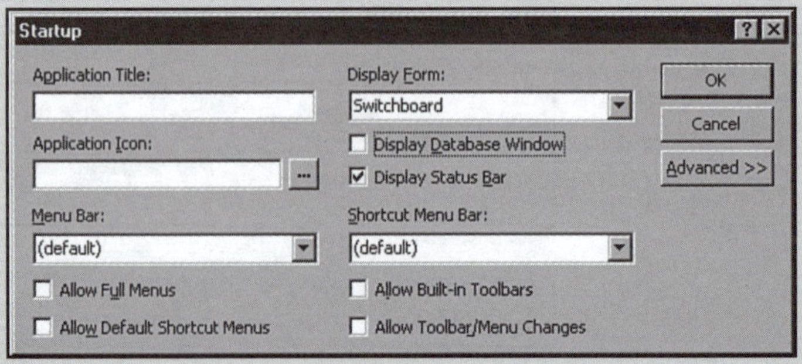

Figure 6.22
The Startup dialog box showing the new settings.

9 **Click OK to close the Startup dialog box. Close the database.**

The next time the Customer-Switchboard database is opened, the startup parameters will be used and the switchboard will be opened automatically.

🔟 **Open the Customer-Switchboard database again.**

The Switchboard form will open automatically. Notice that there are several differences. The menus have fewer choices, the right mouse button does not produce a shortcut menu, and the toolbar is not available (see Figure 6.23).

Figure 6.23
The Switchboard form can be displayed with fewer user options available on the Access menus and the toolbars are turned off.

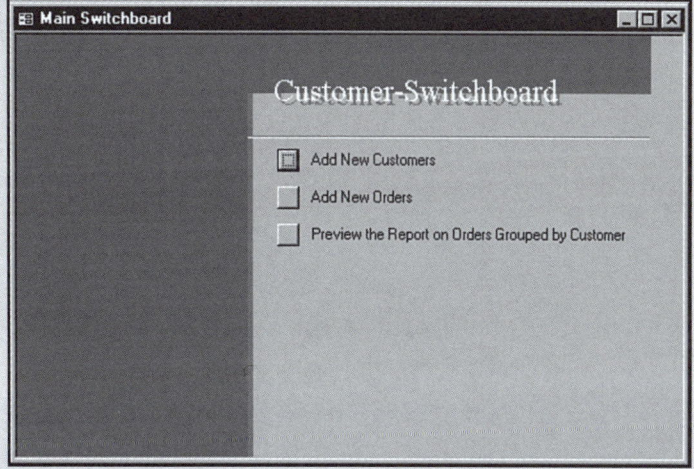

⑪ **Close the Switchboard form.**

The settings from the startup will stay in effect until Access is closed.

⑫ **Close Access.**

When you start Access again, the normal toolbars and menus will be displayed.

Lesson 6: Setting Access Defaults

Startups control the environment of a single database, while Access defaults control the environment for any Access database that is opened from your installed copy of Access. In order to activate the appropriate menus, a database with menus needs to be open.

In this lesson, you learn how to change some of the defaults Access uses.

To Set Access Defaults

❶ **Open the Prices database you used in a previous lesson.**

The Prices database will open, and the menus and toolbars will be visible.

❷ **Choose Tools, Options from the menu.**

The Options dialog box appears (see Figure 6.24).

continues

To Set Access Defaults   (continued)

Figure 6.24
The Options dialog box can be used to set defaults for the Access program.

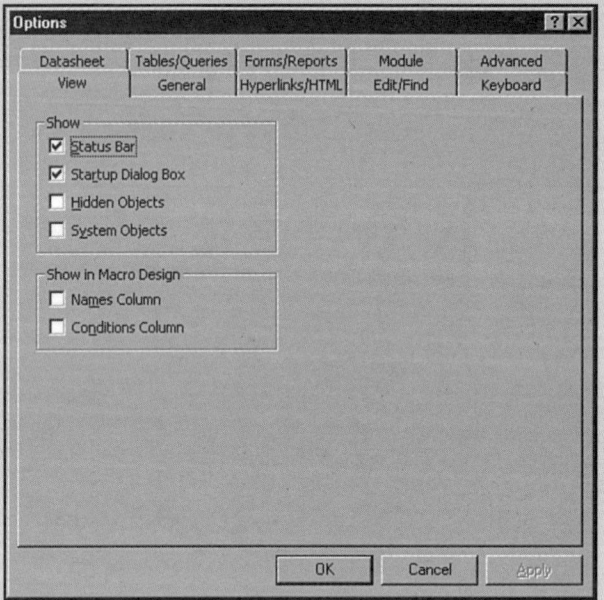

❸ **Click the Keyboard tab.**

The default settings are displayed for movement of the cursor after the ⏎Enter key is pressed or when the arrow keys are used (see Figure 6.25).

Figure 6.25
The Options dialog box can be used to control the movement of the cursor.

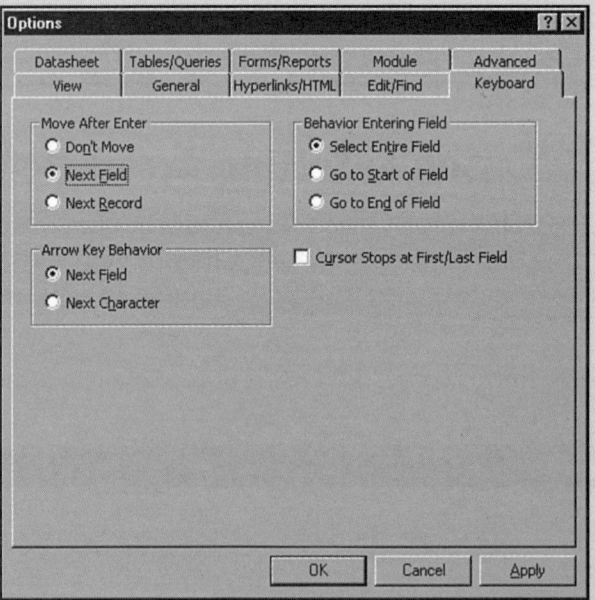

The default setting for movement of the cursor after the ⏎Enter key is pressed is to move it to the next field to the right in the current record. If you are entering or changing the data in one field, it would be more convenient to automatically move to the next record.

4 **Click on Next Record in the Move after Enter area.**

5 **Click the Apply button.**

The cursor will now move down the column of data each time you press the ⏎Enter key when you are in a table view. If you are in a form, the view will page from one record to the next and remain in the same field when you press the ⏎Enter key.

6 **Click the Datasheet tab.**

The default options for the appearance of the datasheet are displayed (see Figure 6.26).

Figure 6.26
The default values for the Datasheet View are displayed.

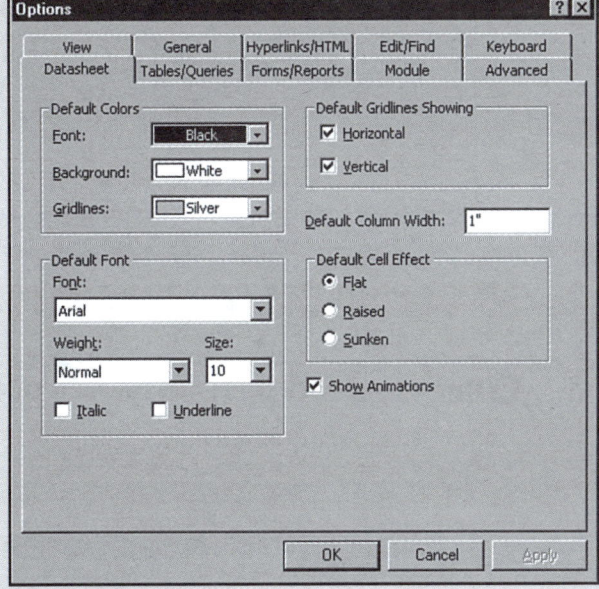

Changes on this form affect the appearance of any datasheet opened in Access.

7 **Change the default colors to White, Gray, and Aqua for the Font, Background, and Gridlines options, respectively. Click the Vertical Default Gridlines check box to deselect it.**

Your Options Datasheet dialog box should look like Figure 6.27.

continues

To Set Access Defaults (continued)

Figure 6.27
The Options Datasheet dialog box displaying the new settings.

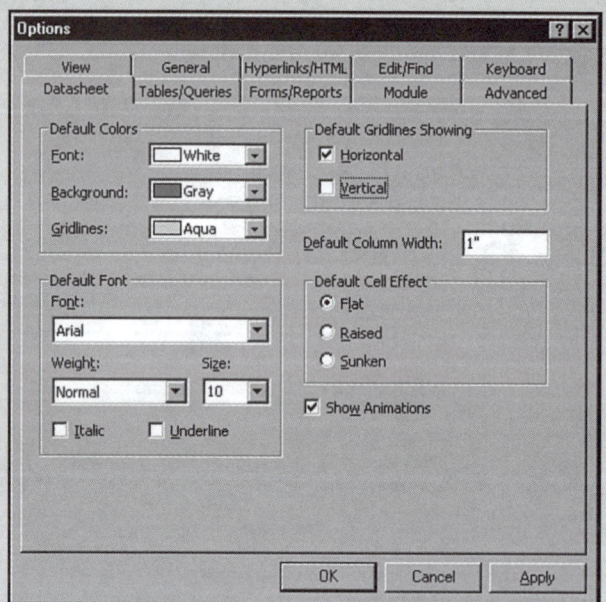

⑧ **Click OK to close the Options dialog box.**

This will also apply the new settings.

⑨ **Open the Stock on Hand table in Datasheet View.**

The new default colors and gridlines settings will be displayed (see Figure 6.28).

Figure 6.28
The Customer table in Datasheet View displays the new default settings.

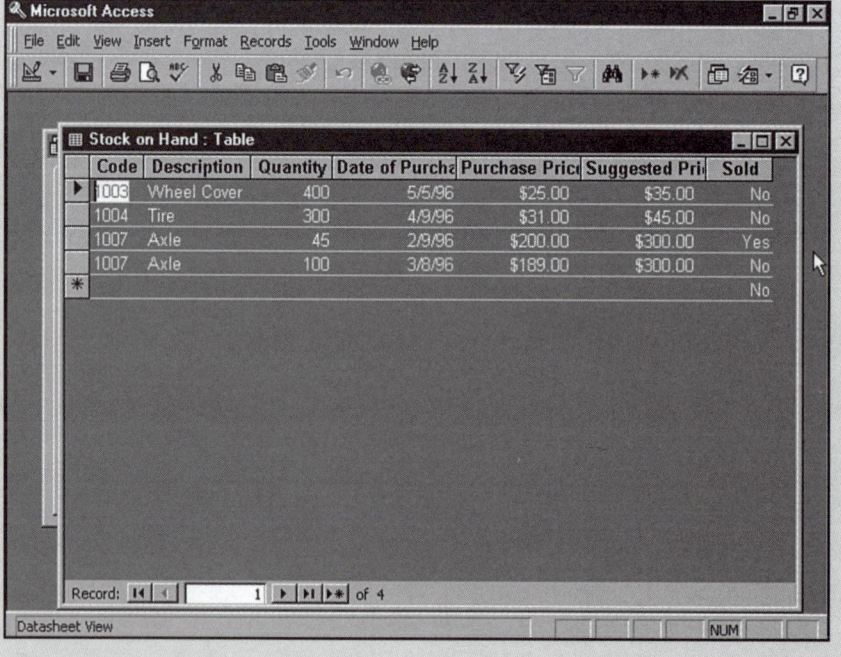

10 **Press the** `⏎Enter` **key several times.**

Notice how the cursor moves down the column, staying in the same field, rather than across the fields.

11 **Close the table.**

12 **Choose Tools, Options from the menu.**

If you share your computer with others, it is important that you return the settings to their original values.

13 **Click on the Datasheet tab. Change the default colors back to Black, White, and Silver for the Font, Background, and Gridlines options, respectively. Click the Vertical Default Gridlines check box to select it.**

14 **Click on the Keyboard tab. Change the Move After Enter option to Next Field.**

15 **Click on OK to make the changes and restore the original settings.**

16 **Close the table and close the database. Close Access.**

Use caution when changing the default Access settings, because they will affect all of your Access databases. If you share your computer with others in a laboratory setting, it would be discourteous to personalize the program without the consent of others who may not know how to change it back. Also, if you are using a copy of Access that is installed on a network server, the defaults will affect anyone else in your workgroup who uses the program. In the previous lesson, we only changed defaults that affected appearance. You could change operational defaults that could affect the function of the program, and you may not remember the original settings. Use this feature with care.

Project Summary

To	Do This
Assign a password to a database	Open the database by choosing the File, Open selecting the Exclusive option. Use the Tools, Security, Set Database Password command to display the Set Database Password dialog box. Enter the password. Enter the password again to verify it. Close the database.
Remove a password from a database	Open the database in exclusive mode using the File, Open command and the Exclusive option. Enter the correct password. Choose Tools, Security, Unset Database Password from the menu. Type the current password and click OK.
Encrypt a database	Start Access but do not open a database. Use the Tools, Security, Encrypt/Decrypt command from the menu. Select the database to be encrypted, and enter a new name for it. Click Save to encrypt and save the new version.

continues

continued

To	Do This
Create a Switchboard	Select a database that already has several forms and reports. Choose **T**ools, Add-Ins, **Sw**itchboard Manager from the menu. Click **Y**es to create a new switchboard. Click **E**dit to add options to the main switchboard. Click **N**ew to add new action buttons. Fill in the resulting dialog box to determine the text to be shown on the switchboard, the action to be taken, and the report or form that is the object of that action. Repeat this process to add more action buttons to the switchboard. Close the dialog boxes. Go to the Forms tab and open the Switchboard form. Click the buttons to test them.
Set Startup parameters	Open the database and choose **T**ools, Start**u**p from the menu. Select the desired form that will be opened when the database is opened, such as the Main Switchboard. Click any other check boxes to set startup parameters like status box. Close the dialog box and the database. Open the database to test the startup parameters.
Set Access defaults	Open the database. Choose **T**ools, **O**ptions from the menu. Make whatever changes are necessary from any of the numerous options. Write down original settings if you may want to reinstate them.

Checking Your Skills

True/False

For each of the following statements, check *T* or *F* to indicate whether the statement is true or false.

__T__F **1.** To add a password to a database, the first step is to open it by double-clicking on its name or icon.

__T__F **2.** To remove the password from a database, you must open it. This implies that you know what the password is.

__T__F **3.** You can only use one switchboard with a database.

__T__F **4.** Encrypting a database prevents someone from reading data in the database by using a word processing program.

__T__F **5.** Default settings are changed with no databases open because they affect all of the databases that are opened with that installation of Access.

Multiple Choice

Circle the letter of the correct answer for each of the following questions.

1. Startup parameters _____.

    a. are set with all of the databases closed

    b. affect all databases opened by that installation of Access

    c. are set after a database has been opened and only affect that database

    d. are used to flash warning messages on the screen if there is too much traffic on the network

2. Which of the following is a parameter setting that you could disable to simplify the appearance of the screen?

    a. Display Toolbar

    b. Display Menus

    c. Display Database Names

    d. Display Title Bar

3. If you wanted to limit the menu choices to those that would be useful for a user but not display those choices a designer would use, you would make which of the following changes to the Startup?

    a. de-select the Allow Built-in toolbars option

    b. de-select the Allow Full Menus option

    c. de-select the Allow Toolbar Changes option

    d. de-select the Display Status Bar option

4. A good password should have the following characteristics to make it hard to guess.

    a. it should be an easy to remember date

    b. it should be an obscure word from the dictionary

    c. it should include a symbol that is not a normal letter or number

    d. it should be the same for all of your accounts

5. If you have set the startup parameters so that they do not allow full menus, the **T**ools option does not appear. How do you change the startup parameters?

    a. reinstall Access

    b. copy all of the data, forms, queries, and reports into a new database

    c. hold down the Control key when you start Access

    d. Close and re-open Access. Hold down the Shift key when you open the database

Completion

In the blank provided, write the correct answer for each of the following statements.

1. Data scrambled and stored in coded form that is not easily read by someone who does not have the code is said to be _____.

2. The term that Access uses for a menu of choices represented by buttons on a form is called a(n) _____.

3. A setting that applies to all of the databases opened in Access is called a(n) _____.

4. A setting that applies to one database and is activated when that database is opened is called a(n) _____.

5. When you want to add or remove a password, the database must be opened in _____ mode.

Applying Your Skills

At the end of each project in *Access 97 Essentials Level III*, you learn how to apply your Access skills to various situations. The following exercises help you practice the skills you have learned in this project. Take a few minutes to work through these exercises now.

Adding a Password to a Database

In the following exercise, you will add a password to protect a database named Books.

To Add a Password to a Database

1. Copy the Proj0603 file and rename it **Books**.

2. Open the Books database in Exclusive mode.

3. Choose **T**ools, Securit**y**, Set **D**atabase Password from the menu.

4. Type the password **Books**.

5. Verify the password by typing it again. Make sure to capitalize the first letter as shown.

6. Close the database and then reopen it. Try typing in the password as **books** to see if capitalization makes a difference. If that does not work, try **Books**.

Removing a Password from a Database

In this exercise, you remove a password from the Books database.

To Remove a Password from a Database

1. Copy the Proj0604 file and rename it **Club**.

2. Open the Club database in Exclusive mode. Use the Password **Club**.

3. Choose **T**ools, Security, Unset **D**atabase Password from the menu.

4. Enter the password **Club**. Click OK.

5. Close the database and then reopen it. Confirm that the password is no longer required.

Adding a Switchboard and Running It Automatically whenever the Database is Opened

In this exercise, you set the startup parameters of a database to open a switchboard whenever the database is opened. In this way, you create a database that a novice can use successfully without having to master the details of the Access program.

To Add a Switchboard and Run It Automatically whenever the Database is Opened

1. Copy the Proj0605 database and rename it **Books with Switchboard**.

2. Open the Books with Switchboard database. Choose **T**ools, Add-Ins, S**w**itchboard Manager to create a switchboard.

3. Edit the existing main switchboard to add two new action buttons:

   ➤ Add a button to open the Quick Entry form in Add mode. Use the text: **Add new books**.

   ➤ Add a button to open the report, Book List. Use the following text: **Preview report on book status**.

4. Close the dialog boxes.

5. Open the Start**u**p parameters dialog box from the **T**ools menu.

6. Choose the switchboard form as the display form opened upon startup.

7. Close the database and reopen it. The switchboard should appear automatically.

Appendix

Why Publish on the Web?

In this Project, you learn:

This appendix was adapted from Chapter 39 of Access 97 Unleashed, *by Dwyane Gifford, et al. (SAMS Publishing).*

This appendix provides an overview of publishing Access objects on the Internet and different ways to access your data from the Web. It also introduces you to the language of the World Wide Web, HTML.

Note: This appendix assumes that you have a working Internet server available to try the techniques presented here. The server can be available to the World Wide Web or just to a local area network, also called an intranet.

Why Publish on the Web?

According to many people, publishing on the Internet, the global computer network, and the intranet, a mini-Internet within a company, is the wave of the future in making information available to end users. The ability to view many different kinds of content through a single application, the Web browser, is quite appealing. The end user never has to guess what application to run in order to view a given bit of content. Similarly, many end users do not want to have to install a large database application such as Access 97 simply to look at a database. In fact, they might not even care to know they're seeing a database at all.

Sometimes you may want to be able to collect information from your users and store the information in your database. You can collect survey responses, merchandise orders, mailing list updates, and so on. The tools available on the Internet let you gather this information, and Access 97 makes an excellent repository for it.

What Do You Want Your Users to Do?

You can let your users do several things with your database from the Web. The following list gives you an overview of the choices:

➤ Display data statically. You control what the user sees and how much data is presented, and the page is not connected to the database in any way but is constructed from the database. The page must be rebuilt any time new data is available.

➤ Display data dynamically. You still control what the user sees, but the page is populated directly from the database. Any time new data is available and the user refreshes the page in the browser, the new data is displayed.

➤ Query the database. This page is similar to the previous page type with some differences. The initial page is a query page giving the user the opportunity to choose selection criteria. The user can retrieve different results based on changing the criteria made available in the query page.

➤ Use a data entry form. This kind of page enables you to collect information from the user and place it in your database. It is similar in construction to the query page except that it does not return results; it inserts data into the database.

Display Data Static or Dynamic?

The first decision to make when you're getting ready to publish a Web page to display data from your database is whether to create a static page or a dynamic page. Understanding the terms will help you determine the right choice for your situation.

A static page is one that simply displays information to the user. It has no connection to a database even though a database might have been used to generate it. Static pages are best used when the information in the database does not change frequently. Store locations or publisher information are good candidates for static pages.

A dynamic page is one that is generated on demand when the user requests the page with a Web browser. The server on which the page sits opens the page and determines that a query needs to be run against the database. When the results of the query come back from the database, the server generates the HTML code on-the-fly and returns it to the browser. If changes are made to the database and the user then refreshes the browser, the query is rerun and the new display reflects all the changes. Dynamic pages are best used when the data in the database changes relatively frequently. Online inventories are excellent candidates for dynamic Web pages.

Static Web Pages

The simplest way to create a static Web page is to choose the object you want to publish—for example, a query named *Catalog*. From the Access menu, choose File then Save As/Export. In the next dialog box, accept the default to save to an external file. In the Save dialog box, select HTML Documents from the Save as type list, then choose a file name. By default, the HTML code is saved in a file with the same name as the object. Listing A.1 shows the HTML file created this way.

Listing A.1 Static HTML from the Query Catalog

```
<HTML>
<TITLE>Catalog</TITLE>
<BODY>
<TABLE BORDER=1 BGCOLOR=#ffffff><FONT FACE="Arial" COLOR=#000000>
➥<CAPTION><B>Catalog</B></CAPTION>

<THEAD>
<TR>
<TH WIDTH="17.2%"><FONT SIZE=2>Last Name</FONT></TH>
<TH WIDTH="17.2%"><FONT SIZE=2>First Name</FONT></TH>
<TH WIDTH="17.2%"><FONT SIZE=2>Book Title</FONT></TH>
<TH WIDTH="31.2%"><FONT SIZE=2>Publisher</FONT></TH>
<TH WIDTH="17.2%"><FONT SIZE=2>Price</FONT></TH>
</TR>
</THEAD>
<TBODY>
<TR VALIGN=TOP>
```

```
<TD><FONT SIZE=2>White</FONT></TD>
<TD><FONT SIZE=2>Johnson</FONT></TD>
<TD><FONT SIZE=2>Prolonged Data Deprivation: Four Case
➥Studies</FONT></TD>
<TD><FONT SIZE=2>New Moon Books</FONT></TD><TD ALIGN=RIGHT>
➥<FONT SIZE=2>$19.99</FONT></TD>
</TR>

<TR VALIGN=TOP>
<TD><FONT SIZE=2>Green</FONT></TD><TD><FONT SIZE=2>Marjorie</FONT>
➥</TD><C2><TD><FONT SIZE=2>The Busy Executive's Database Guide
➥</FONT></TD>
<TD><FONT SIZE=2>Algodata Infosystems</FONT></TD>
<TD ALIGN=RIGHT><FONT SIZE=2>$19.99</FONT></TD>
</TR>

<TR VALIGN=TOP>
<TD><FONT SIZE=2>Green</FONT></TD><TD><FONT SIZE=2>Marjorie
➥</FONT></TD>
<TD><FONT SIZE=2>You Can Combat Computer Stress!</FONT></TD>
<TD><FONT SIZE=2>New Moon Books</FONT></TD>
<TD ALIGN=RIGHT><FONT SIZE=2>$2.99</FONT></TD>
</TR>

<TR VALIGN=TOP>
<TD><FONT SIZE=2>Carson</FONT></TD><TD><FONT SIZE=2>Cheryl
➥</FONT></TD>
<TD><FONT SIZE=2>But Is It User Friendly?</FONT></TD>
<TD><FONT SIZE=2>Algodata Infosystems</FONT></TD>
<TD ALIGN=RIGHT><FONT SIZE=2>$22.95</FONT></TD>
</TR>

<TR VALIGN=TOP>
<TD><FONT SIZE=2>O'Leary</FONT></TD><TD><FONT SIZE=2>Michael
➥</FONT></TD>
<TD><FONT SIZE=2>Cooking with Computers: Surreptitious Balance
➥Sheets</FONT>
➥</TD>
<TD><FONT SIZE=2>Algodata Infosystems</FONT></TD>
<TD ALIGN=RIGHT><FONT SIZE=2>$11.95</FONT></TD>
</TR>

<TR VALIGN=TOP>
<TD><FONT SIZE=2>O'Leary</FONT></TD><TD><FONT SIZE=2>Michael
➥</FONT></TD>
<TD><FONT SIZE=2>Sushi, Anyone?</FONT></TD><TD><FONT SIZE=2>
➥Binnet &amp; Hardley</FONT></TD>
<TD ALIGN=RIGHT><FONT SIZE=2>$14.99</FONT></TD>
</TR>

<TR VALIGN=TOP>
<TD><FONT SIZE=2>Straight</FONT></TD><TD><FONT SIZE=2>Dean
➥</FONT></TD>
<TD><FONT SIZE=2>Straight Talk About Computers</FONT></TD>
<TD><FONT SIZE=2>Algodata Infosystems</FONT></TD>
<TD ALIGN=RIGHT><FONT SIZE=2>$19.99</FONT></TD>
</TR>

<TR VALIGN=TOP>
<TD><FONT SIZE=2>Bennet</FONT></TD><TD><FONT SIZE=2>Abraham
➥</FONT></TD>
<TD><FONT SIZE=2>The Busy Executive's Database Guide</FONT></TD>
<TD><FONT SIZE=2>Algodata Infosystems</FONT></TD>
<TD ALIGN=RIGHT><FONT SIZE=2>$19.99</FONT></TD>
</TR>
```

```
<TR VALIGN=TOP>
<TD><FONT SIZE=2>Dull</FONT></TD><TD><FONT SIZE=2>Ann</FONT></TD>
<TD><FONT SIZE=2>Secrets of Silicon Valley</FONT></TD>
<TD><FONT SIZE=2>Algodata Infosystems</FONT></TD>
<TD ALIGN=RIGHT><FONT SIZE=2>$20.00</FONT></TD>
</TR>

<TR VALIGN=TOP>
<TD><FONT SIZE=2>Gringlesby</FONT></TD><TD><FONT SIZE=2>Burt
➡</FONT></TD>
<TD><FONT SIZE=2>Sushi, Anyone?</FONT></TD><TD><FONT SIZE=2>
➡Binnet &amp; Hardley</FONT></TD>
<TD ALIGN=RIGHT><FONT SIZE=2>$14.99</FONT></TD>
</TR>

<TR VALIGN=TOP>
<TD><FONT SIZE=2>Locksley</FONT></TD><TD><FONT SIZE=2>Charlene
➡</FONT></TD>
<TD><FONT SIZE=2>Net Etiquette</FONT></TD><TD><FONT SIZE=2>
➡Algodata Infosystems</FONT></TD>
<TD ALIGN=RIGHT><FONT SIZE=2><BR></FONT></TD>
</TR>

<TR VALIGN=TOP>
<TD><FONT SIZE=2>Locksley</FONT></TD><TD><FONT SIZE=2>Charlene
➡</FONT></TD>
<TD><FONT SIZE=2>Emotional Security: A New Algorithm</FONT></TD>
<TD><FONT SIZE=2>New Moon Books</FONT></TD><TD ALIGN=RIGHT><FONT
➡SIZE=2>$7.99
➡</FONT></TD>
</TR>

<TR VALIGN=TOP>
<TD><FONT SIZE=2>Blotchet-Halls</FONT></TD><TD><FONT SIZE=2>
➡Reginald</FONT></TD>
<TD><FONT SIZE=2>Fifty Years in Buckingham Palace Kitchens</
➡FONT></TD>
<TD><FONT SIZE=2>Binnet &amp; Hardley</FONT></TD><TD ALIGN=RIGHT>
➡<FONT SIZE=2>$11.95</FONT></TD>
</TR>

<TR VALIGN=TOP>
<TD><FONT SIZE=2>Yokomoto</FONT></TD><TD><FONT SIZE=2>Akiko
➡</FONT></TD>
<TD><FONT SIZE=2>Sushi, Anyone?</FONT></TD><TD><FONT SIZE=2>
➡Binnet &amp; Hardley</FONT></TD>
<TD ALIGN=RIGHT><FONT SIZE=2>$14.99</FONT></TD><C2></TR>

<TR VALIGN=TOP>
<TD><FONT SIZE=2>del Castillo</FONT></TD><TD><FONT SIZE=2>Innes
➡</FONT></TD>
<TD><FONT SIZE=2>Silicon Valley Gastronomic Treats</FONT></TD>
<TD><FONT SIZE=2>Binnet &amp; Hardley</FONT></TD>
<TD ALIGN=RIGHT><FONT SIZE=2>$19.99</FONT></TD>
</TR>

<TR VALIGN=TOP>
<TD><FONT SIZE=2>DeFrance</FONT></TD><TD><FONT SIZE=2>Michel
➡</FONT></TD>
<TD><FONT SIZE=2>The Gourmet Microwave</FONT></TD>
<TD><FONT SIZE=2>Binnet &amp; Hardley</FONT></TD>
<TD ALIGN=RIGHT><FONT SIZE=2>$2.99</FONT></TD>
</TR>

<TR VALIGN=TOP>
<TD><FONT SIZE=2>MacFeather</FONT></TD><TD><FONT SIZE=2>Stearns
➡</FONT></TD>
```

```
<TD><FONT SIZE=2>Computer Phobic AND Non-Phobic Individuals:
➡Behavior Variations</FONT></TD><
TD><FONT SIZE=2>Binnet &amp; Hardley</FONT></TD><TD ALIGN=RIGHT>
➡<FONT SIZE=2>$21.59</FONT></TD>
</TR>

<TR VALIGN=TOP>
<TD><FONT SIZE=2>MacFeather</FONT></TD><TD><FONT SIZE=2>Stearns
➡</FONT></TD>
<TD><FONT SIZE=2>Cooking with Computers: Surreptitious Balance
➡Sheets</FONT></TD>
<TD><FONT SIZE=2>Algodata Infosystems</FONT></TD><TD ALIGN=RIGHT>
➡<FONT SIZE=2>$11.95</FONT></TD>
</TR>

<TR VALIGN=TOP>
<TD><FONT SIZE=2>Karsen</FONT></TD><TD><FONT SIZE=2>Livia
➡</FONT></TD>
<TD><FONT SIZE=2>Computer Phobic AND Non-Phobic Individuals:
➡Behavior
➡Variations</FONT></TD>
<TD><FONT SIZE=2>Binnet &amp; Hardley</FONT></TD><TD ALIGN=RIGHT>
➡<FONT SIZE=2>$21.59</FONT></TD>
</TR>

<TR VALIGN=TOP>
<TD><FONT SIZE=2>Panteley</FONT></TD><TD><FONT SIZE=2>Sylvia
➡</FONT></TD>
<TD><FONT SIZE=2>Onions, Leeks, and Garlic: Cooking Secrets of the
➡Mediterranean</FONT></TD>
<TD><FONT SIZE=2>Binnet &amp; Hardley</FONT></TD><TD ALIGN=RIGHT>
➡<FONT SIZE=2>$20.95</FONT></TD>
</TR>

<TR VALIGN=TOP>
<TD><FONT SIZE=2>Hunter</FONT></TD><TD><FONT SIZE=2>Sheryl</
➡FONT></TD>
<TD><FONT SIZE=2>Secrets of Silicon Valley</FONT></TD>
<TD><FONT SIZE=2>Algodata Infosystems</FONT></TD><TD ALIGN=RIGHT>
➡<FONT SIZE=2>$20.00</FONT></TD>
</TR>

<TR VALIGN=TOP>
<TD><FONT SIZE=2>Ringer</FONT></TD><TD><FONT SIZE=2>Anne</FONT></TD>
<TD><FONT SIZE=2>The Gourmet Microwave</FONT></TD>
<TD><FONT SIZE=2>Binnet &amp; Hardley</FONT></TD><TD ALIGN=RIGHT>
➡<FONT SIZE=2>$2.99</FONT></TD>
</TR><C2>
<TR VALIGN=TOP>
<TD><FONT SIZE=2>Ringer</FONT></TD><TD><FONT SIZE=2>Anne</FONT></TD>
<TD><FONT SIZE=2>Is Anger the Enemy?</FONT></TD>
<TD><FONT SIZE=2>New Moon Books</FONT></TD><TD ALIGN=RIGHT>
➡<FONT SIZE=2>$10.95</FONT></TD>
</TR>

<TR VALIGN=TOP>
<TD><FONT SIZE=2>Ringer</FONT></TD><TD><FONT SIZE=2>Albert
➡</FONT></TD>
<TD><FONT SIZE=2>Is Anger the Enemy?</FONT></TD><TD><FONT SIZE=2>
➡New Moon Books</FONT></TD>
<TD ALIGN=RIGHT><FONT SIZE=2>$10.95</FONT></TD>
</TR>

<TR VALIGN=TOP>
<TD><FONT SIZE=2>Ringer</FONT></TD><TD><FONT SIZE=2>Albert
➡</FONT></TD>
```

```
<TD><FONT SIZE=2>Life Without Fear</FONT></TD><TD><FONT SIZE=2>
➡New Moon Books</FONT></TD>
<TD ALIGN=RIGHT><FONT SIZE=2>$7.00</FONT></TD>
</TR>
</TBODY>
<TFOOT></TFOOT>
</TABLE>
</BODY>
</HTML>
```

The resulting Web page should look something like Figure A.1 in your Web browser.

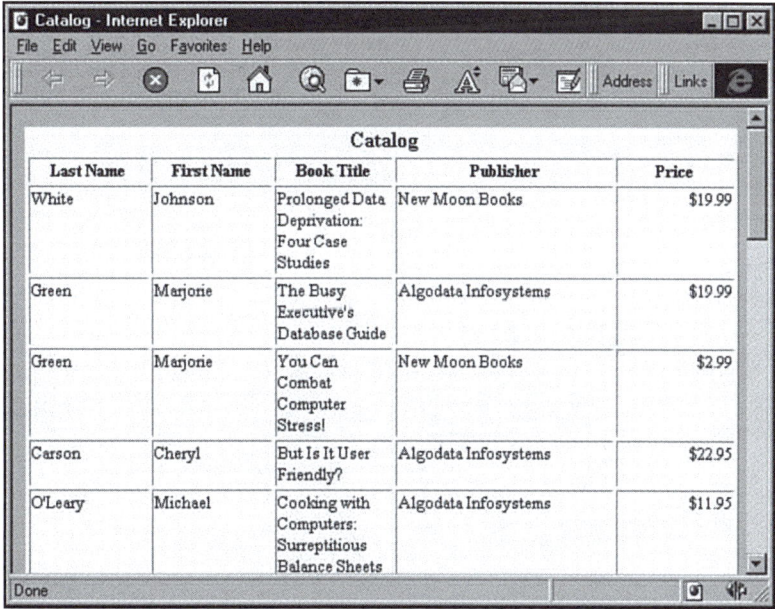

Dynamic Web Pages

Creating a dynamic page is similar to creating a static page. You need to take some additional steps before the results will actually work. Specifically, you must create an ODBC datasource for each Access database you want to publish with dynamic Web pages.

To use Access 97 as the datasource for a dynamic Web page requires that Access 97 be installed on the Web server. It also requires an ODBC datasource for the database you want to publish.

There are two kinds of dynamic pages you can create: Microsoft IIS and Microsoft ActiveX Server. The choice of which one to use depends on what your Web server will support. By default, an NT server with the Internet Information Server installed will support IIS pages. NT version 4.0 installs version 2.0 of the Internet Information Server.

The Microsoft ActiveX Server extends the basic IIS functionality beginning with Internet Information Server version 3.0. It uses ActiveX Server page

(ASP) files to retrieve data from an ODBC data source. Besides script code that is run on the server, an ASP file will also contain ActiveX controls and VBScript code.

To create a simple dynamic page, choose the object you want to publish—for example, a query named Catalog. From the Access menu, choose File | Save As/Export.

In the next dialog box, accept the default to save to an external file. This dialog box is shown in Figure A.2.

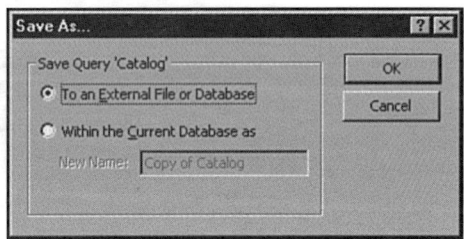

In the Save File dialog box, as shown in Figure A.3, select either Microsoft IIS 1-2 or Microsoft ActiveX Server from the Save as type list, then choose a file name.

Figure A.3
The Save File dialog box.

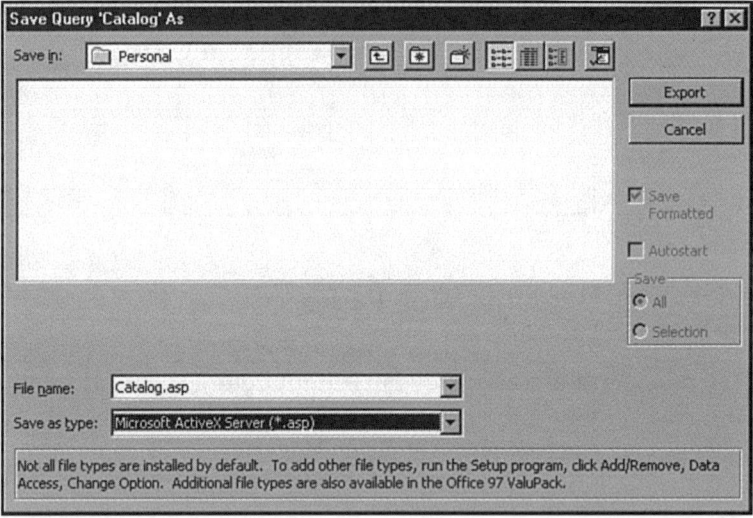

If you choose Microsoft IIS 1-2, two new files will be created: one with the .IDC extension and the other with the .HTX extension. Using the Catalog query as an example, you should now have a file called Catalog.IDC and one called Catalog.HTX.

If you choose Microsoft ActiveX Server, a single file is created with the .ASP extension, for example, Catalog.ASP.

The file extension stands for Internet Database Connector. It contains the connection and query information needed to generate results to display. Listing A.2 shows the IDC file that results from generating a dynamic page for the query Catalog.

Listing A.2 IDC File for the Query Catalog

```
Datasource:Publications
Template:Catalog.htx
SQLStatement:SELECT authors.au_lname AS [Last Name],
+authors.au_fname AS [First Name],
+titles.title AS [Book Title],
+publishers.pub_name AS Publisher,
+titles.price AS Price
+FROM ((authors INNER JOIN titleauthor ON authors.au_id =
➥titleauthor.au_id)
+INNER JOIN titles ON titleauthor.title_id = titles.title_id)
+INNER JOIN publishers ON titles.pub_id = publishers.pub_id;

Password:
Username:
```

The file extension HTX stands for HTML Extensions. An HTX file is a template for how the results of the query referenced in the IDC file will be displayed. Listing A.3 shows the HTX file that results from generating a dynamic page for the query Catalog. It uses a table to organize the display of data. Listing A.4 shows the ASP ActiveX file for the query Catalog.

Listing A.3 HTX File for the Query Catalog

```
<HTML>
<TITLE>Catalog</TITLE>
<BODY>
<TABLE BORDER=1 BGCOLOR=#ffffff><FONT FACE="Arial" COLOR=#000000>
➥<CAPTION><B>Catalog</B></CAPTION>

<THEAD>
<TR>
<TH WIDTH="17.2%"><FONT SIZE=2>Last Name</FONT></TH><TH
➥WIDTH="17.2%"><FONT SIZE=2>First Name</FONT></TH>
<TH WIDTH="17.2%"><FONT SIZE=2>Book Title</FONT></TH><TH
➥WIDTH="31.2%"><FONT SIZE=2>Publisher</FONT></TH>
<TH WIDTH="17.2%"><FONT SIZE=2>Price</FONT></TH>
</TR>
</THEAD>
<TBODY>
<%BeginDetail%>

<TR VALIGN=TOP>
<TD><%Last Name%></TD><TD><%First Name%></TD><TD><%Book Title%></TD>
➥<TD><%Publisher%></TD><TD><%Price%></TD>
</TR>
<%EndDetail%>

</TBODY>
<TFOOT></TFOOT>
</TABLE>
</BODY>
</HTML>
```

Listing A.4 ASP ActiveX File for the Query Catalog

```
<HTML>
<TITLE>Catalog</TITLE>
<BODY>
<%
```

```
Param = Request.QueryString("Param")
Data = Request.QueryString("Data")
%>
<%
If IsObject(Session("Publications_conn")) Then
    Set conn = Session("Publications_conn")
Else
    Set conn = Server.CreateObject("ADO.Connection")
    conn.open "Publications","",""
    Set Session("Publications_conn") = conn
End If
%>
<%
If IsObject(Session("Catalog_rs")) And Not (cstr(Param) <> "" And _
        cstr(Data) <> "") Then
    Set rs = Session("Catalog_rs")
Else
    sql = "SELECT authors.au_lname AS [Last Name], authors.au_fname AS
    sql = sql & "[First Name], titles.title AS [Book Title], "
    sql = sql & "publishers.pub_name AS Publisher, titles.price AS Price"
    sql = sql & "FROM ((authors INNER JOIN titleauthor ON
➥authors.au_id = "
    sql = sql & "titleauthor.au_id) INNER JOIN titles ON
➥titleauthor.title_id "
    sql = sql & "= titles.title_id) INNER JOIN publishers ON
➥titles.pub_id = "
    sql = sql & "publishers.pub_id;  "
    If cstr(Param) <> "" And cstr(Data) <> "" Then
        sql = sql & " WHERE " & cstr(Param) & " = " & cstr(Data)
    End If
    Set rs = Server.CreateObject("ADO.Recordset")
    rs.Open sql, conn, 3, 3
    If rs.eof Then
        rs.AddNew
    End If
    Set Session("Catalog_rs") = rs
End If
%>
<TABLE BORDER=1 BGCOLOR=#ffffff CELLSPACING=0>
<FONT FACE="Arial" COLOR=#000000><CAPTION><B>Catalog</B></CAPTION>

<THEAD>
<TR>
<TH BGCOLOR=#c0c0c0 BORDERCOLOR=#000000 >
<FONT SIZE=2 FACE="Arial" COLOR=#000000>Last Name</FONT>
</TH><TH BGCOLOR=#c0c0c0 BORDERCOLOR=#000000 >
<FONT SIZE=2 FACE="Arial" COLOR=#000000>First Name</FONT></TH>
<TH BGCOLOR=#c0c0c0 BORDERCOLOR=#000000 >
<FONT SIZE=2 FACE="Arial" COLOR=#000000>Book Title</FONT></TH>
<TH BGCOLOR=#c0c0c0 BORDERCOLOR=#000000 >
<FONT SIZE=2 FACE="Arial" COLOR=#000000>Publisher</FONT></TH>
<TH BGCOLOR=#c0c0c0 BORDERCOLOR=#000000 >
<FONT SIZE=2 FACE="Arial" COLOR=#000000>Price</FONT></TH>
</TR>
</THEAD>
<TBODY>
<%
rs.MoveFirst
do while Not rs.eof
 %>
<TR VALIGN=TOP>
<TD BORDERCOLOR=#c0c0c0 ><FONT SIZE=2 FACE="Arial" COLOR=#000000>
<%=rs.Fields("Last Name").Value%><BR></FONT></TD><TD
BORDERCOLOR=#c0c0c0 >
<FONT SIZE=2 FACE="Arial" COLOR=#000000>
```

```
<%=rs.Fields("First Name").Value%><BR></FONT></TD><TD
➥BORDERCOLOR=#c0c0c0 >
<FONT SIZE=2 FACE="Arial" COLOR=#000000><%=rs.Fields("Book
➥Title").Value%>
<BR></FONT></TD><TD BORDERCOLOR=#c0c0c0 ><FONT SIZE=2 FACE="Arial"
COLOR=#000000><%=rs.Fields("Publisher").Value%><BR></FONT></TD>
<TD BORDERCOLOR=#c0c0c0  ALIGN=RIGHT><FONT SIZE=2 FACE="Arial"
COLOR=#000000><%=rs.Fields("Price").Value%><BR></FONT></TD>
</TR>
<%
rs.MoveNext
loop%>
</TBODY>
<TFOOT></TFOOT>
</TABLE>
</BODY>
</HTML> <SB BOX>
```

The IDC, HTX, and ASP files must be in an executable directory on your Internet server. Internet Information Server creates a scripts directory at the same level as the wwwroot directory for this purpose.

The Publish to the Web Wizard

Sometimes you may want to publish several database objects at once. For instance, you might want to publish a book catalog, a listing of current authors, and the publishing houses you deal with. Using the preceding steps for each one of these objects can be a bit tedious. To simplify this process, Access 97 comes with the Publish to the Web Wizard.

The Publish to the Web Wizard, which is an easy-to-use component of Access 97, enables you to create complete Web pages from Access database objects. It lets you create pages from tables, queries, forms, or reports. You can choose a template to provide a specific look and feel for your pages. You can quickly build a home page that lets your users locate all your pages through a single location.

From the Access menu, start the Publish to the Web Wizard by choosing File and then Save As HTML. Access spends a few moments setting up the Publish to the Web Wizard, which looks like Figure A4.

Figure A.4
The Access 97 Publish to the Web Wizard.

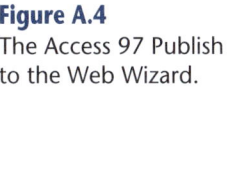

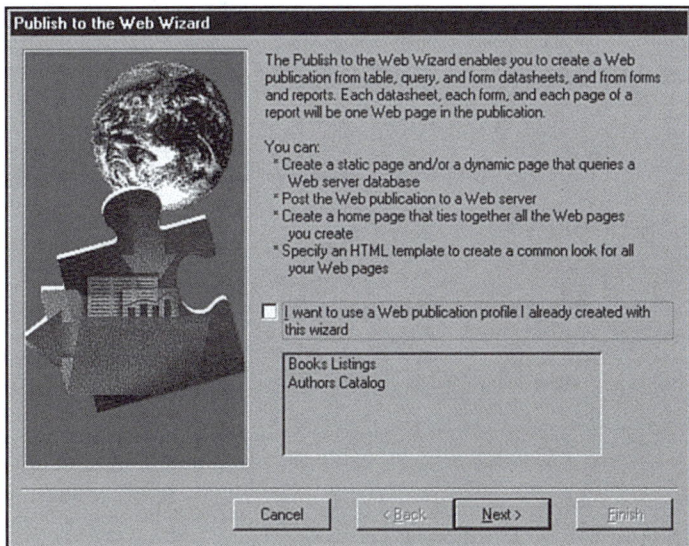

Choosing Database Objects to Publish

The Access 97 Publish to the Web Wizard enables you to publish any combination of objects. For the example, you can use three queries: Catalog, Authors Directory, and Publisher List. The wizard object selector looks something like Figure A.5.

Figure A.5
Choosing database objects for publication.

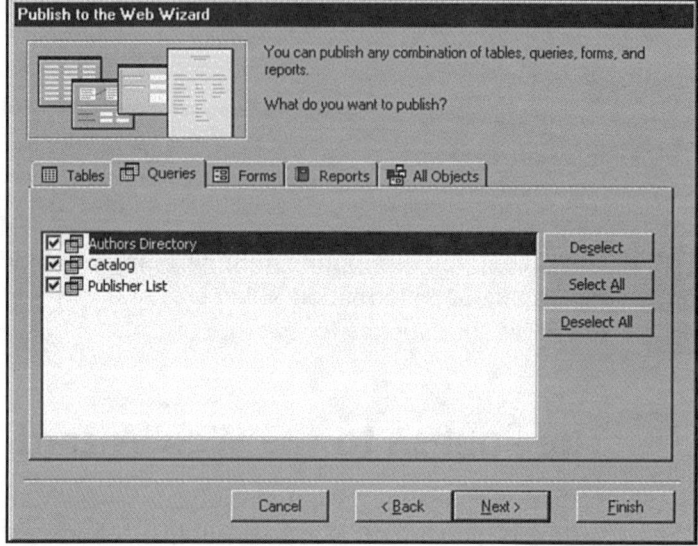

Templates

Using templates, you can easily create Web pages that have a uniform look and feel from Access database objects. You might want to have a formal look for business-related pages and have a more casual look for recreational pages. You can use as a template any existing Web page that has the desired look and feel.

To use an existing template, click the Browse button in the Web Wizard, shown in Figure A6. Locate the desired template file and select it. When you choose to complete the page, the Publish to the Web Wizard uses the selected template to create the appearance of the page.

Figure A.6
Selecting a template.

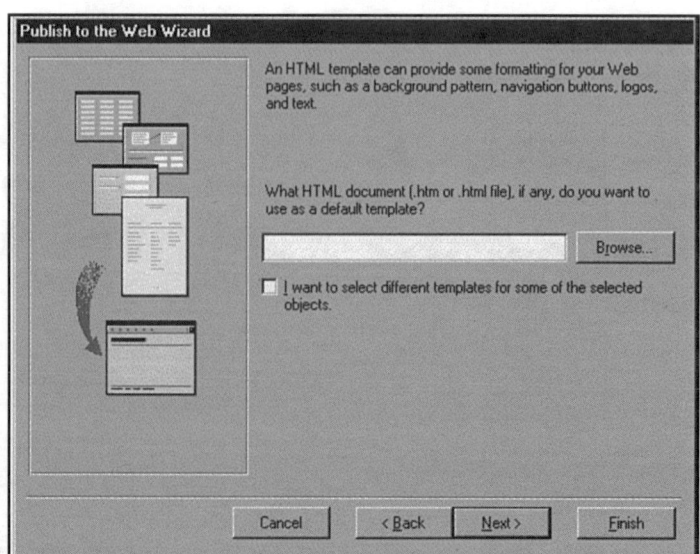

Selecting a Page Type

The Publish to the Web Wizard next lets you select a page type, as shown in Figure A.7. Here, you can choose whether to publish all the objects as static or dynamic.

Figure A.7
Selecting a page type.

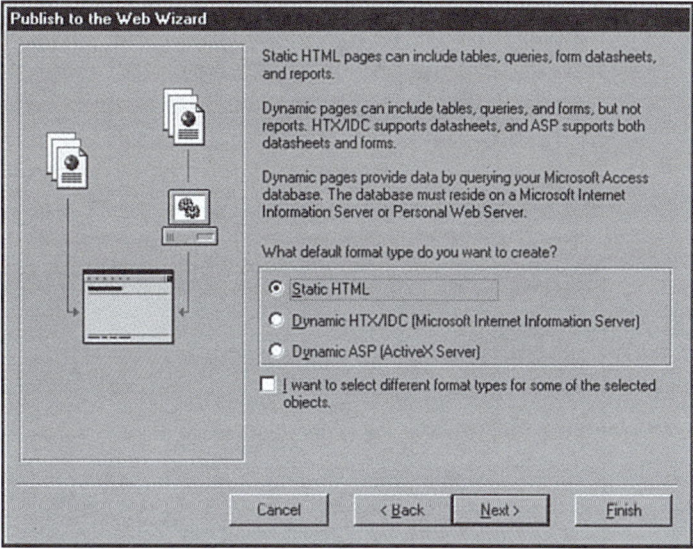

Choosing a Publication Location

In the next wizard dialog box shown in Figure A.8, you can choose where the wizard will place all the files it generates. Normally, you choose a default directory on your own machine. If you don't want to use the default directory, simply select the desired destination.

You also can choose to launch the WebPost Wizard so that you can easily register the new pages with your Internet server. WebPost copies all the files the Web Wizard creates to the virtual root of the target Internet server.

Figure A.8
Choosing a publication location.

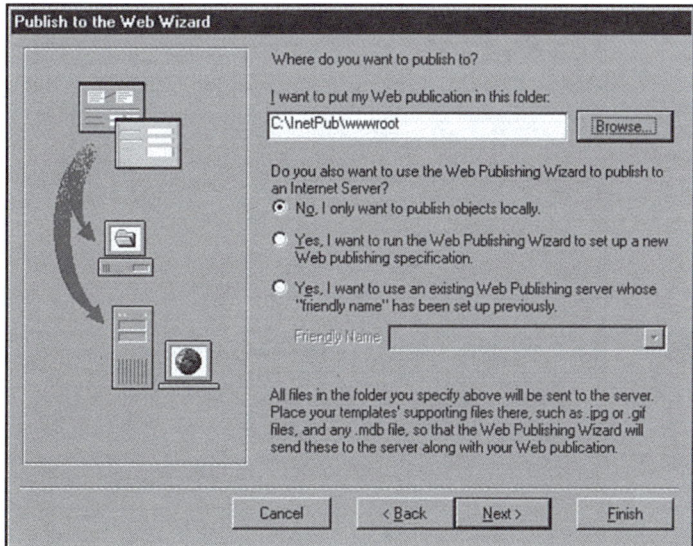

Creating a Home Page

If you're publishing several database objects, having a page that ties them all together is a good idea. The Web Wizard can create a home page that contains a table with links to all the pages it creates.

Typically, a home page is called default.htm by the Web Wizard. This way, a user can refer to the so-called "virtual directory" of the site rather than have to also remember the filename. For example, a full Uniform Resource Locator (URL) called http://access97/authors/default.htm can be referred to in the browser as http://access97/authors/. If you want to name your home page something other than default.htm, you are free to do so on the section of the wizard shown in Figure A.9.

Figure A.9
Creating a home page.

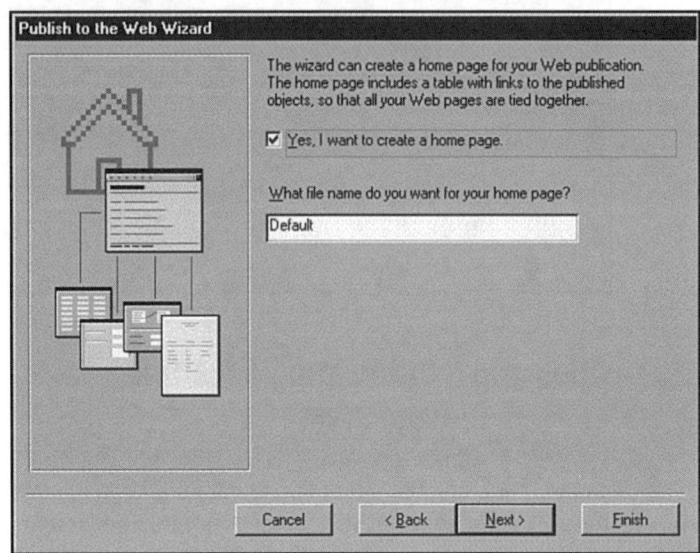

Figure A.10 shows a home page created with the Web Wizard for the three queries in MyDb39.MDB.

Figure A.10
A home page.

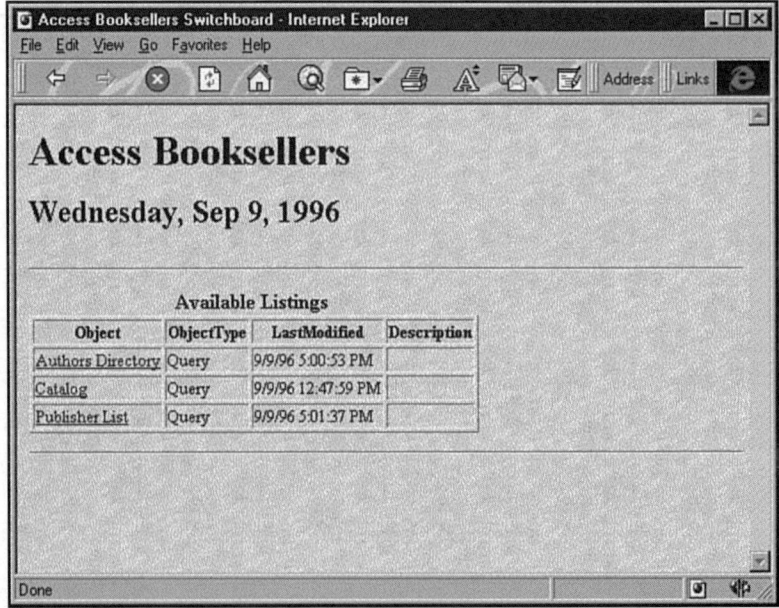

Saving Your Publication Specification

To save work in the future, you can save the specification for this publication in the wizard dialog box shown in Figure A.11. This feature is most useful if you're creating a set of static pages. In most cases, after you create a set of dynamic pages, you probably do not need to re-create the pages again.

Figure A.11
Saving a publication specification.

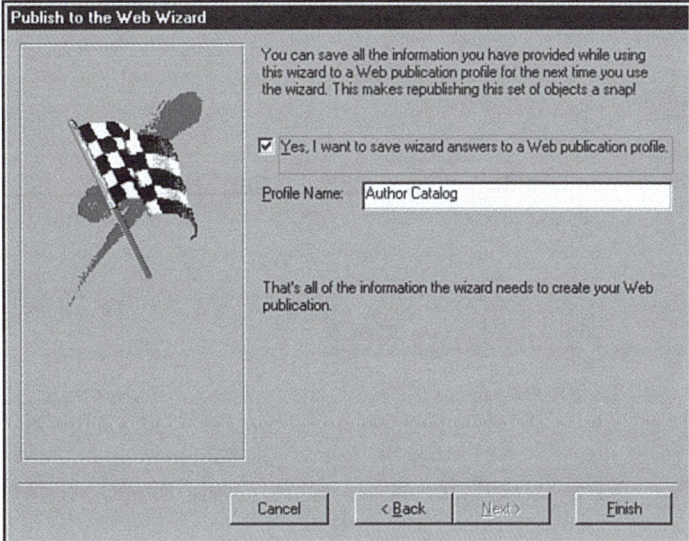

You have now gone through the tools Access 97 provides to make Web publishing easy. You still have much more to explore, such as creating your own Web pages, using page templates, and setting up Web-based data entry for your Access 97 database.

Database Query Forms

Often, showing the entire contents of a database table or query in a single Web page is impractical. To help users find the information in which they're interested, you can allow them to run a query against the database. You can create a Web page that lets your users build and submit a query and then display the small result set from the query rather than all possible records.

The downside is that, as of this writing, Access 97 does not have a tool to easily create this kind of page. Doing so, however, is not difficult. In the next few sections, I walk through building such a page, introducing you to writing your own HTML code. You can use any text editor for creating HTML files, including Notepad. Some reasonably good HTML editors and assistants such as the Microsoft ActiveX Control Pad are also available.

Creating a Simple Page

The first step in building a Web-based query form is to create a simple Web page to use as the basis for the query form. Later, you can add features such as headings, images, links to other pages, and so on.

Use your favorite text editor to create a page like the one in Listing A.5.

Listing A.5 Creating a Simple Web Page

```
<HTML>
<HEAD>
<TITLE>Order</TITLE>
</HEAD>
<H1>Find an Author</H1>
<BODY>
Use this form to locate author information.
When you are done, click on Submit to run your query.
</BODY>
</HTML>
```

Be sure to try this page in your Web browser just to prove that it works. It's always a good idea to build Web pages in small stages and test them as you go.

Adding Entry Fields

Now add several entry fields to your page, as shown in Listing A.6. An entry field is identified with the <INPUT> tag. You need to supply a name for the field, what kind of field it is, and how long it is if it is a text field. Refer to the "HTML Quick Reference" section later in this chapter to see the parameters for the <INPUT> tag.

Listing A.6 Start with a Simple Web Page

```
<HTML>
<HEAD>
<TITLE>Order</TITLE>
</HEAD>
<H1>Enter Order Information</H1>
<BODY>
Use this form to enter a new book order.
When you are done, click on Submit to send your order to us.
<HR>
<FORM METHOD="POST" ACTION="MyDb39.IDC">
<P>Author Last Name <INPUT TYPE="TEXT" NAME="LName" SIZE="20"
➡MAXLENGTH="20">
<P><INPUT TYPE="SUBMIT" VALUE="Run Your Query">
</FORM>
</BODY>
</HTML>
```

Creating an Internet Database Connector File

You now need to create an Internet Database Connector (IDC) file to contain the SQL code for the query and identify the template file to use for displaying the results. Listing A.7 shows such a file. It is almost identical to the dynamic page shown in Listing A.2, so if you want, you can use a copy of that file as the basis for this new one. Note that the query now has a WHERE clause with LName surrounded by the percent sign (%). This tells the server to replace %LName% with the value the user enters into the query form field called Lname.

Listing A.7 IDC File for a Database Query Form

```
Datasource:Publications
Template:Catalog.htx
SQLStatement:SELECT authors.au_lname AS [Last Name],
+authors.au_fname AS [First Name],
+titles.title AS [Book Title],
+publishers.pub_name AS Publisher,
+titles.price AS Price
+FROM ((authors INNER JOIN titleauthor ON authors.au_id =
➥titleauthor.au_id)
+INNER JOIN titles ON titleauthor.title_id = titles.title_id)
+INNER JOIN publishers ON titles.pub_id = publishers.pub_id
+WHERE aulname like '%LName%*';

Password:
Username:.
```

Creating a Results Display Template

You now need to create an HTX file that the IDC file can use as a template for displaying the results of the search. The example in Listing A..8 fits this bill. It uses a table to organize the display of data, although you can display the data any way you want. Note that it is also the same file as the HTX file shown in Listing A.3 for the basic dynamic page.

Listing A.8 HTX File for the Search Results

```
<HTML>
<TITLE>Catalog</TITLE>
<BODY>
<TABLE BORDER=1 BGCOLOR=#ffffff><FONT FACE="Arial" COLOR=#000000>
➥<CAPTION><B>Catalog</B></CAPTION>

<THEAD>
<TR>
<TH WIDTH="17.2%"><FONT SIZE=2>Last Name</FONT></TH><TH
➥WIDTH="17.2%">
➥<FONT SIZE=2>First Name</FONT></TH>
<TH WIDTH="17.2%"><FONT SIZE=2>Book Title</FONT></TH><TH
➥WIDTH="31.2%">
➥<FONT SIZE=2>Publisher</FONT></TH>
<TH WIDTH="17.2%"><FONT SIZE=2>Price</FONT></TH>
</TR>
</THEAD>
<TBODY>
<%BeginDetail%>

<TR VALIGN=TOP>
<TD><%Last Name%></TD><TD><%First Name%></TD><TD><%Book Title%></TD>
➥<TD><%Publisher%></TD><TD><%Price%></TD>
</TR>
<%EndDetail%>

</TBODY>
<TFOOT></TFOOT>
</TABLE>
</BODY>
</HTML>.
```

You now have a basic query form, database connector, and results display template. You're now ready to try querying your database from the Web.

Data Entry from the Web

You can allow users who access your Web pages to add data directly to your database from the Web. Access 97 does not yet provide a tool to help you create a data entry form, but the process is not difficult. You use an IDC file to make the connection, so in the following example, I assume your Internet server is running Microsoft Internet Information Server on Windows NT.

Start with a Simple Page

The first step is to create a simple Web page to use as the basis for the data entry form. Later, you can add features such as headings, images, links to other pages, and so on.

Start with a page like the one in Listing A.9.

Listing A.9 Start with a Simple Web Page

```
<HTML>
<HEAD>
<TITLE>Order</TITLE>
</HEAD>
<H1>Enter Order Information</H1>
<BODY>
Use this form to enter a new book order.
When you are done, click on Submit to send your order to us.
</BODY>
</HTML>
```

Be sure to try this page in your Web browser just to prove that it works. It's always a good idea to build Web pages in small stages and test them as you go.

Adding Entry Fields

Now add several entry fields to your form. An entry field is identified with the <INPUT> tag. You need to supply a name for the field, what kind of field it is, and how long it is if it is a text field. Refer to the "HTML Quick Reference" section to see the parameters for the <INPUT> tag.

You need to include a way to invoke the database connector to get the data into the database. You do so by using a Submit INPUT TYPE control. You also want to include a button to let the user clear all the fields and start over again. This button is a Reset INPUT TYPE control.

Listing A.10 shows a simple data entry form.

Listing A.10 Adding Entry Fields and Action Buttons

```
<HTML>
<HEAD>
<TITLE>Order Entry</TITLE>
</HEAD>
<H1>Enter Order Information</H1>
<BODY>
Use this form to enter a new book order.
When you are done, click on Submit to send your order to us.
<HR>
```

```
<FORM METHOD="POST" ACTION="MyDb39.IDC">
<P>Customer ID <INPUT TYPE="TEXT" NAME="CustID" SIZE="12"
➥MAXLENGTH="12">
<P>Book ISBN <INPUT TYPE="TEXT" NAME="ISBN" SIZE="13"
➥MAXLENGTH="13">
<P>Quantity <INPUT TYPE="TEXT" NAME="Qty" MAXLENGTH="4">
<P><INPUT TYPE="SUBMIT" VALUE="Submit Your Order">
<P><INPUT TYPE="RESET" VALUE="Clear Entries">
</FORM>
</BODY>
</HTML>
```

You now have a basic data entry form. What remains is to connect it to your database.

Web Data Entry IDC File

To your data entry form to your datasource requires an IDC file, discussed previously in the section "Dynamic Web Pages." If you have created a dynamic Web page, you can use that IDC file as the basis for the new one. The key to making this IDC file work for a data entry form is the SQLStatement line in the file. Your new IDC file should look something like Listing A.11.

Listing A.11 IDC File for a Data Entry Form

```
Datasource:Publications
Template:Catalog.htx
SQLStatement:
+INSERT INTO Orders (CustID, ISBN, Qty)
+VALUES('%CustID%', '%ISBN%', %Qty%)
Password:
Username:
```

How you type the fields in the Values list is very important so that you can avoid datatype mismatch errors. Delimiters tell the Access ODBC driver what kind of information is coming in. Text fields must be delimited by single quotation marks, dates must be delimited by pound signs (#), and numbers do not use delimiters.

Also note that you must have the same number of variables coming from the entry page as you have database field names on the INSERT INTO line. Listing A.12 shows the HTX file that will be shown after the user clicks on the Submit button.

Listing A.12 HTX File for the Data Entry Page

```
<HTML>
<TITLE>Order Entry</TITLE>
<BODY>
<%BeginDetail%>
<%EndDetail%>
<HR>
<P>
Thank you for your order.
It will be processed within 24 hours.
<P>
<HR>
<A HREF="Entry.htm">Return</A> to order entry form
</BODY>
</HTML>
```

You are now ready to try data entry from the Web. After you click Submit on the Web page, you can easily verify that it worked by doing a quick Access query on the table to which you added the new record.

If you've tried any of the exercises from the preceding sections, be sure to look at the results with your Web browser. Experiment with different templates. Try customizing some of the HTML and HTX files that Access creates by adding headings, images, and other enhancements.

If you're not yet familiar with HTML, which is the language of the Web, go ahead to the next section. You learn what goes into a Web page, especially what Access puts into a Web page.

HTML Basics

In the following sections, I give you some background in HTML. I do not intend this information to be an exhaustive discussion of all the HTML tags available but to be a description of the ones used most often and especially those used by Access 97 to generate your Web pages.

What Is HTML?

HTML stands for HyperText Markup Language. It is the language understood by today's Web browsers such as Netscape or Microsoft's Internet Explorer. A Web page is defined by a text file—I'll call it an HTML file—containing HTML code and text content. To create a Web page, you can use any text editor, such as Windows Notepad, or any one of a growing number of Web authoring tools.

You also can use an existing Web page as the basis for a new one you want to create. Pages for the Web are often built this way. For instance, you can add many enhancements to the pages created by Access 97. You can even use the pages generated by Access 97 and the Web Wizard to create other pages.

Listing A.13 shows a simple Web page using just a few HTML tags.

Listing A.13 Simple Web Page

```
<HTML>
<HEAD>
</HEAD>
<BODY>
This is a sample web page constructed using HTML.
</BODY>
</HTML>
```

The contents of an HTML file can become quite complex as the content to be presented to the user becomes more complex and, hopefully, more appealing. Listing A.14 shows a much richer Web page.

Listing A.14 Rich Web Page

```
<HTML>
<TITLE>Access Booksellers Switchboard</TITLE>
<BODY bgproperties="fixed" background="bgwhite.jpg">
```

```
<A NAME = "top"></A>
<H1>Access Booksellers</H1>
<H2>Wednesday, Sep 9, 1996</H2>

<HR>
<TABLE BORDER=1>
<FONT FACE="Arial" COLOR=#000000>
<CAPTION><B>Available Listings</B></CAPTION>

<THEAD>
<TR>
<TH WIDTH="22.7%"><FONT SIZE=2>Object</FONT></TH>
<TH WIDTH="17.0%"><FONT SIZE=2>ObjectType</FONT></TH>
<TH WIDTH="26.3%"><FONT SIZE=2>LastModified</FONT></TH>
<TH WIDTH="34.0%"><FONT SIZE=2>Description</FONT></TH>
</TR>
</THEAD>
<TBODY>
<TR VALIGN=TOP>
<TD><FONT SIZE=2 COLOR=#0000ff>
<A HREF="Authors Directory.htm">Authors Directory</A></FONT></TD>
<TD><FONT SIZE=2>Query</FONT></TD>
<TD><FONT SIZE=2>9/9/96 5:00:53 PM</FONT></TD>
<TD><FONT SIZE=2><BR></FONT></TD>
</TR>

<TR VALIGN=TOP>
<TD><FONT SIZE=2 COLOR=#0000ff>
<A HREF="Catalog.htm">Catalog</A></FONT></TD>
<TD><FONT SIZE=2>Query</FONT></TD>
<TD><FONT SIZE=2>9/9/96 12:47:59 PM</FONT></TD>
<TD><FONT SIZE=2><BR></FONT></TD>
</TR>

<TR VALIGN=TOP>
<TD><FONT SIZE=2 COLOR=#0000ff>
<A HREF="Publisher List.htm">Publisher List</A></FONT></TD>
<TD><FONT SIZE=2>Query</FONT></TD>
<TD><FONT SIZE=2>9/9/96 5:01:37 PM</FONT></TD>
<TD><FONT SIZE=2><BR></FONT></TD>
</TR>

</TBODY>
<TFOOT></TFOOT>
</TABLE>

<HR>
</BODY>
</HTML>
```

HTML Quick Reference

The following pages contain a quick reference to the most commonly used HTML tags. It is organized by functional area so that you can quickly find out how to accomplish the desired task.

In the following reference, the ellipses...indicate where user-defined text or tag parameters are to be placed in actual code. Tags that appear as a pair, such as <HTML>...</HTML> affect everything in between the pair. If a tag accepts parameters, the valid parameters are listed below the tag and indented.

Basics

The tags in this section are the basic building blocks for a successful Web page. All Web documents have the <HTML>, <HEAD>, and <BODY> tags.

<!...>	Creates a comment. For example, <!This is a comment>.
<HTML>...</HTML>	Encloses the entire HTML document.
<HEAD>...</HEAD>	Identifies the head of the HTML document.
<BODY>...</BODY>	Encloses the remainder of the Web document. The opening tag can have a number of parameters that refine the appearance of the page, including colors, background image, and so on.
<TITLE>...</TITLE>	The title of the Web document as it will appear in the browser caption. The title typically is included inside the <HEAD>...</HEAD> tag.

Headings

Heading tags provide a convenient way to format text in a kind of outline format on your page.

<H1>...<H6>	Headings 1 through 6. Heading 1 is formatted with the largest characters, decreasing in size with each subsequent heading tag.

Paragraphs

A paragraph tag tells the browser to place text that follows the tag on a new line.

<P>...</P>	Creates a simple paragraph. The </P> tag is optional— most of the time, you'll see <P> by itself to identify a line break.

Links

Links are the basic Web navigation mechanism provided by Web pages.

<A>...</A>	Creates a link to another Web document. This is also called an anchor to the page named in the HREF argument.
HREF="..."	Indicates the URL of the document this link points to. This can be a full URL to another site or a relative URL to another page on the current site.
NAME="..."	Indicates the name of this link.

Character Formatting

You may frequently want to change the appearance of characters in your document to draw attention to important information or minimize the "fine print."

<EM>...</EM>	Emphasis
<STRONG>...</STRONG>	Stronger emphasis.
<CODE>...</CODE>	Source code listing.
<KBD>...</KBD>	Text to be typed from the keyboard.
<VAR>...</VAR>	Variable.
<SAMP>...</SAMP>	Sample.
<CITE>...</CITE>	Citation.
<B>...</B>	Boldface.
<I>...</I>	Italic.

Other Formatting

There are many other formatting tags provided by the HTML standard.

<HR>	Draws a horizontal rule across the page.
 	Adds a line break.
<BLOCKQUOTE>..</BLOCKQUOTE>	Indicates long quotes or citations.
<ADDRESS>...</ADDRESS>	Displays information about the author of the Web document.
<FONT>...</FONT>	Changes the font properties for all the enclosed text.
SIZE="..."	Indicates font size, from 1 through 7. This number is the incremental size relative to the base font for the page.
<BASEFONT...>	Sets the default size of the font for the current page.
SIZE="..."	Indicates font size, from 1 through 7.

Images

Images are perhaps the most appealing part of a Web page. You can insert an image tag inside a link to make the image clickable.

<IMG...>	Inserts an image into the Web document.
SRC="..."	Indicates the URL of the image file to use.
ALT="..."	Sets the text to display if the browser is not capable of displaying Web images.
ALIGN="..."	Sets the alignment of the image within the Web document.
VSPACE="..."	Sets how much empty space to display above and below the image.
HSPACE="..."	Sets how much empty space to display to the left or right of the image.

Tables

Access 97 uses HTML tables to contain the results of queries in the Web pages it creates.

<TABLE>..</TABLE>	Begins the definition of a Web table.
BORDER="..."	Determines how wide a border to use for the table.
<CAPTION>... </CAPTION>	The caption for the table. This tag is optional. Often, Web designers use text elements outside the table to describe the contents of the table.
ALIGN="..."	Determines the position of the caption. Possible values are TOP and BOTTOM.
<TR>...</TR>	Defines a row in the table.
ALIGN="..."	Determines the horizontal alignment of the contents of the cells in the row. Possible values are LEFT, RIGHT, and CENTER.
VALIGN="..."	Determines the vertical alignment of the contents of the cells in the row. Possible values are TOP, MIDDLE, and BOTTOM.
<TH>...</TH>	Table heading cell. It identifies the contents of the column it occupies.
ALIGN="..."	Determines the horizontal alignment of the contents of the cells in the row. Possible values are LEFT, RIGHT, and CENTER.
VALIGN="..."	Determines the vertical alignment of the contents of the cells in the row. Possible values are TOP, MIDDLE, and BOTTOM.
ROWSPAN="..."	Tells how many rows the heading covers if it applies to more than one row.
COLSPAN="..."	Tells how many columns the heading covers if it applies to more than one column.
<TD>...</TD>	Creates a table data cell.

Forms

Data entry forms are easy to construct, but a number of tags are involved in setting them up.

<FORM>...</FORM>	Defines the enclosed block as a data entry form.
ACTION="..."	Indicates the URL of the file that handles the data sent by the Submit button.
METHOD="..."	Determines how data is sent to the file identified by the ACTION parameter. Possible values are GET and POST. For Access databases using IDC files, POST is the proper value.
<INPUT...>	Sets up a data entry control on the Web page.

TYPE="..."	Identifies the kind of data entry control. Possible values are CHECKBOX, HIDDEN, RADIO, RESET, SUBMIT, TEXT, TEXTAREA, or IMAGE.
NAME="..."	Indicates the name of the data field as sent to the file identified by the ACTION parameter.
VALUE="..."	Indicates the default value to use if the user does not supply one for a TEXT or HIDDEN control. For RESET or SUBMIT buttons, it is the text to display on the button face.
CHECKED	Equivalent to the user selecting the control for CHECKBOX and RADIO controls.
SIZE="..."	Indicates the display size of a TEXT control.
MAXLENGTH="..."	Limits the number of characters that can be entered into a TEXT control.
ALIGN="..."	Determines how the text and image will align for images on forms. It is the same as ALIGN in the <IMG> tag.
<TEXTAREA>...</TEXTAREA>	Identifies a multiline text control.
NAME="..."	Indicates the name of the data field as sent to the file identified by the ACTION parameter.
ROWS="..."	Indicates the number of text rows to display.
COLS="..."	Indicates the number of text columns, or characters, to display.
<SELECT>...</SELECT>	Creates a menu or scrolling list of items from which to choose.
NAME="..."	Indicates the name of the data field as sent to the file identified by the ACTION parameter.
MULTIPLE	Allows more than one item in the list to be selected.
<OPTION>	Identifies a single item within a SELECT control.
SELECTED	Selects the given OPTION by default.
VALUE="..."	Indicates the value to submit for the SELECT control if this OPTION is selected.

INDEX

Notes

Notes

Notes